CLIFTON'S

AND

CLIFFORD CLINTON

Our door's unlatched
for every guest
Let he who enters
find peace and rest

Clifford and Nelda Clinton cut the ribbon at the opening ceremonies of their chain of cafeterias, this time at Clifton's Century City, 1965.

Opposite: Clifford Clinton looks out his front door on 5470 Los Feliz Blvd. He never locked the front door, and the welcome mat was always out.

Clifton's Pacific Seas added a bit of island kitsch to downtown Los Angeles after its redecoration in 1938, a look that lasted until its demolition in 1960.

A huge crowd of revelers gathered in front of Clifton's Brookdale—as if it were the Times Square of Los Angeles—a central place to celebrate the end of World War II, 1945

ANGEL CITY PRESS

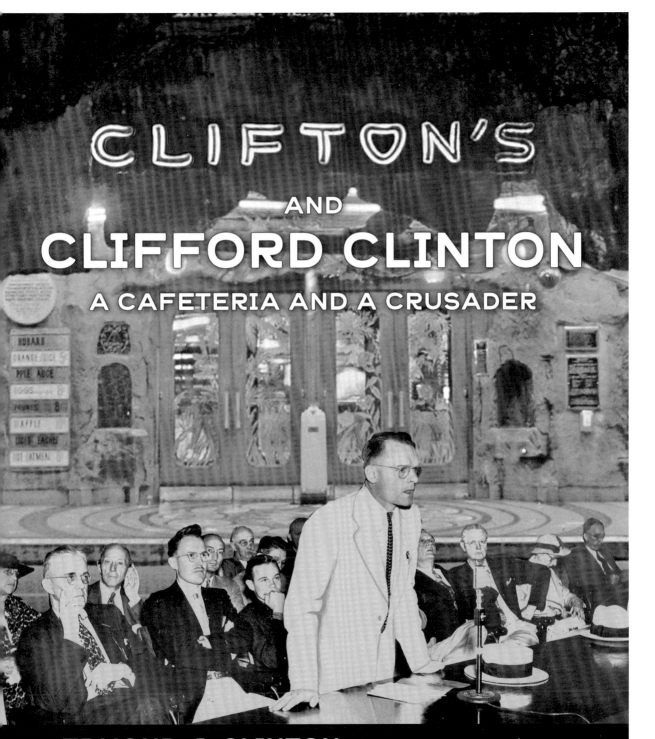

CLIFTON'S

AND

CLIFFORD CLINTON

A CAFETERIA AND A CRUSADER

EDMOND J. CLINTON III WITH MARK VIEIRA
FOREWORD BY TOM SITTON, Ph.D.

Clifton's and Clifford Clinton: A Cafeteria and the Crusader
By Edmond J. Clinton III with Mark A. Vieira

Copyright © 2015 Edmond J. Clinton III

Design by Amy Inouye, Future Studio Los Angeles

ISBN-13 978-1-62640-022-1

Printed in Canada

Library of Congress Cataloging-in-Publication Data is available

Published by Angel City Press
2118 Wilshire Blvd. #880, Santa Monica, California 90403
+1.310.395.9982
www.angelcitypress.com

Image Credits

Unless otherwise noted, photographs and Clifton's Cafeteria ephemera in this book are from the Clinton family collections. The author and publisher are grateful to individuals and institutions listed below for permission to reproduce images on the following pages:
California Historical Society: 130 bottom; **David Davis:** 137 (badges); **Natural History Museum of Los Angeles County:** 139 top left; **Los Angeles Public Library Photograph Collection:** 5, 9, 10, 108, 133 top, 135 top left, 136 top and bottom left, 140 bottom, 142 top left; **J. Eric Lynxwiler:** image of Clifton's Cafeteria tray; **Mary Mallory:** 134 bottom; **Seaver Center for Western History Research, Los Angeles County Museum of Natural History:** 139 top left; **UCLA Charles E. Young Research Library Department of Special Collections, Clifford Clinton Papers:** 4, 12, 18, 138 middle, 141 top; **University of Southern California Doheny Memorial Library, Special Collections, "Dick" Whittington Photography Collection:** 137 top, 138 top left and bottom.

For my father and grandmother,
Edmond Jackson Clinton II
and Nelda Mae Clinton

Clifton's BROOKDALE

DOORS
Lona Mae Dorman

Some doors have hearts, it seems to me,
They open so invitingly:
You feel they are quite kind–akin
To all the warmth you find within.

Some doors, so weather-beaten, grey
Swing open in a listless way,
As if they wish you had not come;
Their stony silence leaves you dumb.

Clifton's PACIFIC SEAS

Some classic doors stand closed and barred,
As if their beauty might be marred
If any sought admittance there,
Save king or prince or millionaire.

Oh, may mine be a friendly door;
May all who cross the threshold o'er,
Within, find sweet content and rest,
And know each was a welcome guest.

Interior of Clifton's Pacific Seas, circa 1940.

CONTENTS

Clifford Clinton in his home office, late 1940s.

FOREWORD

MAYBE THE SUNSHINE CAST AN ESPECIALLY POSITIVE LIGHT ON SOUTHERN CALIFORNIA. Ambitious young newcomers like budding entrepreneur Clifford Clinton saw Southern California as a land of opportunity. When he first laid eyes on Los Angeles in 1931, in the early years of the Great Depression, it was the fifth-largest city in the U.S., and soon to be much more populous. Some of its citizens had arrived in periodic waves since the late nineteenth century; others had come recently in the booming 1920s. Some came for their health and the salubrious climate or for a new start in life. Most were hard-working citizens in search of better opportunities, maybe a more promising place to raise a family.

The entire nation was experiencing tough times: massive unemployment, bank business failures, questionable political panaceas, and social dislocation. Los Angeles was no exception. But even though Los Angeles businesses suffered in the early 1930s, the local economy was strong. The city was the county seat of Los Angeles County, the national leader of all counties in agricultural production in the first half of the twentieth century, as well as the leading manufacturing center on the Pacific coast. Even in a depression, major industries—motion pictures, petroleum refining, secondary automobile assembly and airplane body parts, machinery manufacturing, furniture, and others—created many opportunities for workers and for those who would provide meals for them and their families in eating establishments.

Clinton expected to raise his family and build his cafeteria business in Los Angeles. Like others in his situation, the struggle and successes of just that would be challenge enough. For a while it was. In fact, in the early 1930s he had little thought, if any, of engaging in municipal politics. And little did he expect what he would soon experience in that world.

In 1931, the political structure and operation were the products of the Progressive reform movement at the turn of the century. Like major cities throughout the nation, Los Angeles elections in the early 1900s were fought by political parties, which chose candidates and campaigned for them, filled city offices with their members, and decided how to vote on issues. In most major cities, well-known city bosses—men often aligned with the underworld that financially supported them—dominated the process. Like their counterparts in other cities, Los Angeles reformers fought for devices such as nonpartisan elections, civil service, direct democracy (initiative, referendum, and recall), and at-large elections to reduce the power of party bosses. The Los Angeles group was successful with all of these measures by 1909, when one of its own, former County Supervisor George Alexander, was elected mayor, and the reformers then moved to eliminate vice operations in the city.

With the political parties limited in both city and county politics, however, there was a vacuum in acquiring and holding power as political strategists organized alliances of special interest groups. By 1930, Los Angeles politics was generally contested by three major coalitions: business organizations such as the Chamber of Commerce, and Old Guard Republicans with *Los Angeles Times* publisher Harry Chandler and his paper as its voice; a 1920s alliance of liberals, municipal ownership advocates, and unions led by former Mayor George Cryer and his mentor, Kent Kane Parrot; and a fundamentalist minister, Reverend Robert "Fighting Bob" Shuler, and his growing Protestant congregation which elected Mayor John Porter in 1929.

The liberal alliance defeated Mayor Porter and the business alliance in 1931; former County Supervisor Frank L. Shaw then assumed the office of mayor. Shaw was a depression fighter while he was a supervisor; as mayor he was successful in bringing a large number of federal projects to the city to reduce unemployment and build infrastructure. His administration, however, included some corrupt individuals (as did previous administrations) who cooperated with underworld figures and managed a crooked police department. To many, the Shaw regime resembled the corrupt leadership of New York, Chicago, Atlantic City, and other major cities in the Great Depression decade, so it wasn't long before another Los Angeles reform movement would replace it.

The new reform crusade started off slowly, as it had plenty of competition for the mayor's attention. The mid-1930s saw heightened labor unrest and resistance from the Los Angeles Police Department and its Red Squad, which countered the advances of unionists and radical groups such as the Socialist and Communist parties. Right-wing organizations such as the Ku Klux Klan were active, although the Klan was only a shadow of what it had been when it was on the rise in 1920s Los Angeles. Novelist and social critic Upton Sinclair's End Poverty in California (EPIC) campaign for governor in 1934 and the plan for old-age pensions promoted by Dr. Francis Everett Townsend, a retired Long Beach physician, were major movements to improve the economic situations of residents and generate their financial support. Other organizations advocating panaceas for making the world a better place, such as Technocracy and the Utopian Society, were also in the spotlight. Many of the groups held monthly meetings in Clifton's

Cafeteria, "the rendezvous of all intransigents with plans for a new world," as described by two authors who analyzed these groups. Whether or not these meetings in his cafeterias influenced Clinton in his coming political activism is unknown.

Clinton was brought into the budding urban reform movement of the 1930s and became a major force with his consistent leadership, his mastery of the media in his political campaign, and his pocketbook. Although there were many leading figures in the reform movement, Clinton was the indispensable character in its 1938 electoral success in removing Frank Shaw from office. In defeat, Mayor Shaw followed Charles Bowles of Detroit in 1930 to become at least the fourth mayor of a major American city to be recalled in the twentieth century.

Having grown up as the son of Christian missionaries, Clinton was deeply religious and especially considerate of the less fortunate, as evidenced in his business principles and his unique methods in feeding Angelenos and later, the world. It was a testament to his personal mission in life that no one should ever go hungry. Clinton's passion and persistence in this cause is clearly evident in his political reform campaigns, which continued into the 1940s.

Clinton's legacy as a Los Angeles political reformer before and during World War II is much more than just substantial. He played a pivotal role in the city's political development at the beginning of the era in which Los Angeles emerged as a modern municipality in its economy as well as its politics; it would move forward even more in the next few decades. Some of his opponents— and there were many—saw him as an opportunist who was damaging the city's reputation; others thought he was just naïve in thinking he could bring about major change. But Clinton actually believed that he could reform things in City Hall and was willing to sacrifice his time and his money in this crusade.

This is Clifford Clinton's own story based on his memory of events and the research and the interpretation of those events and that life by his grandson. This fascinating narrative reveals a wealth of information and insights that contribute to our understanding of Clinton's background, his ambition, and his subsequent activism. Edmond Clinton offers new evidence of his grandfather's political agenda and his role in the urban reform movement. This biography of a man whose name is remembered more for his eatery than his important political contributions also adds a new dimension to our knowledge of the growth of Los Angeles during one of the most important periods of the city's maturity.

Tom Sitton, Ph.D.
Curator Emeritus, Natural History Museum of Los Angeles County
2015

PREFACE

THE UNIVERSITY OF SOUTHERN CALIFORNIA'S KECK SCHOOL OF MEDICINE IS A GLEAM-
ING NEW FACILITY IN THE BOYLE HEIGHTS DISTRICT OF LOS ANGELES. Behind it sits a
venerable stone-and-steel building, its Art Deco-esque profile instantly recognizable.
A fictional hospital in numerous movies and television programs, its real-life significance is far
greater. Opened in 1933 as Los Angeles County General Hospital, when I graduated from USC
Medical School in 1974, it was the Los Angeles County-USC Medical Center. I spent my internal
medicine internship in it. I remember wondering how such a massive, complex structure could
have been built during the Great Depression.

My years in this structure were the most trying, challenging, and educational of my adult life.
As I struggled to endure them, my thoughts often turned to someone else whose life was changed
by this facility: my grandfather, Clifford E. Clinton. He had died just a few years before I began
my residency, but I vividly recalled a story he had told me when I was a child. In 1936, he discovered that this magnificent facility was being mismanaged. He saw evidence of graft and waste.
Someone else might have left it at that, rationalizing that patients were, after all, receiving care
and nutrition. In 1937, my grandfather resolved to do something.

Nearly forty years later, my memories of the oral history I received during my time with my
grandparents still seem fresh and ready for the telling. Because Clifford Clinton was a big part
of my life, I tell the story from an insider's perspective. Though one of thirteen grandchildren, I
was greatly influenced by Clifford and my grandmother Nelda. My grandparents possessed a deep
understanding of what it took to help raise young ones. They enlightened us with reading, in-
struction, and discussions. They probed our minds and helped each of us develop character. They
set us on the road to the future. To this day, my grandfather exerts a profound influence on me.
No surprise? He exerted an influence on everyone who met him. And he influenced Los Angeles.

Writing a biography is a daunting prospect, doubly so for a physician like me. I wanted to tell the story of a complex, controversial figure, one who was as important to this city as it was to him. I thought this would be a straightforward task. Before long, I realized I was writing about important aspects of the history of Los Angeles, and then it became an even more daunting experience. I had spent years with Clifford E. Clinton. I grew up near him in the Los Feliz district. I spent summer evenings at the Griffith Observatory, the Hollywood Bowl, and the Greek Theatre, and summer days busing tables at the Clifton's Cafeteria on Hoover Street in the old Westlake District. I thought I knew Clifford Clinton and his adopted city. I discovered that writing about both of them was anything but straightforward. It has taken five years and the assistance of many. I wish to thank the following institutions, archives, and individuals for helping me.

I thank the Los Angeles City Historical Society for access to books and documents dealing with the reform movements; the Special Collections Library at University of California, Los Angeles, for access to the Clifford Clinton papers; the University of Southern California for access to documents and photographs.

I thank Christina Rice of the Los Angeles Public Library for help in acquiring rare photographs of Clifford Clinton; Bill Frank, curator of the Huntington Library in San Marino, for access to the John Anson Ford and Fletcher Bowron files. Thanks also to Jennifer Byrd of the Salvation Army for information on my great-grandparents' service.

I thank the eminent Los Angeles historian Tom Sitton, Ph.D., for sharing his knowledge and for mentoring me. His published works and doctoral dissertation helped bring understanding and clarity to the Clinton saga. Having his foreword included in this book is an honor for me.

I am deeply grateful to my uncle, Donald H. Clinton, who is Clifford Clinton's surviving son. Uncle Don shared his collection of clippings and photographs with me, and took the time to improve the manuscript with details and editing suggestions.

I thank Mark A. Vieira for helping me tell the **story** of a lifetime, of several lifetimes, with skill and sincere enthusiasm. I am grateful to Jed Smith of Angel City Press for his insights and guidance and to Todd Berger for his critical and careful eye. I thank Paddy Calistro and Scott McAuley, publishers of Angel City Press, for their faith in this project and for their determination to get me to write the most complete story that I could.

I owe a very personal thank you to my wife Diane. She is an indefatigable research assistant, and she encouraged me while I organized the material into a manuscript. I had my memories and I had historical accounts, but they didn't tell the full story of this man. Then I was fortunate to gain access to his unpublished memoir. This made it possible for me to see the events of years ago through his eyes, but I still needed help. Diane's insights, both sensitive and objective, improved the manuscript at every stage of its preparation, and my journey of discovery finally reached its destination.

Edmond J. Clinton III

The restaurant sponsored a courtesy sightseeing bus and picked up passengers in front of Clifton's Pacific Seas, late 1930s.

CLIFTON'S CLIFFORD CLINTON

MOST PEOPLE HAVE NEVER HEARD OF CLIFFORD CLINTON. If they have lived in Los Angeles for more than a decade, they most likely have heard of his famed cafeteria, Clifton's. Many who open this book have had a meal there or even had a family tradition of celebrating at Clifton's. The downtown landmark was always a testament to good eating and good intentions, yet the cafeteria itself doesn't adequately tell the story of how its founder almost singlehandedly saved a city that was rife with corruption, a city on the verge of destroying itself in its prime.

Clinton moved to Los Angeles to run a business with service foremost and to raise his family in a place filled with opportunity. Given this great chance to live the life he had dreamed of, he felt he owed a debt to the city. When he was asked to address the graft and waste in the L.A. County Hospital budget, he had no idea of the political hornet's nest he was about to disturb. When appointed to the 1937 Grand Jury (a governmental body he'd never heard of until he was asked to join it), he agreed to do his best, his duty as a citizen. He didn't know it was his first step down a long road of championing reform.

He was warned "You can't fight City Hall" and was frequently reminded that he had much to lose. But his sense of civic responsibility became a sort of sacred calling. In the words of historian Kevin Starr, Clinton had "a creative response to the social challenges of his time." The impetus, successes, and tribulations of the 1930s moral reform movement became his cross to bear.

His unpublished memoir, penned in 1957 while on a round-the-world trip with his wife Nelda and preserved by his family, is the source for many of the details and quoted material that follow in this book. You will read his descriptions of recollected moments, scenes and conversations throughout this book, indented, like his words that follow here. About these extended recollections, Clifford Clinton wrote:

> It has been genuinely surprising that taking pencil in hand, I find pictures and words flowing onto these sheets of paper, even scenes that were witnessed by a seven-year-old boy more than fifty years ago.

Clinton Cafeteria on Powell at Market Street in San Francisco, 1921.

E.J. AND GERTRUDE

THE WINTER OF 1932 WAS BRUTAL. The United States was in the grip of the worst economic depression it had ever known. Nearly one-third of its working population was out of work. Even in Los Angeles, where a displaced person need not freeze to death when caught without a roof over his head, the situation was grim. The hopeful throngs who had come looking for a new life found the Big Orange squeezed dry. Downtown Los Angeles, which had once been a hub of commerce, was riddled with breadlines and food riots, and gradually, the once-colorful paradise had become a monochromatic purgatory. At least there was one place where people could get something to eat. Everybody could.

Into this economically depressed dystopia had ventured Clifford Clinton and his fledgling family, full of hope for a new business and a new life. Like many Angelenos, he was a transplant and might have subconsciously viewed the city as a larger metaphor for rebirth and rejuvenation. In 1931, with only two thousand dollars in his pocket, his first move had been to take over the Olive Street cafeteria of his longtime rivals, the Boos brothers. He called this new cafeteria Clifton's, a portmanteau of his first and last names, to emphasize a clean break from his father's "Clinton's Cafeteria Company" up north in the Bay Area.

Armed with 2,400 recipe cards and an operations manual he had assembled while still working for his father in San Francisco, he rapidly assembled his cafeteria. He instituted the "Cafeteria of the Golden Rule" policy, where employees were treated as "associates" and customers became "honored guests in our home." He instituted the twin policies of "Pay What You Wish" and "Dine Free Unless Delighted." He had a third policy that he maintained throughout his life: "No guest need go hungry for lack of funds."

Though these ideals attracted customers to the new cafeteria, many who came had no way to pay for their meals. This put a strain on the Olive Street Clifton's, with so many needy coming through the doors, and created a dilemma for Clinton. Should he change his policies of providing for the hungry in his new city? After prayerful consideration, he came up with a solution, and he would later reflect that every problem he ever faced would eventually have a solution if he prayed enough. Instead of allowing the cafeteria to go bankrupt, in 1932, he opened a second cafeteria he called the Penny at Third and Hill Streets, where poor people would find a nutritious meal for a single cent. Before long, the Penny Cafeteria was serving four thousand meals a day. Miraculously, it survived through the worst years of the Great Depression, ultimately serving two million meals.

Clinton had accomplished what he set out to do; by feeding the indigent population as well as those who could pay, he had applied his ideals in a practical and helpful way. Though in other parts of Los Angeles, restaurateurs like Bob Cobb and Billy Wilkerson were focused on wooing well-heeled movie stars with the continental luxuries of the Brown Derby and the Trocadero, Clinton was content to offer simple, economical meals for simple folks and to spread his message of hope.

Los Angeles was a terminus shared by many Midwesterners whose forebears began the gradual drift west in the late nineteenth century. For thirty-one-year-old Clinton, as for many, this was the land where new ideas could be explored. His success in the service of his fellow man would not have been possible, however, had his ancestors not taken a chance on the West Coast.

In 1888, a Southern Pacific train traveled from Joplin, Missouri, carrying David Harrison Clinton, his blind mother, his cousin Mollie, his three daughters, and sixteen-year-old son, Edmond Jackson Clinton. The family had paid a dollar a head to get to Los Angeles. After settling in, David went into the hospitality business near the Santa Fe Depot. E.J., as friends and family called him, worked at his father's restaurant while attending Los Angeles High School, at Temple and Broadway. His days in class were brightened when he met Kansas-native Gertrude Hall, eighteen months his junior.

After E.J. graduated from high school, he worked on the Atchison, Topeka and Santa Fe Railway as a fireman and motorman while Gertrude joined a newly popular church, William Booth's Salvation Army. Gertrude persuaded E.J. to accompany her to her church at the local "corps," and it wasn't long before they became "officers." When Maude Ballington Booth, daughter-in-law of the founder, was conducting a downtown tent meeting in November 1895, the two were married to the dulcet tones of a sixteen-piece military brass band. The next year they were commissioned as captains and sent into the field.

E.J. and Gertrude spent five years serving in Southern California, and finally realized it was time to postpone the charitable life and start making some money to live on. They moved to Berkeley and, following in his father's footsteps, entered the restaurant business. E.J. opened a small restaurant, the Puritan Dining Room, but it quickly failed, so he took a position at Dennett's Restaurant in San Francisco, earning seven dollars a week.

Elmira Hall wanted to be near her daughter Gertrude, so she donated her East Los Angeles farm to the Salvation Army and followed the young Clintons to Berkeley where she bought a house. The Halls' Southern California home and land would eventually become Booth Memorial Hospital, a home for unwed mothers. The move afforded Gertrude's sister Lillian and brother Burton the opportunity to attend the University of California at Berkeley. Her other sister, Mabel, graduated from the Boston School of Music.

On August 3, 1900, another son was born to E.J. and Gertrude. They could not decide on a name for "Baby Clinton," until Gertrude's sister Mabel christened him Clifford. Gertrude added Edmond, in honor of his father.

By 1903, E.J. was running not only the Dennett's location on Market Street where he started, but the entire chain. He was earning a respectable seven thousand dollars a year, and by 1905, he had saved enough to buy the whole operation, the Dennett's International Surpassing Coffee Company. Having secured his family's well-being with a modicum of business success, he and his wife returned to their interrupted passion of missionary work. The couple applied to the Presbyterian Missionary Board and offered their service, but they were denied for reasons unknown. Undaunted, they applied to a Quaker missionary, Horace W. Houlding, who was outfitting an expedition to northern China. Its purpose was twofold: to reinforce the Chinese economy with agricultural technology, and to spread the Christian spirit through their philanthropic work. Houlding accepted the application, perhaps because E.J. was pledging his salary to the cause. The Clintons were off to China.

By 1905, China was recovering from the Sino-Japanese War and the ongoing slaughter of Chinese Christians and Westerners of the past five years. E.J. and Gertrude decided to help the Chinese make a transition to "enlightened" Western ways. They packed twenty shipping cases with food, medical and dental supplies, and everything that a family of six would need in a far-off and uncertain land. By now there were four Clinton children: Evangeline, Clifford, Marguerite, and Catherine. The Clintons boarded the S.S. *Mongolia* in San Francisco and sailed for Shanghai. Five-year-old Clifford would years later recall "the thrill as we children looked ahead to a month in which to romp and play on this great ocean liner." This pleasant journey stood in stark counterpoint to their arrival in Shanghai.

The family was to embark on a train to Tientsin and Peking (Tianjin and Beijing today), since their mission was located in northern China. They were brought to the railway station by rickshaw, a carriage pulled by a bevy of "thin, almost naked men in wide straw hats." This was Clifford's first encounter with the results of the paucity and famine endemic to post-Boxer China. Gertrude hustled her children onto the train while E.J. made sure that the luggage was being loaded. Then, suddenly, the Clintons felt the train moving. It was pulling out of the station—without E.J.

> Mother was frantic. Father had the tickets, the money, the information concerning our stopover, and a magic piece of paper on which were Chinese characters to aid us in arriving at our correct destination. There were hysterical efforts to stop the train. "Send someone back!" But who? We children huddled around Mother for comfort. And Mother prayed.

2

CHINA

G ERTRUDE AND FOUR SMALL CHILDREN WERE RIDING TO PARTS UNKNOWN, ON A CROWDED
TRAIN IN A STRANGE COUNTRY. They spoke no Chinese, had no food, and were terribly
frightened. When porters came asking for money, Gertrude attempted to convey to
them that she had none. This was the first time that Clifford had seen his parents lose control of
their environment.

> All was confusion. The feeling which still possesses me in times of crisis, or problems,
> is the urge—the necessity—to have a personal part in putting things right. Unrest and
> insecurity overwhelm me. Where there is disorder or lack of plan, I cannot be relaxed
> or quiet within myself.

But stuck on the speeding train, the Clintons could only turn to prayer. An empathic English-
man eased the Clintons' disaster, on the crowded train car by reassuring Gertrude that a mission
station was just ahead. Upon learning this, Gertrude prepared her brood and gathered their meager remaining luggage to wait. When the train slowed to pull into the station, they shoved their
suitcases through the windows and onto the platform. Amidst the protestations of the porters,
Gertrude pulled her children off the train and grabbed the suitcases. A group of missionaries saw
Gertrude and the children and led them through a crowd of anti-missionary, hostile Chinese.
When she reached the mission station, she was told that word would be sent back to her husband,
assuring him of their safety and relative well-being. She collapsed in relief.

> Mother looked strange to us lying in the great bed with its thick quilted puffs. A great

rattan fan hung from the ceiling, running the length of the room. A Chinese child pulled on a rope to keep the fan moving, cooling the air, and chasing flies. Paper walls were new to us. We put our childish fingers on them, gently testing each small square. The floors were covered with matting. They felt smooth and soft to our bare feet.

If little Clifford found this town unusual, its citizens found him downright exotic. The missionaries informed Gertrude that a crowd of curious Chinese was outside, asking to see the "little old man." Clifford was a towhead.

> The Chinese never saw fair hair on youths, only on the aged. The noisy crowd seemed threatening. The missionaries felt there was danger. A wave of fear swept over us again. People pressed close to me. They touched my hair and felt my clothing. I trembled at their touch. Just then, a soldier came and told the people to leave.

The anti-missionary sentiment that had fueled the Boxer Rebellion was still in the air, and Gertrude was uncertain of the crowd's intentions. What might the Chinese do to a small boy? As the crowd was pushing against the door of the station, the missionary hostess pointed to a motto that hung on a wall: "Trust and Believe."

E.J. arrived the next day and the family set off once more. One leg of the journey took place in a Chinese *junk*—a flat-bottom boat with a short-mast and a triangular sail—on the waters of the Yangtze Kiang River, thick with yellow mud and silt. At times, the sail caught the wind and pulled the boat, while at other times, male and female laborers pulled the boat from the shore with long ropes. As the craft passed other *junks* and *sampans*, Clifford stared in wonder at their occupants, and they stared back at him. When the family stopped at towns, children would yell: "*Fahn qui Zai!*" (Foreign devils!) The lingering resentment was palpable, since only a few years earlier, soldiers of the Eight-Nation Alliance had come through this region, looting, raping, and killing under the auspices of suppressing the Boxers. The next three weeks of the journey were experienced from the back of donkey-pulled covered carts. E.J. and Gertrude looked askance as Chinese worshiped at roadside shrines, in unfamiliar religious ceremonies.

> People came bowing and praying with folded hands in front of the idols. Many lighted a punk-stick, which gave a fragrant odor, and left bowls of food for the idols. Father and mother told us it was wrong for people to pray to idols stating that of course idols could not smell sweet incense or eat food. Our parents said we had come to tell of Jesus so they would not have to pray to the idols anymore.

Though the Clintons experienced the grandeur of rural China, passing grand pagodas and striking temples, not all of the sights were beguiling. China was a country in distress. The afflictions of body and spirit paled in comparison to the gruesome military justice meted out by the roving bands of the Eight-Nation Alliance. They happened upon the gruesome sight of a group of robbers beheaded by the soldiers.

> The deepest impression made on our childish minds was of people lying alongside the road, too sick to walk. There were many poor people, some with great sores on their gaunt faces, both adults and children. Their villages had been cursed with poor land and meager crops. There were lepers sitting by the roadside. . . . We stood aghast looking at those heads hanging on a pole by the hair, their yellow faces, black hair and eyebrows, bulging eyes, open mouths showing their teeth, and their severed necks, which were still dripping blood.

At last the Clintons arrived at the Houlding mission in Tai Ming Fu, in the interior of northern China. They were welcomed by an advance party and escorted to their new home, a two-story stone structure. One of their first duties was to pay respects at the graves of missionaries murdered by Boxers. As the family settled in, prayers and Bible study commenced amidst hard and charitable work. E.J., who had a natural disposition toward first aid, unpacked his instruments and established a first-aid station, laying out forceps, extractors, dental tools, and scalpels for the morning clinic at his dispensary. He had used these instruments caring for his own family regularly.

Although Gertrude and the children quickly mastered Mandarin, the language of the north, E.J. found it difficult. He watched with frustration as his children spoke Chinese and played with other children in the mission compound. E.J. also had trouble acclimating to the chain of command in the Houlding Mission. There were disagreements, after which Gertrude diplomatically explained to the children that their father felt he could be of greater service to God at another mission.

In 1905, the Yangtze Kiang flooded, ruining crops and causing further famine in the villages that lined its banks. That winter, E.J. carried food and a medical kit and trekked across the icy terrain, going from village to village. Clifford accompanied him and saw sights that would haunt him for the rest of his life.

> I saw people bending down in their black padded clothes, scratching and digging at the frozen soil for roots, as the leaves—and all else above ground—had long since gone. Some became so desperate that they ate the soil itself to fill their empty bellies. These were the objects of our visits. . . . Sometimes in a hovel Father would inquire after a patient and then be told that he had been put out to die. In one instance, Father treated a man for a carbuncle by applying an oatmeal poultice. On the next visit, Father learned that the man had been put out to die—without the oatmeal poultice. "He must give it to the living," a relative told him. It was eaten. . . . This was a period of challenge, danger, and economy. To this day I cannot see waste or misuse of food or of any material thing.

E.J. and Gertrude each wrote to their own parents, asking them to send money. One day in April 1906, E.J. received a cable from his partners in San Francisco. It read simply: "Earthquake and fire. San Francisco and your business destroyed. Come at once."

3

EARTHQUAKE AND SHUI HING

U PON RECEIVING A LOAN FROM HIS BERKELEY RELATIVES, E.J. IMMEDIATELY SAILED
TO SAN FRANCISCO, DETERMINED TO SAVE HIS DECIMATED BUSINESS AND SHATTERED
FINANCIAL AFFAIRS. Gertrude would eventually receive money from home to return
to California with the youngest children. Since Clifford and his older sister Evangeline would
remain in China until E.J. could afford their return voyage, one of the missionary associates
arranged for the two young children to attend a British school in China. There, the youngsters
soldiered on, without their family, until they could return, despite considerable anti-American
rhetoric and bullying by the other children.

The San Francisco earthquake and the resulting fire was more than a professional and financial tribulation for E.J. It was one of the worst disasters in American history. At 5:13 A.M.
on April 18, 1906, San Francisco was shaken by a temblor that lasted nearly a minute and has
been estimated at a magnitude of 7.8. As a result of the shaking and fire, more than twenty-five
thousand buildings were destroyed, and nearly three thousand people perished. In a letter to his
family, E.J. described walking over the ruins of a once-bustling metropolis. Even after ninety
days, the ashes were still smoldering.

> Nothing of Father's business had been saved, except some tableware, a wagonload of
> papers, and the contents of the safe, which held the receipts of only a few days' business.
> He was staggered.

The family was reunited when Clifford and Evangeline arrived in San Francisco after an adventurous sea voyage under the care of their close friend, missionary Moore Gordon. The whole Clinton clan moved into a little green house on Channing Way in Berkeley (where the earthquake caused virtually no damage), while E.J. worked to reestablish the business. It had a front lawn, a backyard, a "real bathroom," and even a guest room, which was occupied by a Chinese youth who was studying in the U.S. under the peace plan that followed the Boxer Rebellion. Grandma Elmira Hall lived nearby at 2018 Parker St., sharing the house with Gertrude's unmarried brother Burton and her married daughters Mabel and Lillian, both of whom were separated from their husbands but had children to raise. Elmira's home was a haven for her family and a "rock of security" for Clifford. He grew close to Burton, his "Uncle B," who was a former teacher but had been unemployed since a nervous breakdown.

> He often came to stay when mother was away, to look after us, and it was Uncle B who spent many hours talking with us, listening to our chatter, our ambitions and dreams.

As San Franciscans began to rebuild their city, E.J. opened a new restaurant, the Puritan Dining Room, at 749 Market St., with a partner named Mr. Goodbody, his full name lost to history. A cook in a tall chef's hat stood in the Market Street window, theatrically flipping pancakes in the air over an eight-foot griddle, then served a stack on china plates. E.J. worked six days a week, from early morning until late—he took a 7:00 A.M. train to the Berkeley ferry terminal and then sailed to San Francisco on a ferryboat, returning home about 10:00 P.M.

> Tension in the Clinton home was due at least partly to Gertrude's concern about finances.

> Mother was silent and distraught when she went to Grandma's one day. When she returned, she seemed to be encouraged. While she waited for Father, we waited in our beds. Then, around ten, we heard Father come in. In a while there were bright voices. We knew that Grandma had saved the day with the mortgage on one of her properties. Father's solvency was the concern of the entire family.

The loan made a huge difference. By 1908, E.J.'s restaurant was doing well enough to warrant the opening of another, the Quaker Dining Room and Bakery. In 1910, he opened a second Quaker Dining Room and Bakery, this one at the busy intersection of Mission and Sixteenth Streets.

> One of my real pleasures was to accompany father, on Saturdays and spend the day in the bakery, nibbling at almonds and icings, playing at work, and climbing into the loft where the flour and sugar was stored in great sacks.

Not long after it opened, the Quaker burned down, but E.J. rebounded with a partnership in a Polk Street candy store. Clifford remembered his father's resilience.

You can well understand that "Polk Street" soon became the favorite visiting spot for us children on Saturdays. We learned how to make sodas and other fountain items, to help in cutting the simple, but colorful, sugar candies and in packing them in boxes.

Despite his success, what E.J. desired most was to return to China. He had been setting money aside, but it was taking too long. Frustrated, he pushed himself to work longer hours. He expected the same of his workers and of his children.

> Father's orders were obeyed without question. A Puritan—almost Spartan—attitude prevailed.

Ten-year-old Clifford had his own problems. He was unusually self-reliant for his age, but at the same time he was insecure about his ultra-pale complexion. He had a difficult time at the McKinley School, becoming increasingly introverted and withdrawing from school life.

> I was slow to learn. I could not quickly grasp a question and give an answer. School defeated me.

In third grade, he was traumatized by two incidents. In the first, his foot became lodged in a desk. When he had to remove his shoe, his classmates saw that his sock had a huge hole in it. They derided him mercilessly. The second, and more severe embarrassing situation happened when he forgot to button his fly and inadvertently exposed himself to the whole classroom.

> Within this small boy's world all was over, lost, black! No amount of persuasion, even from Father, could get me back into that classroom.

E.J. was a practical man with little patience, and Clifford's Uncle Burton was the opposite sort, a man who, although he was always typing up a new draft for a play in his room at Grandma Hall's home, came to Clifford's aid in a quiet, caring way.

> "What does Burton know, he never even earned his own living, never sold a successful play; he is a failure and a phodist. An idealist can never be practical," according to father. . . . But it was [Burton] now, who comforted and encouraged me, and working with the school, suggested an alternate classroom. He went along with me during the first hard days, gradually setting those timorous feet, back on the road to education. But though Uncle Burton tried, tutored, and got the outward processes in motion, something had happened inside. Three terms had to be spent in the third grade. Promotion only came eventually, because of his intervention, and suggestion that encouragement might be the needed element. Adding to [my] internal confusion, was the oft overheard conversations of the elders who would say, "There must be something wrong with Clifford."

Uncle B was kind and understanding and knew how to listen to a young boy who had no one to talk to about his confusion and embarrassment. He remained nonjudgmental and took Clifford for walks in the hills of Berkeley, gently guiding him from fear to hope. Gradually Clifford began to regain his confidence.

> With Uncle B's love and perseverance, life became worth living. In this simple, but wise way, he awoke within me the desire to work toward a full life, and these were the beginnings of a framework upon which to hang hopes and dreams of the future.

Burton also began to teach Clifford a philosophy that was separate from his religious upbringing. As they hiked through eucalyptus groves, Uncle B told him: "You will do well in life if you daily strive to do good." Clifford took these words to heart, and, in the process, he bonded with his uncle in a way that he never had with his father. Sensing this, E.J. grew resentful but was unable to reach out to his son. Though he included Clifford in weekend excursions to his restaurants, he was otherwise distant.

> Our love for Father was diluted by fear and by awe. When some wish was to be presented to him, Mother was our intermediary. We scarcely dared ask him for anything. We tiptoed and whispered. We did not read the funny papers on Sunday. We sat straight in our chairs, so as not to be told: "I will put braces on your shoulders if you do not stand more straight."

When E.J. came home from work, he was always tired and never in a good mood. Clifford was terrified that his father would be told of some misbehavior. Gertrude was in uncertain health, so E.J. would administer punishment.

> I remember lying in bed for hours dreading the moment when the front door would open and father would hear of my misdeed and then come to my room with the razor strop. There were times when his methods may have been justified, yet they were mostly too severe and not always fair.

Burton helped Clifford get through his childhood, enabling him to develop a friendship with a Japanese neighbor boy, and to foster his unrealized aspirations toward charity, by caring for stray cats.

> One day I found a kitten. It was lost and friendless. When it cuddled against me, purring, it won my heart. I made a home for it in my backyard. One cat led to another. Eventually there were thirteen, all equally loved. This and the companionship of my newfound friend helped me to heal.

The makeshift menagerie attracted attention, first from the neighbors, and then from E.J., who ordered Clifford to get rid of them.

The loss of the cats was painful. I was always searching for something to love, searching to satisfy that inexpressible yearning.

By 1910, E.J. had finally saved enough money to fund a second trip to China. In preparation, he and Gertrude were ordained and his restaurants left under the aegis of business associates. The Clintons packed twenty-two cases and departed for China on the Japanese liner *Chiyo Maru*.

E.J. had volunteered the services of the Clinton family to Edwin Palmer Burtt and his wife, who operated a school for orphans and blind girls in Shui Hing, in the southern China province of Canton (Guangdong today). Shui Hing was a walled city. There were watchtowers along its walls and large, spiked gates that were opened by day for travelers and closed at night to keep out warlords and bands of robbers. The Clintons were staying outside the city walls, in the mission compound, which housed the only white people for hundreds of miles. The mission had a building with a large overhanging porch that overlooked an idyllic communal water well and a chapel, surrounded by blossoming lychee trees. Years later, Clifford described the lychee as tasting like a combination of grape, pear, and peach.

Mr. Ah, the mission pastor, taught Clifford and his friend Victor (the son of another missionary) to speak Cantonese by shouting out their lessons in singsong fashion. E.J. operated his dispensary and acted as financial manager, soliciting donations from travelers and local residents. Although he ministered to everyone, the sixty students from the nearby Blind Girls' School were his primary patients. These girls had been cast out of their homes after birth and left to die because of their disability. Clifford spent time with these girls, took them on walks in the countryside, and tried to make them feel like part of his family.

> Some were blind, some even deaf and blind. Some were grotesque, with great unseeing eyes, opaque with cataracts, and some had twisted, misshapen features. I saw them as beautiful. Their faces seemed to shine with an inner radiance, especially when given recognition. They would pass their sensitive fingers lightly over our faces, our hair, and our clothes, chattering excitedly about each discovery.

One day Mr. Ah's little daughter fell into a well. E.J. yelled for Clifford to bring a special rope and help him rescue her. Though he was at first paralyzed with fear, Clifford did as he was told when E.J. said he was going to lower him into the well. "Hold her with all your might," E.J. ordered him. "Don't let her fall." Clifford performed bravely, and the girl was saved. The reaction in the community was unexpected: how amazing that a man would risk a "precious" son to rescue an "unworthy" daughter. Clifford would remember the event for two reasons. First, he experienced the honor and confidence of being relied upon by E.J., and second, he internalized his father's calm handling of a crisis. From that point on, the boy resolved to emulate him.

Gertrude became pregnant again, but when she gave birth this time, with no doctor available, an amah—a housemaid—served as midwife. The child—named Grace Shui Hing Clinton to honor her birthplace—was born healthy, but Gertrude's recovery was protracted, an early indication of her poor health. Clifford doted on the baby and secretly put sweets into her bottle. While he immersed himself in Cantonese, China once again was in the midst of upheaval.

Although the Manchu Dynasty remained in power in 1911, rebel forces were mobilizing. Sun Yat-sen, the Chinese revolution leader, had been trying for years to transform China from a feudal empire into a constitutional monarchy. Yat-sen lived for a time in the United States and admired its democratic government. When the Yangtze Kiang flooded and killed one hundred thousand Chinese, it was spoken of as an omen against the dynasty. On October 10, a military uprising took place in Wuchang (Wuhan today) heralding a sequence of rebellions that precipitated sixteen provinces seceding, with Yat-sen serving as provisional president of the Republic of China.

Dinner conversation at the compound was dominated by talk of revolution. Before long, American gunboats had dropped anchor off the river near Shui Hing.

> One day Mr. Ah and the servants came running in. An American sailor was at the gate, asking that father and Mr. Burtt come down to the gunboat and talk with the captain.

E. J. was warned that Americans could be caught in the crossfire between revolutionaries and loyalists, and then the gunboat departed, its captain promising to return. Clifford went on a medical trip to a nearby village with his father and Mr. Ah. On the way, they stopped to see a crowd gathering. The boy pushed through the throng and saw a row of men kneeling on the ground.

> Their arms were tied behind them, and their necks were bared. A man stood above them with a great two-handled blade, awaiting a signal. As I stood, riveted to the ground, the signal came. The blade dropped on the first man. His head rolled to the ground, and blood spurted from his neck.

On the way home, Clifford asked what the men had done to deserve such awful punishment. "They were rebels," Mr. Ah said quietly. The army of New China was advancing.

The citizens of Shui Hing grew tense. Clifford and Victor found shop doors slammed in their faces. One day a crowd gathered, yelling "foreign devils" and began chasing them. The boys ran down granite streets, jumping over open sewers. As they zigzagged through the city, they collided with a tiny bathtub, laying in the sewage-ridden gutter. The infant in the tub was thrown to the ground. Though blood flowed, Clifford was never able to find out what happened to the child. The boys barely escaped the angry mob with their lives.

Struggling for a shred of normalcy, despite the turmoil surrounding them, the residents of the mission celebrated Christmas. Clifford helped to decorate the chapel with colored wood-and-paper lanterns made in the shape of boats, temples, and pagodas. Students sang at the services. Afterwards Clifford and Victor conducted their own service, and Clifford delivered a sermon based on his father's preaching.

> I wondered about my future and whether I should be a minister. There was a conflict, though, between my shyness—fear almost—and my mischievous audacity. My real desire was to be a leader.

When the gunboat returned, E.J. and Burtt sailed on it to the city of Canton to see exactly how things stood. While they were away, news reached Shui Hing that Canton had fallen. While awaiting his father's return, Clifford saw an opportunity to do something he had never done before—earn money. The local Chinese men were desperate to look like the revolutionary army soldiers, who did not wear the traditional braids the Manchus forced upon the Han Chinese, in an effort to differentiate themselves from China's monarchical past. Clifford and Victor set up a barbershop. Using scissors and E.J.'s clippers, they cut off hundreds of the townsmen's queues, until business was interrupted by an alarm.

> Victor and I saw soldiers coming toward the city, marching in endless lines. When the city gates were locked against them, the soldiers began setting fires. The first buildings to go up in flames were outside the walls.

Because the mission compound was also outside the walled city of Shui Hing, the adults at the mission began making plans. They would go behind the compound and stand in the stagnant lake. As buildings burned, citizens began to flee Shui Hing. Clifford could not find Victor, but he needed to know how much time the mission had. His father had not returned. He feared for his family. Maybe his father was at the river. He had to do something.

> I ran to the river amid the confusion. Crowds carrying bundles of their possessions were flocking from the city, fleeing the fires and the soldiers. I saw some go back for their possessions. Soldiers shot them down. Return shots came from the watchtowers on the city walls. I knew I must return and warn the mission. I found myself stumbling, falling, crawling underfoot, and then rising and running as if in a dream.

Clifford got back just as the entire mission population was running to hide behind the lychee trees at the lake; it was dark except for the reflected light of the fires. Then the first soldiers arrived, carrying torches, and stood staring at them. Gertrude, again in poor health, Mrs. Burtt, and Victor's mother Mrs. Robinson, sent Mr. Ah ahead to ask the officers if he could speak with them. To his surprise, they politely acquiesced. They looked at the women and blind children and offered to provide a New China Guard for the mission compound.

> The next morning with the New China Guard at our gates, the citizens saw a new day was dawning, and even more came to request us to cut off their queues. We American Boy Hair Stylists were again hurried into business, cutting hair as fast as our fingers could fly. A long line of eager customers formed. . . . When Father and Mr. Burtt returned and read a crude sign on our gate, in Chinese characters, "American Style Haircuts, ten cents," it puzzled them as much as did the New China guard at the gates. The Barber Business came to an abrupt end when father took in the situation, and saw us using his precious scissors and clippers. He drove the customers away, and confiscated our box and bottle full of coins and gave the bitterest scolding that I can remember. . .Several tried to help us explain, but he would not listen, and to this day, I can't imagine why he was so angry. He had no word of praise for our efforts to aid the family in time of dan-ger. . .The money, too, loomed large in our eyes, as it was the first money we had ever earned, and we felt it had been taken from us unjustly.

Before long, E.J. was faced with another crisis. His restaurants could send no more money. In desperation, he cabled his father. Nothing arrived, so the Clintons had no choice but to leave the mission and wait in Macao. It was there that a cable finally arrived from David Clinton. It said: "Business near insolvency. Best you return. Elmira and I raising passage money all family." E.J. Clinton surrendered to the inevitable. He would have to again bury his dream of mission work and return to the restaurant business.

4

CLIFFORD COMES OF AGE

ONCE AGAIN THE CLINTON FAMILY RETURNED FROM A CHARITABLE EXPEDITION, DIS-APPOINTED AND BELEAGUERED. Though they had no home to return to, Elmira Hall opened Parker Street to them. There were now nine Clintons—E.J., Gertrude, and seven children. Hall gave them the main floor of Parker Street and moved upstairs, where she continued to raise their daughter Ann. Clifford moved into the work shed with Burton Hall.

In time, Gertrude gave birth to a child named David, and Clifford assumed responsibility for diaper washing and early-morning feeding while he was setting the table. In the backyard shed, Clifford made some rudimentary furniture to sell in order to help with home expenses. He also transformed a portion of the old shed into a workout facility, with rings and a chin-up bar. He focused on building a stronger body.

The Puritan Dining Room faced financial ruin, so E.J. closed it and sought a new situation. The Boston Good Eats was an old café located at 731 Market St., in the basement of the Bancroft Building, one of the few structures left standing after the earthquake. The lease was available, but before signing it, E.J. did some research. He had heard of a new restaurant concept in Los Angeles, four successful siblings, the Boos brothers, were causing a stir with their new *cafeteria*.

The term *cafeteria* was coined in 1893 by Chicago restaurateur John Kruger to distinguish the new stand-in-line and serve-yourself concept from the Swedish smorgasbords that inspired it. In 1905, Los Angeles saloonkeeper Helen Mosher joined the name to the modern idea of the cafeteria; she was widely believed to be the first to have her patrons choose items at a counter, put their selections on trays, and carry their own meals to their tables. She emphasized the visibility of the food and the invisibility of waiters. "Food You Can See" and "No Tips" were her slogans.

The Boos brothers—Horace, Henry, John, and Cyrus—were the next to popularize the cafeteria concept in Los Angeles. Horace, the eldest, saw the cafeteria as more than a one-location novelty, so he built a chain of them, feeding crowds of people with this new fast-food concept. In 1906, they opened their own cafeteria at 211 West Second St., three blocks from Miss Mosher's place. Horace's original idea of placing a plank along the front counter of the deli provided both a support and a path for small trays that carried food. He targeted workingmen whose lunch break was too short for the luxury of a waiter.

By 1911, E.J. had heard about the Boos Bros. Cafeteria and believed he could adapt the business model to his diners in the City by the Bay. E.J. traveled to Los Angeles to see for himself what the new style restaurant was like. By then, there were four Boos Bros. Cafeterias in Los Angeles, all popular and all profitable. Upon his return to San Francisco, E.J. borrowed more money, signed a lease, and opened the first cafeteria in San Francisco, the Quaker Cafeteria, where the Good East once stood.

From the start, the Quaker was handicapped by its downstairs location. Despite this, E.J. attempted to improve on the winning formula the Boos family had created. There was a short-order kitchen at the beginning of the service line and a conveyor belt to transport dishes from the dining room to the dish room. To aid digestion, there was also an all-girl orchestra playing soft music. A number of E.J.'s former employees, including Chef Hersey, joined him at the Quaker. Due in part to its out-of-the-way location and the minimal evening foot traffic, the cafeteria did not fare well financially, although customers agreed the restaurant had good food and entertainment. The average wage of the employees was $2.80 per week, so E.J. cleared fifteen to eighteen dollars per week.

Because his big family's cost of living was so high, E.J. could not afford to buy a house. Hall came to the rescue again, and this time she rented a property at 1907 Haste St. for the family. Everyone except Ann moved into the new house; she stayed with Hall. Clifford worked as much as he could at the Quaker after school.

> I felt grateful to Father for being allowed to help. I began to take an especial interest in the storeroom, the hub of the eating business.

He would soon work a ten-hour day, six days a week for the employee's standard $2.80 a week. This was what he had wanted since he visited the candy store with this father. That Clifford was identifying so strongly with this core aspect of the restaurant business indicated he saw his future in it. Still, he was perceived as having a learning disability, despite Uncle Burton's continued faith in him. Although Burton persisted in tutoring and counseling him, other members of the family continued to whisper "What's wrong with Clifford? Why can't he learn his lessons?"

In 1914, there was a moving-picture theater on Market Street near the Quaker called the Silver Palace. When Clifford's mother condemned moving pictures, he asked why. "Because the people who make them are bad and lead wicked lives," she answered. He countered that some of the prophets, even King David, had been wicked, but God had forgiven them. "Father and I think they are bad," Gertrude said, ending the conversation. Clifford was, of course, intrigued.

> I found the pictures adventurous and entertaining, and I saw no evil in them, but there was always the guilt feeling because of my defiance. I kept my going a secret.

Clifford was not a devious child. He was devoted to his parents, and worked assiduously at his chores. On one occasion he mobilized his sisters into a cleanup committee so that Gertrude could come home to a spotless house. The children cleaned the entire dwelling, washed every glass and chandelier shade, and scrubbed every cupboard shelf.

> Then we breathlessly awaited mother's step on the porch. When we welcomed her with hugs, she knew something was afoot, and when she saw the results of our efforts, she told us that she genuinely appreciated our work, but more so that we had thought of her.

Clifford entered adolescence without the benefit of a gentle talk with his father. E.J. rarely spoke with his son about business, much less about the facts of life. Clifford was growing and improving his appearance via his exercises in the makeshift gymnasium. Although he looked like a young adult, he was not too old to enjoy roughhousing with his siblings. One day after school, he was resting on his bed when one of his sisters came in and wanted to play. He extended his feet and lifted her there, tossing her up and down in a rocking horse motion. The girl laughed so heartily that Gertrude heard her and came in. She reacted with a look of shock, then composed herself and ordered the girl out of the room. Then she turned on Clifford and berated him, "Clifford, I am ashamed that you could be so nasty." Clifford later wrote that he was devastated and unaware of what he did to incur such wrath. She confined him to his room and deprived him of dinner. It was after ten o'clock when he heard his father approach. When the door opened, Clifford saw the razor strop. He cringed and tried to ask what he had done.

"You know very well," answered E.J. Then the beating began. It was the worst Clifford had ever endured. He was never able to communicate to his parents about the unfairness of the incident. Their reluctance to discuss human sexuality had thusly been beaten into their son.

> Only years later, after I had learned sex from backyard talk, did I realize that mother must have felt I was satisfying some sex urge with my sister. This was as close to any sex education as I received from my parents. Their punishment, unjustly given, was a turning point in my life. From then on I never had a full and complete confidence in them. I loved and respected them, of course. But never again did I give them the spontaneous devotion of my childhood.

One night, E.J. came to Gertrude with the news that the Boos brothers had leased the main floor of the Bancroft Building for their first San Francisco cafeteria. They had engaged the noted architect Charles F. Plummer and were spending one hundred thousand dollars to create a spectacular restaurant. The new restaurant would be ultramodern in design with a sparkling chrome-and-glass interior and a sumptuous dining room. No expense was spared to bring in the most modern equipment. When the new Bancroft cafeteria was finally finished, E.J. and his children attended the opening, marveling at the beauty of the reconstruction and the hand-painted Einar Petersen murals. The restaurant was a noteworthy addition to the city and a true showplace.

E.J. was discouraged. He had not repaid his debts, business was still poor, and this competition, only a floor away, would surely destroy the Quaker. To make matters worse, union organizers began talking to the Quaker's employees, trying to recruit them. When the workers rejected their offers, E.J. stood behind them. A local newspaper reported union trouble at the Quaker. Pickets marched in front of the entrance to the downstairs cafeteria. Labor forces threatened to close it down. E.J.'s restaurant survived the siege, but both he and Clifford retained a lifelong distrust of organized labor.

As the Quaker struggled to survive in the shadow of the grand new Boos brothers installation upstairs, Clifford saw E.J. in desperate need and offered him eighty dollars in gold pieces he had saved up from his independent business ventures in San Francisco—from cleaning homes and yards. E.J. eagerly accepted the money. Later when arrangements were being made to move to the new location, Clifford helped his father by packing food supplies including candy and gum. One day, he found his father searching his room for some missing boxes of gum!

> I dared not believe that Father suspected me. But he did. And his lack of trust widened the gulf between us.

The solution to the Boos crisis was a new location. A few blocks away, at 136 O'Farrell St., was a failed restaurant called the Rex. It had a carpeted dining space and a mezzanine, and its décor featured mirrored walls, mirrored columns, and twelve chandeliers. E.J. kept the dining room but added a two-counter cafeteria service in a partitioned-off area. He brought back the all-girl orchestra. He also named this new venture the Quaker Cafeteria, though unlike its predecessor, it was at the right place and the right time. The right place was the theater district. The right time was 1915, and the opening of the Panama-Pacific International Exposition, which would bring eighteen million tourists to celebrate San Francisco's return from the ashes and the completion of the Panama Canal. The Quaker Cafeteria became so popular that it had to stay open on Sundays.

But, in the midst of E.J.'s slowly burgeoning success, Clifford experienced another disaster. His mother was suffering a difficult pregnancy. She had to be hospitalized for the birth of her tenth child, Daniel. When she was released, she was ill again, probably from an infection caught in the hospital.

Just about one month later, on December 8, 1915, Gertrude Hall Clinton died. She was only forty-two years old.

Clifford struggled to reconcile the loss of his mother with her purposeful life. Even in death Gertrude was made to sacrifice.

> Our poor, dear Mother, who so longed to give her full measure of life on the altar of foreign service was forced to serve instead in the lives she gave her children. When Mother was laid to rest in the Sunset View Cemetery, there was insufficient money for a headstone. Father's debts were heavy, and his business needs required every penny.

As the Quaker was now open seven days per week, E.J. was no longer able to spend even a day a week with his family. To fill the vacuum left by E.J.'s absence, their grandfather David Clinton and other Parker Street relations came to spend time with the children, who looked forward all week to these visits. This gave Uncle Burton an opportunity to spend more time with Clifford, tutoring him in mathematics and talking to the young man about his dreams and plans.

On rainy Sunday afternoons, Burton gathered the family around the fireplace and moderated fireside chats. Anyone who happened to drop in was welcome. A topic had been chosen the previous week and the group discussed it at length. Topics included "Which is most important: the sun or the moon?" and "What is the most important thing in the world?" Both adults and children participated in these free-for-all discussions, and everyone was encouraged to express his or her viewpoint.

Occasionally, Burton would share more of his own philosophy. He was known to be a vegetarian, and while Clifford enjoyed sitting with him at Elmira's drop-leaf walnut table, eating nuts and dried fruit, he wanted to understand better why his uncle espoused this diet.

> Uncle B's answer was simple, so like his gentle spirit. He could not sanction the killing of living creatures for food when God had provided so much in abundance otherwise.

One of Uncle Burton's questions that lingered in Clifford's young mind was "Was not helping others the greatest thing a man could do?" Once Clifford quoted Burton in front of E.J. "What does Burton know?" snarled E.J. "He has never sold a play—never even earned a living. He is a failure." Clifford had heard talk that Burton had lost his only gainful employment—a position at a boys' school—to a nervous breakdown, and he came away from E.J.'s tirade trying to understand how he could hold both his father and Burton in equally high esteem.

And so, I began to discern that right or wrong, a man must answer his conscience, and that the answers are not always as clear as black and white. They vary from person to person, from people to people, and from time to time.

E.J. was contemptuous of his brother-in-law, but he was also wise enough to stop short of forbidding his son to spend time with him. Though Clifford respected his father, his feelings for Burton were much stronger.

> There was never any drastic command by Father to sever relations with Burton. If there had been, open rebellion would have been the result.

Following the end of the 1915 Pan Pacific Exposition, the Bancroft began to lose many of the tourists who came to eat while they were visiting the fair, which prompted E.J. to congratulate himself on relocating the Quaker. His cafeteria continued to thrive. Burton encouraged Clifford to attend Berkeley High School, and although he agreed to, his heart was in the family business. After a year, he dropped out and went to work full-time in the restaurant storeroom. There Clifford conquered his "learning disability" by acquiring applied knowledge in counterpoint with the nurturing support and education he received from his caring uncle at home. Clifford mastered the storeroom and then other jobs; mechanic, electrician, plumber, steam boiler operator, and even carpenter.

> The store was a hard but invaluable school. I finally seemed to be able to learn.

Clifford learned other aspects of food service and the fundamentals of business, and was probably unaware that he was turning very spare moments into a profitable experience. E.J.'s managers became Clifford's real teachers. From a former dining-car caterer he called Mr. Cady, Clifford learned how to make relishes and sauces, how to select cheeses to pair with other foods, how to marinate fish, assemble seafood cocktails, and prepare oysters on the half shell. He also learned cuts of meat and how to mix and garnish fine salads.

> I could do every job except office work. For my efforts, I was proud to receive eighteen dollars a week. I began to feel a sense of security and confidence.

Clifford's confidence did not extend beyond the walls of the cafeteria. He attended church, but at social events, shyness kept him on the sidelines. He was intimidated by young women, no matter how badly he wanted to meet them. The only friendships he knew were at work, where he was on safe ground and made friends with female coworkers as easily as with men.

> One was a strong boisterous girl. We tested each other's strength. It was innocent enough but when Father saw us, he felt otherwise, and she was fired. Later, I became smitten with a young woman who had previously been married and had a child. Our friendship

consisted of little more than talking together occasionally, but Father said if it were not broken off, she too would be fired. In a "heroic" gesture to save her job, I quit mine. This was the first real stand I took against Father.

Making a break with his father, however symbolic or temporary, gave Clifford time to see the world outside the Quaker. He was sixteen, developing a life philosophy, and he needed a neutral environment in which to cultivate ideas. He traveled to Mount Hermon, California (near Santa Cruz), where E.J. owned a small cottage. Clifford read newspapers and magazines and learned of the Great War in Europe, which was turning into the greatest armed conflict in the history of the world. When President Woodrow Wilson declared war on Germany in April 1917, Clifford was only seventeen and forced to wait until August 1918 when, with his father's tepid blessing, he enlisted and was sent to Camp Colt in Gettysburg, Pennsylvania, for basic training. Major Dwight Eisenhower was forming the first army tank corps, and Clifford was inducted into it for training as a tank gunner. He escaped the influenza epidemic and in less than three months was sailing to France on the S.S. *Leviathan* with the 336th Battalion. As he had so many years before, Clifford passed the voyage getting to know his fellow passengers.

> In each life there is an anchor of love. I felt this as the men talked of their sweethearts and wives. I had no love of this kind. The pride and affection I felt for Father, the love for the children and my dear aunts, uncle, and grandmother did not fill the need of young manhood I was feeling so keenly.

After some weeks, Clifford arrived in Liverpool, England, and then went to Southampton for training as a machine gunner with special courses in gas warfare. Clifford adapted well to military life, later noting that it was a period that shaped his adult life.

> Men are pulled out of a familiar environment, subjected to new pressures and lack of restraints. Some have religion and home to give them moral strength. Others succumb to temptation. As a newly commissioned sergeant, I was responsible for my men, some of whom, after drinking and carousing, could not find their way back to quarters. I felt it my duty to help them home. Food, drink, and women were the regular routine, and occasionally I witnessed sordid, wholesale affairs. Prostitutes were remarkably casual in their service. There was one horrible old woman who operated above the bar and served all comers within sight of the whole company. I was shocked and shamed by all I saw. It was a side of life of which I had known nothing but the secret talk of small boys.

Not all of Clifford's time at the front was picaresque. Most of it was miserable.

> For all my memories of France, those that remain are the rain, the mud and the very bitter cold.

While in France, Clifford began corresponding with Nelda Mae Patterson, a girl he knew from church back home in Northern California.

In November, he and his battalion were finally on their way to General John J. Pershing's headquarters at Chaumont, France, near the Marne River. They were within hearing distance of the big guns and could see biplanes.

> It was customary for us to get our news from the men returning on the adjoining tracks. This morning we suddenly realized that all was strangely quiet. The next passing train was filled with men shouting: "*Fini la guerre*!" (The war is over!). We were about as deflated as it is possible for men to be. We felt cheated.

Clifford spent months in a camp on the Girronne River in France, waiting to be sent back, and then, suddenly, he was marching to Bordeaux, where he was put on a Spanish steamer bound for New York. Once there, he was put on a train to San Francisco.

> Our move had been so sudden that there had been no time to send word of our coming. Now in San Francisco again, I was determined to wait the last ten days until my discharge at the Presidio before calling Father and surprising him.

Clifford had been receiving letters in France. In one, E.J. had said: "We'll welcome you home with a band." In others Clifford read that E.J. had met and married a wonderful evangelist named Rose Potter Crist. Unhappily for E.J., his oldest child, Evangeline, had taken an instant dislike to Rose and had even proposed to raise the other children herself. E.J. would have none of it. Evangeline defied him and brought the feud to their church, where the congregation took sides. Then Evangeline married a man named Paul Mills. Although this was the scene Clifford observed when he returned home, his mind was not on family squabbles.

> The nineteen-year-old soldier who awaited his discharge was a different person from the inexperienced lad who had gone out only a year earlier. I was ready to start life.

Before this could happen, he had to visit his father, and resolve his past. Instead, he impulsively went to reminisce at the old homestead on Haste Street. There was a new family living there. "We're the Pattersons from the church," said a woman who was—by a weird coincidence—the mother of the same Nelda Mae Patterson who had been writing to Clifford while he was stationed in France. Without giving him a chance to explain, they hailed his sister Evangeline, who happened to be nearby. Then the telephone rang. His father had somehow heard that Clifford was there. "If you want to come home at all," said E.J., "come right now." His harsh tone of voice shattered the otherwise joyous mood.

My dreams of a happy homecoming vanished. And I felt a return of the abysmal despair that always accompanied conflicts with father.

Clifford's anxiety was not misplaced. E.J. was in a cold fury. As usual, he turned a deaf ear to his son's explanations. He refused to listen to why Clifford had seen Evangeline first, and all he cared about was that Clifford had. Accidental or not, it amounted to the same thing—taking sides with Evangeline. E.J. had left the church because its members would not let Rose preach there. Having just come from a real war, Clifford knew nothing of the petty battles of Berkeley, but he was caught in the crossfire nonetheless. Clifford couldn't forget his father's words:

> "I dreamed of your coming home," he told me. "And of all it could mean, but it is plain to see that you have no regard for my feelings or respect for your home. I wish now that you had never come home."

Clifford spent a short, sad, awkward period at his father's new home, but soon found shelter with the Pattersons, who made a space for him in his old bedroom. He was fond of the Pattersons, yet maintained an air of shy formality. During a picnic, Nelda helped Clifford discover his tender, playful side by coaxing him out of his discomfort from a swollen tooth with flirtatious teasing. The two began courting.

> We usually ended our evenings with one of the marvelous ice cream concoctions at Haas's confectionery. . . . I was shy, dour, and old at twenty. Nelda's love and understanding were the balancing qualities I needed.

The Clinton-Patterson wedding took place on September 7, 1920, at the Friends Church in Berkeley. The couple chose it because it was neutral territory, and they hoped that the ceremony would not be spoiled by family quarrels. The reception was held at the Pattersons'.

> Father and Rose surprised us all by attending. They brought refreshments and a most charming touch: the ladies' orchestra from the cafeteria. Animosity was laid aside, and it seemed as if the dissent and strife had begun to heal.

E. J. was about to open the Clinton Cafeteria in the basement of the Flood Building on Market Street. He offered his son the position of manager in the new restaurant. As a gesture of reconciliation, Clifford agreed, but before he could assume the position, his father capriciously gave it to a cousin. Clifford was forced to settle for being assistant manager in the old restaurant.

> I was deeply disappointed, but I accepted this, as I had responsibilities, and our first child was expected.

Despite his disappointment, Clifford used his time at the new Clinton Cafeteria Company for self-improvement. He threw himself into his duties and focused on efforts to develop a system of operations and quality controls throughout the company. He took an economics extension course at University of California and a correspondence course in business law. He also wrote articles for trade journals. Unlike the missionary culture in which he was raised, where communication was personal and within small groups, written communication could reach far greater numbers of people and had the potential for a much wider impact.

Clifford occasionally filled in at the new cafeteria as relief manager, but it became obvious that his father had no intention of promoting him. He dreamed of a time when he could start his own business, a time when he would allow employees increased responsibilities and earnings—he even made personal loans to men and took ailing workers into his home, where Nelda helped them convalesce.

> I did not have my way made easier by being the boss's son. I wanted to make suggestions but was not permitted expression. I knew what it was to work long hours for a small paycheck, to be docked because of illness, to be ordered about and criticized. . . . I see now that gradually a whole philosophy had taken shape. It was during these years that I felt the urge to do something for those of my employees whose health or financial problems were interfering with their work.

In August 1921, Clifford turned twenty-one. He was officially an adult, and Nelda Clinton had given birth to their first son just months before. Though he was a married man, a father, and a rising restaurant professional, his filial conflicts continued. E.J.'s dress code for managers required them to wear white shirts. One day, Clifford dared to wear a pale blue shirt and was summarily fired.

5

STRIKING OUT ON HIS OWN

CLIFFORD CLINTON WAS NOT ONE TO SPEND TIME LICKING HIS WOUNDS. He returned to his odd jobs, assisted at times by Nelda's father, Fred Patterson. He had received severance pay from E.J. Rather than spend it on a new home, Clinton considered ways to invest it. He and Nelda had befriended a former employee named Rowe, a self-proclaimed stock market expert and a state-proclaimed ex-convict. Rowe convinced the Clintons to invest their entire savings of two thousand dollars with him in the market. With the profits that were sure to ensue, Rowe told them, Clinton and Uncle Burton would be able to open a cafeteria in the Oakland Federal Building. Clinton turned the cash over to Rowe and waited for the good news to come from New York. It never came. Clifford never heard from Rowe again.

Clinton and his wife struggled for a time. They had to sell their Milvia Street cottage and move back in with the Pattersons at 1907 Haste. To pay room and board, Nelda cooked and cleaned. Clinton worked on the construction of the University of California football stadium in the Berkeley hills.

> I pushed a wheelbarrow over narrow planks on high walls. I helped pour cement. Physical work always brought me satisfaction. I went into it in a frenzy of joy. A strange energy burned within me.

In 1923, the Clintons were blessed with a second child, Jean Marion. They were content to live with the Pattersons—theirs was a happy home. E.J., however, had moved Rose and his children to the Fruitvale district of Oakland, and theirs was neither happy nor loving. Evangeline reported that Robb Crist, Rose's son from a previous marriage, had taken up residence at E.J.'s. The prodigal son received the affection that Rose denied E.J.'s children.

> Robb was a clever, polished young man with a smooth manner. His quick repartee and easy use of language made me envious.

Before long, E.J. began to feel neglected, too; he confronted Rose. It was bad enough that he was giving Robb free lodging, lending him money for stock speculation, and paying to repair the family car, time and time again following Robb's periodic drunk-driving accidents, but Rose was spending all her time with her high-living son, and none with her husband or his children. E.J. wanted Rose to explain, and she was only too happy to clarify.

> Father had a rude awakening. Rose actually told him that she put her son, Robb, first in her affections, and put her husband second. The children, we knew, were an added burden. Now that her son was back, she poured out upon him all the indulgences she had been unable to lavish, during his years of travel, and wayward life. . . . After his disillusionment, [Father] spent more and more time at his business, making Rose resentful of the very thing that provided her with the luxuries of life. She often urged him to sell out. In confidence, one day, he told Nelda and I of his realization of his mistake in marrying, but said the marriage vows that he took would not permit him to abandon the marriage and that he would support Rose as long as she lived. But his heart was not in it anymore. Most pitiful was the gradual realization in E.J.'s heart that his children had slipped away, and he had not the ability to reach them, nor had he ever.

Clifford was taken aback when E.J. invited him to his office. He was even more surprised when his father offered him a job in his new cafeterias.

> When I was working there, and tried to go in and offer suggestions, I was brushed aside and told to come back later. I was surprised at this welcome. Father sat behind his double mahogany desk. I sat on the other side, facing him for the first time as an independent person. He went on to explain that he had an opportunity to expand. He had been offered the two Boos Brother locations, and he might consider one or two more places, thus making a Clinton chain of cafeterias in San Francisco. He offered me the position of supervising manager, if I would come and help to build this new Clinton Company.

Clifford was flattered by the offer, but he had been contemplating his goals and thought it was time to act, not simply react. He wanted to go to Los Angeles and study the intricacies of the cafeteria business from the ground up. E.J. realized that he was speaking to an adult. He had no choice but to let his son go.

> Since severing our connections with the cafeteria and E.J. in business, I felt free as I had never felt before. [Now] my basic desire was for a business of my own which I would operate on Christian principles.

Clinton had been thinking about a restaurant tour of Los Angeles as a way to formulate the best plan for a successful food-service business. He checked into a $3-a-week hotel downtown on Hill Street and proceeded to canvas the district. His first stop was the Boos Bros. Cafeteria at 618 South Olive. There were other inspiring restaurants in downtown Los Angeles as well, but the Boos Bros. Cafeteria intrigued him.

Horace, Henry, John, and Cyrus Boos had come to Los Angeles from Missouri in 1909 to open a delicatessen on Hill Street. Located in the center of the business district, the deli attracted workingmen who needed a convenient lunch establishment where they could sit and eat their noon meal. Horace, the brains of the outfit, came up with the idea of placing a plank along the front counter of the deli, providing small trays for customers to use after they had selected their menu choices. The chain had started there, and they had been very successful expanding their chain throughout the city.

Clinton applied for a low-level job. He was soon bussing tables. He was also taking notes on operations, policies, and management. To get an idea of how other cafeteria locations functioned, he attempted to move to another Boos Bros. Cafeteria at 648 South Broadway, though no jobs were posted. Because he was willing to work for meals and the secret education he was receiving, he was put to work cleaning tiled floors and walls. He was so diligent that he was offered a job in the storeroom. He declined it, seeking to peer behind the veil of yet another cafeteria, and summarily moving to Leighton's Cafeteria in the Arcade Building, where he held various jobs before being recognized by the manager, a former San Francisco restaurateur.

> We had a good laugh together, but I felt it was time to move on.

Clinton then visited the La Palma Cafeteria, and he was given a tour by its owner, James Manspeaker. The way the restaurant presented its food was a revelation to Clinton. Instead of white-enameled pans, there were cut-glass bowls and colorful pottery.

> The food counter was a thing of beauty. The difference between this and ours was as radical as that between a hospital ward and a trellised garden. . . . There was molded gelatin, tall bright glasses of whipped puddings, cakes dripping with luscious icings, warm fruit pies, and even freshly baked cake layers, ready to be topped with mouth-watering chocolate, caramel, nuts, and creams. The salads, meats, vegetables, and hot breads all reflected the same perfection, and were all seasoned with real butter or cream.

As eager as Clinton was to start his own business in balmy Southern California, he had neither the funds nor the opportunity to do it. And he had a wife and two children to support. After a month in Los Angeles, he returned to San Francisco and turned to his father for a job.

Again. This time, Clinton found that E.J. had made some changes in the executive structure of his business. James Gilchrist was still vice president, but Paul Mills, Evangeline's husband, was now secretary, and Robb Crist was now chief buyer. Clinton began working as a relief manager for the two Clinton locations. In 1926, a third child, Donald, was born to Clifford and Nelda.

At the same time, E.J. began eyeing the Boos Bros. Cafeterias at 725 and 1059 Market St. E.J., who had two successful restaurants, some stocks, and some sideline ventures, was able to secure sufficient bank credit to accumulate one hundred thousand dollars, which he used to purchase both Boos Bros. locations, along with the dining room of the Hotel Sutter at 48 Market St., the Crystal at 762 Market St., and a small satellite outlet at the YMCA. During this period of expansion, Clifford Clinton further developed a system of controls and established uniform operations between all the locations. He also studied trade journals and took economics courses. When he was invited to write an article for a journal, he felt publicly vindicated for all those years of being labeled a slow learner.

By late 1928, E.J. was operating seven restaurants. Even though the 1920s were boom years, only two of his shops were consistently profitable, and it became clear that he was not an effective manager. He was preoccupied with get-rich-quick goldmine schemes and his wife's incessant financial demands. She had made him give up his estate near Oakland for a small home on Forty-Second Avenue in San Francisco. Rose had insisted that by living in San Francisco, E.J. could save time and money by eliminating the train and ferry commute. Also, he would be closer to her son Robb, who could live with them. In addition to giving up his large comfortable home in Fruitvale, E.J. was forced to constantly placate her with trivial entertainments. At fifty-six, E.J. appeared to be vital and healthy, but seemed to Clinton to have become frustrated and worn down with constant worry about the success of his business and the dissatisfaction with his marriage to Rose.

At the same time, Clifford had finally acceded to the post of general manager. He hoped to have some freedom to apply the many lessons he had learned, but he was hamstrung by E.J., Mills, and Crist.

> I found myself unable to move freely in major policy issues. My function was limited to that of a steward, watching employees and maintaining standards of cleanliness.

Still seeking a way to advance his cause, Clinton worked with Uncle Burton to draft a proposal in which he could buy the two profitable restaurants from E. J.

"If I ever sell," E.J. sighed, "it will be everything. I will not sell the business to you alone. If I ever decide to sell, it will only be to Paul, Robb, and you. And it will only be for cash."

This was the signal for which Clinton had been hoping. He pulled Mills and Crist into a series of conferences. Little by little, they devised a way to buy the company. They used its liquid assets to buy shares of stock from E.J., Gilchrist, and the other shareholders in order to pay cash to E.J. for his stock. The three new owners were "up to our ears" In debt.

> We three each held equal interest. I was president and general manager, Paul Mills was secretary and treasurer, and Robb Crist was vice-president and purchasing agent. We had been given the finest thing any young man could ask—a chance.

Clinton threw himself into the business, brainstorming policy, a stock purchase plan for employees, and even a medical plan. He instituted an advertising program and an in-store publication; leaflets were placed on tables for customers to read while dining. He also began to build a comprehensive recipe file to ensure uniformity in weight and size of portions. Writing the file cards took months, and he could be seen scribbling away on the porch at Mount Hermon while his children played in the sun. He also undertook the repayment of bank loans.

> We had given ourselves substantial salaries, equal between the three, and we had disposed of several of the unprofitable stores. In the first year, we consolidated our strength, cut overhead and made a profit.

Yet little could have offset the damage from what was to happen in the last quarter of 1929.

E. J. owned a sizable portfolio of Bank of America stock. He borrowed against it in order to finance a new venture. A veteran Klondike miner named Billy West sold E.J. on the idea of reviving Bodie, California, which had been a booming goldmine in the 1870s.

> The old and rotting cabins and buildings of a hundred years ago, were falling down and were inhabited only by termites and spiders.

Though the bank had advised E.J. to sit on his stock, E.J. abandoned family and good sense alike for his ghost town.

In 1929, Clinton and Nelda were enjoying their prosperity and their newfound stability in family. Nelda's cousin, Charles Gowanlock, and his wife Lillian became part of the Clintons' life on Haste Street. Every Saturday night the Gowanlocks would join the Clintons in conversation, bridge, and dessert. The dessert would invariably be ice cream, Clinton's favorite. The two men would each eat a pint, but Clinton's rigorous exercise kept him slim and fit. Yet even innocent pleasures such as these would have unforeseen consequences.

On a Sunday afternoon in 1929, Clifford took his family to the Oakland Estuary to see some out-of-commission Navy craft. He spied an old destroyer waiting to be scrapped, and, after asking a bystander he assumed to be a watchman, took his family aboard. They came across a few unsalvaged items they thought would make fine souvenirs. As Clinton returned to the dock, an irate stranger strode over, shouting that he would make an example of these thieves. Despite

Clinton's attempts to explain, the whole group was taken to the Oakland jail. The children were released, but Clinton was fingerprinted and incarcerated. Maintaining his innocence, he refused to pay the fine. When it looked as though he would have to stay overnight, Nelda posted bail and he was released. Clinton appeared the next day before a judge, who threw the case out, but not before headlines screamed "Cafeteria President Jailed Robbing Destroyer."

The roar of the 1920s reached its crescendo on October 29, 1929. On that Black Tuesday, the stock market crashed. In one day, 16,410,030 shares were dumped and fourteen billion dollars melted into nothing. E.J.'s portfolio dropped 190 points. What cash he had left was tied up in Bodie, and soon evaporated. E.J. was wiped out. Clinton had been investing, too, in Miller and Lux, Union Oil, Security Bond and Finance, and Palos Verdes Estates. He had also bought land in East Oakland and acreage for a house in the Trestle Glen district of Oakland.

Meanwhile, the lease on the O'Farrell Street restaurant expired, so when the Clinton Company decided on another location, Clinton renewed his acquaintance with the Boos brothers' architect Charles Plummer.

> I worked closely with him on the plans, and went occasionally to his Los Angeles office. He was as handsome as he was likable. I was proud to have him for a friend.

Clinton met daily at lunch with the other directors on the board, Mills and Crist. But he couldn't convince them that investing in a new location was exactly what would increase the declining sales. His partners couldn't see beyond the dwindling revenue, feared spending any money, and voted no. As the economic situation worsened, the partners found it increasingly difficult to reach a consensus.

> I was still tantalized by the idea of my own place where I could test my unconventional ideas, but our heavy indebtedness made any change unlikely.

The new location had to be abandoned. Plummer was given a cash settlement for his work on the aborted project. As he left for Los Angeles, Clinton took him aside.

> If you ever come across a likely location, I want to get into business for myself.

In the bleak financial landscape of 1930, this request was a long shot. So Clinton busied himself with marketing research and efficiency projects. When he and his partners had taken over the business, its recipes existed only in the form of a chef's memory. If a chef departed, crisis ensued. Clinton determined that he could standardize the menu, offset staff turnover, and most importantly, introduce predictable uniformity to portion sizes—a revolutionary idea.

> We were serving 90,000 portions a day. Over-serving a quarter of an ounce per portion would waste $220 per day. Such an amount could spell the difference between profit and loss.

He tackled the problem by having wax models created for employees to match. Scales were introduced and sets of photographs mounted in albums. Clinton had just come up with the concept of portion control, something that would change the cafeteria business, and most restaurant businesses forever. Lastly, he began to write in a loose-leaf binder, articulating his ideas into what he called a "Manual of Operation."

Despite all his efforts, Clinton felt he was still losing ground. The freewheeling Crist had married a young woman in his own department. Mills was having trouble with Evangeline, who bitterly resented the partner setup. In long telephone conversations with Nelda and Clinton, she complained bitterly, claiming that although her husband was a one-third owner, she should have part of the business herself. For a time, Nelda suffered these tirades, but Clinton finally intervened. He would later say that he should have put his arm around her and tried to help her, but he was also feeling thwarted. So instead, he raged to his sister:

> I never want you to call our home again. I never want to speak to you again!

This turn of events did not improve the atmosphere at the office.

> I did not blame my partners for my dissatisfaction. They were by nature conservative. I was not.

It was a welcome surprise, then, when Clinton opened a telegram from Los Angeles. "Would you consider the 618 Olive St. location? Boos giving it up—signed Charles Plummer." Clinton did not wait to be asked twice. He boarded a train to Los Angeles.

As it transpired, the Boos brothers had sold their interests for eight million dollars to New York's esteemed Childs Company, which then misjudged both the market and the economy. The restaurant at 618 South Olive St. was losing six thousand dollars a month, a fortune in 1930.

> This was not the booming city I had visited five years before. The depression that followed the stock market crash had brought business low. Even the skyrocketing Leighton chain had been sold to a securities syndicate.

After sizing up the restaurant, Clinton traveled to New York and got a tentative agreement from the Childs management. He then returned to Los Angeles to meet with James G. Warren, who owned the property. Clinton was happy to learn that Warren was a Christian, and sympathetic.

He was a round and twinkling sort of man. He respected this young chap who was willing to gamble so heavily. I had only my dreams, but Mr. Warren had a losing business on his property. He needed a tenant who could bring it to life.

They signed a ninety-nine-year lease. "I will give you the lease," said Warren, rapidly. "I hope you make a lot of money—and make me a rich man!"

With things moving so quickly, Clinton had little time to think. When he finally did, the reality of the situation hit him. How would he present this to Mills and Crist? Would this restaurant fit the Clinton structure? After turning it over in his head, he decided that the best proposal was this: he would start a separate Clinton Company in Los Angeles, one that would be affiliated with the San Francisco Clinton, but one in which he would have full control of operations and policy. He resolved to present this to Mills, who was the more approachable of the two partners.

Before Clinton had even left for San Francisco, he received a telegram. "At a meeting of the board of directors, it was decided that your position and salary as general manager are hereby terminated." The telegram was signed by Paul Mills and Robb Crist. By a majority vote of two of the three board members, they felt they could terminate the third member.

6

EACH WAS A WELCOME GUEST

WHEN CLIFFORD CLINTON RETURNED TO BERKELEY, THE FIRST THING HE DID WAS SIT DOWN WITH NELDA AND THE CHILDREN FOR A FAMILY CONFERENCE. He wanted to know if his wife and children were willing to take a chance on a new business in Los Angeles. It could be the biggest gamble of their lives. When he saw that he had their support, he was ready to face his former partners.

He confronted Paul Mills and Robb Crist, saying that no meeting of the board was legal without proper notification. They might succeed in replacing him, but they had no right to deprive him of his share of the company's earnings. When he used the phrase "cause for legal action," the mood shifted. There were handshakes and assurances that his salary would continue for six months.

Before Clinton could move his family from Berkeley to Los Angeles to start his new cafeteria in the building at 618 Olive St., he and Nelda had to settle some financial issues and determine what was left after the market crash in 1929 to start this new venture. Their holdings in Miller and Lux, Security Bond and Finance, and Palos Verdes Estates were worthless. Their Union Oil stock had also declined dramatically when forty oil wells caught fire.

> We seemed a jinx to the whole stock market. Other than the cafeterias, our financial efforts were miserable failures.

Forced land sales in East Oakland and Trestle Glen brought a fraction of their original value. After liquidating all assets, Clinton came up with three thousand dollars, but at least a third of that was earmarked for moving and living expenses until income from the new place started to come in. He and Nelda needed the full three thousand dollars to secure the lease with James Warren. Charles Plummer agreed to donate one thousand dollars to the cause, becoming a twenty-five percent partner. Clinton borrowed additional money and was then able to sign the lease for 618 South Olive.

At dawn on June 27, 1931, an old Studebaker rolled south. It carried two employees and three Clintons: Clinton, Nelda, and Clinton's brother Joe. It was loaded with luggage, the Manual of Operation, and 2,500 recipe cards. No kids. The family had decided that the Clinton children would stay in Berkeley until their parents got on their feet in L.A. No Uncle Burton. His health was fragile, so he stayed behind.

Emblematic of their hopes for guidance and protection on their new frightening undertaking, the group had tied six special angel cake tins to the rear bumper. This trip to Los Angeles was made with the stark knowledge of the risks and unknown future that awaited them in this new city. Clinton summed it up:

> Though we often see in luminous brilliance the distant goal, the great challenge is to overcome the actual obstacles as they inevitably appear in real life among the most difficult being other men's objections and fears. . . . On this trek, we were living in stark reality. Angel cake tins were fine. What we really needed were angels.

The clan arrived in Los Angeles on June 28, 1931, three days before the new lease on the restaurant space was to begin. The temperature hovered in the mid-eighties, the first sign that things would be decidedly different from Berkeley. After settling into the Winton apartment building at 219 South Flower St., Clinton turned his thoughts to naming his new establishment. It had to be different from the Clinton Company in San Francisco, and yet Clinton wanted some connection with the past. He found it in *Clifton*, which combined his two names, *Clif*ford and Clin*ton*, just as this venture combined commerce with ideals.

> My challenge was to make this enterprise conform to the goal that had for so long been the driving factor of my life. Clifton's Cafeteria would be a successful business because it would give service to others, and through it we could express Christian philosophy.

He vowed to keep that philosophy always in the forefront of the business. The Manual of Operations laid out policies, all based on the Golden Rule: "Do ye therefore unto others that which ye would have them do unto you." He planned to implement these policies through the Wheel of Service, which applied the Golden Rule to all the spokes of the wheel. These included: (1) the customer (the "guest"); (2) the employee (the "associate"); (3) the business; and (4) the community.

There was much to do in preparation for the opening. The space had deteriorated some in the interval since the time the Boos brothers vacated and sold out to the Childs Company. Clinton had wired architect Charles Plummer while still in San Francisco to purchase equipment and necessary furnishings, but placement of stoves, food preparation and storage equipment, and arrangement of the dining room had to be accomplished. Plummer was in charge of restoration and redecorating. The firm of Miller and Petersen was hired to put the plans into action amidst scaffolding and drop cloths. The dark Moorish interior was enhanced with brighter colors, and palm trees and a central fountain added interest. (The original exterior was plain and uninspired. This would not change until the remodeling in 1938.) By one hour past midnight on July 1, 1931, everything was completed.

Despite the renovations, Clifton's was open for business. Four hundred guests, including curious passersby and many former loyal Boos Bros. customers, came the first day.

> Landlord James Warren came to wish us well. He kept a sharp eye on the remodeling and on the customer count. Nelda stood near the front door, greeting each patron. She also brought water and the morning paper to each table, and expressed her heartfelt appreciation to each patron We prized every one and directed both the employees who had come from San Francisco and the staff who had remained from Boos Bros. to give each guest the maximum value for the lowest price."

Clinton affixed a poem called *Doors* to the blotter on his desk, a poem that expressed his feelings about the entrance to his new restaurant at 618 South Olive. The work by an anonymous poet remained there for the rest of Clinton's life.

> Some doors have hearts, it seems to me,
> They open so invitingly;
> You feel they are quite kind—akin
> To all the warmth you find within.
> Some doors, so weather-beaten, gray
> Swing open in a listless way,
> As if they wish you had not come;
> Their stony silence leaves you dumb.
> Some classic doors stand closed and barred,
> As if their beauty might be marred
> If any sought admittance there,
> Save king or prince or millionaire.
> Oh, may mine be a friendly door;
> May all who cross the threshold o'er,
> Within find sweet content and rest,
> And know each was a welcome guest.

Like Warren, Plummer caught the spirit of the venture. He visited daily at lunchtime, greeting patrons.

Mr. Plummer's good looks were truly an asset. He became such a familiar sight on the floor that he was known as "Mr. Clifton." Because of my innate shyness, I was glad to have it so.

Regardless, Clinton was too busy managing to be a greeter. His manual was constantly open as he approached each facet of his cafeteria's presentation. Drawing on years of research, he prettified the food display, adding color and texture, and then lowered prices. Breakfasts were twelve cents, lunches nineteen cents, and dinners twenty-four cents. After installing an ice cream plant, he opened a fountain and milk bar. "All You Wish" ice cream was ten cents. A milkshake too thick for a straw cost twelve cents.

Clinton strove to make Clifton's Cafeteria a place that served more than just food. A sign hung near the cashier's desk that read: "Food for the Soul Is Important, Too." To lighten Depression blues, Clinton introduced entertainment that he had known in San Francisco. He purchased an organ, and St. Louis organist Julius Johnson started playing. Hired on a temporary basis, Johnson became so popular with guests that he was soon permanently employed. On Friday and Saturday evenings, he played old favorites such as "The Old Rugged Cross," while he conducted sing-a-longs with guests.

It gave one and all a moment's pause. Many of our guests stayed late to enjoy these evenings, which provided free entertainment at a time when money was scarce. On Saturday nights, talented guests and local groups performed.

College students performed choral music, which brightened moods and encouraged guests to stay longer at their tables and converse with other diners. This more than anything created a homey environment, which attracted many newcomers to Los Angeles who had left their social networks behind. The entertainment continued until World War II, when an entertainment tax was levied on restaurants, putting an end to the concerts.

The word began to spread in local businesses and hotels that the new cafeteria was something special. In its second week, Clifton's served more patrons each day. The next week five hundred meals were served, then six hundred, and finally the week arrived in which one thousand meals were registered. Clifton's had begun to gain in daily receipts, but still, neither Clinton nor Plummer was drawing a salary. When the time arrived that one thousand meals were served in a single day, it was cause for celebration, even though the dining room was still festooned with tarpaulins and cluttered with ladders. Once up to speed, Clifton's employed 150 associates and served an average of eight hundred guests daily.

The Manual of Operations that Clinton had begun writing when he was still in San Francisco emphasized the practical application of the Golden Rule to the cafeteria business, and it was this thinking that drove his policies at Clifton's. Applied to his guests, the principle dictated guests be treated the way he wanted to be treated—as honored guests in his home. For his employee "associates," this meant equality and broad benefits. He listened to associate concerns by creating representative committees, provided wages on par with other business, and provided a medical plan, a groundbreaking concept in the restaurant industry at the time. The plan paid for all surgical, medical, and prescription costs, as well as a week's free hospital care for each year of service. In 1938, Clinton purchased a large home on the corner of Los Feliz and Western Avenues in Los Angeles. He converted an upstairs porch or solarium into an illness-recovery suite. He and Nelda cared for several cafeteria employees while they were recovering from illness. He provided employees half-price meals, even on days off.

To say that Clinton's philosophy was unusual would be an understatement. One had only to look at his competitors—teashops, cafés, speakeasies, and swank hotel restaurants—to see that Clifton's Cafeteria was unique. Clinton knew he was odd.

Sometimes my approach was just too radical!

No one else would dare put this sign at the entrance: DINE FREE UNLESS DELIGHTED. No other eatery had this printed at the bottom of its checks:

This is our estimate of the value of your meal. Please pay what you wish.
Dine Free Unless Delighted.
Please pay what you wish.

One morning the restaurateur was standing by the register when a thin young man stepped up to him. He recognized him as an employee of a nearby drugstore. "Mr. Clifton," the man said, "I've lost my job. Will you help me get by? I will pay you when I get work." Clinton knew that this man was eating only the smallest meals. Could he morally turn him away? *"No guest shall go hungry for lack of funds."* Putting his arm around him, he assured him that Clifton's would carry him. Within two months the man was working again. He became a staunch Clifton's booster.

To Clinton this was not just a business policy, but rather a humanitarian obligation. He had not forgotten the starving faces he saw in China. He had not forgotten Charles Sheldon's *In His Steps*. Written in 1897 by the Congregationalist minister who later helped lead the Social Gospel movement, the novel put the teachings of Jesus Christ in an urban context. "What would Jesus do," wrote Sheldon, "about the army of unemployed who tramp the streets and curse the church? Would He go His way in ease and comfort?" Clinton would ask those questions, as would generations long after him.

Clinton believed that profits earned by Clifton's Cafeteria could help feed the needy. As his unorthodox policy became known, more destitute people found their way to Clifton's, lining up early in the morning on Olive Street and blocking the way of paying customers. In Clifton's first

CLIFTON'S AND CLIFFORD CLINTON

three months of operation, ten thousand people were served under this policy, for the Great Depression was worsening. Faced with a surge of unhappy, unkempt, sometimes unscrupulous humanity, Clifton's began to lose momentum. Clinton continued to feed the poor, but his business began to suffer. He was losing twenty cents on each person who asked for a free meal. At this rate, he would soon be unable to meet his day-to-day expenses, let alone pay his creditors.

One of Nelda's breakfast customers told her, "I expect to see you in my court one of these days." She learned he was a judge in bankruptcy court.

> We did not believe that the Golden Rule required us to be destroyed. Our joining the breadline would not help the hungry. The answer to a problem always awaits us.

The answer came in the form of a large basement. Clinton leased an old cafeteria at Third and Hill Streets, and, on October 10, 1932, in addition to a convention cafeteria on the main floor, he opened his latest innovation, the Penny Cafeteria, which was quickly nicknamed the "caveteria" by locals, and sneeringly by the *Los Angeles Times*, because of its underground setting. In the Penny, the poor and hungry could buy a portion of food for one cent. The menu was simple, with wholesome, nourishing foods: macaroni, beans, stews, thick soups, salads or slaws, bread, dessert, coffee. The average meal cost just four cents.

To make this possible, suppliers sold their food to the Penny Cafeteria at cost. Langendorf Bakery supplied day-old bread for one cent a loaf. Markets supplied fresh produce at a negligible cost; some even gave their product free. Many people volunteered services; artists, musicians, and florists contributed to this humanitarian project. Tickets were printed in one-cent denominations and sold at the 618 South Olive restaurant. Guests and charitable agencies purchased and then gave away these tickets. During the service hours, there was always a queue down the block. His Golden Rule approach wasn't received well by his critics, so much so that he submitted an editorial to local newspapers:

> We have been severely condemned for our operation of the Penny. There was fear it would cause more drifters to remain in our city.

The fear was unfounded. When the worst of the Depression had passed, he determined that the Penny had served its purpose. By 1934, the underground spot had served two million people. Clinton closed its doors.

Even with the relief provided by the Penny, Clifton's on Olive was not prospering. Even when the daily count of guests reached one thousand, things began to look truly hopeful, but there were still no profits to share; all money in excess of bills had gone to improvements.

A certain amount of skepticism of Clinton's Golden Rule policy remained in the public's mind. As kind-hearted and giving as it seemed, many people wondered whether Pay What You

Wish and No Guest Need Go Hungry for Lack of Funds were too naïve or trusting to work. The question of individuals taking advantage of or abusing this kindness often arose.

> There was a very small percentage who tried to defraud us. A young man ate day after day, and to the enormous amount of fourteen dollars. He then would walk out saying, "I'm not paying." Managers spoke to him. He said the food and service were alright, but he wasn't going to pay. We decided to test the policy, in the interest of preserving it for the good of all. Our policy is a guarantee of satisfaction, not an invitation to a free dinner. This young man had stated his determination to pay nothing—after declaring that both food and service were satisfactory. In the presence of a police officer, he was again asked if they were satisfactory. He said yes but still refused to pay. He was arrested, charged with intent to defraud, and soon convicted. Upon his release, he commenced to park his car in front of our business. His car was plastered with signs slandering Clifton's. He would stand in front of it for hours, passing out circulars containing derogatory statements. In time he was made to desist.

In late 1933, as a result of President Franklin D. Roosevelt's policies, the economy started improving. About the same time, Clifton's operating expenses began to fall in line, and Clinton saw that his business was going to survive. Nelda was able to come home in the afternoons. The long days of struggle were shortened. It was time to relax a bit. Up to this time, Clinton and Nelda's sole escape had been to drive through the city at midnight, stopping for the watermelons displayed on Beverly Boulevard under a cascade of ice water.

> Life took on new meaning now. On Saturdays our children came down to work on the service counter, fill glasses, and do other chores in the family business. This was what I had done in my early days.

After expanding Clifton's to Third Street, Clinton opened a unit at Hollywood Boulevard and Western Avenue called the Holly Western, and then a little unit in Whittier called Clifton's Whittier. And, 618 was doing a great business. Sometimes it was so busy that Clinton himself had to bus tables. A customer watched him bustling about and commented to one of his associates, "That new busboy is working too hard. If he keeps up that pace, he won't live very long."

"That's the owner," the associate told the customer.

"It can't be true," said the customer. It was true, of course. And, like so much at Clifton's, it flew in the face of convention. As the word spread, there came the inevitable pooh-poohing. This Clifford Clinton was just too good to be true. His ideas were outlandish, impractical, naïve. But they worked.

DRAWING FROM THE SILENCE

A VERY POPULAR FEATURE AT CLIFTON'S CAFETERIA WAS A WEEKLY BROCHURE CALLED *FOOD FOR THOT* THAT WAS PLACED ON EACH TABLE, AIMED AT THE SOLITARY DINER. It contained verses, inspirational paragraphs, and articles about Clifton's latest innovations. But the success of the eatery was due in large part to Clifford Clinton's willingness to listen. He was, in fact, very eager to hear opinions, especially if the ideas would improve his customer counts. For that reason, *Food for Thot* (which was often titled *Food 4 Thot*) included a section called "Guest Voice" which encouraged patrons to submit criticism. In the next issue, Clinton could answer the patrons. Clinton wanted the leaflet to promote discussion, and it did. He delighted in printing disapproving letters that were usually anonymous and sent with the challenge: "You won't dare print this." That he did spoke volumes of his sense of fair play.

Los Angeles was racially diverse, but dominated by white Anglo-Saxon Protestants. As many food service establishments violated state antidiscrimination statutes by discouraging the patronage of blacks and Asians, Clifton's color-blind policy was forthright and controversial. One guest wrote to *Food for Thot*: "I have always liked Clifton's, but yesterday while I was having lunch, two Negroes came and sat at my table. After that the food tasted like sawdust. I like the Negro people, but I refuse to eat or sleep with them. I will hereafter go where they do not have Negroes."

In his response, Clinton expressed regret at the loss of a valued friendship, but stood firm:

> It is our duty to serve all who enter our doors and conduct themselves within their
> legal rights.

Clinton would later comment that it was "easier to smash an atom than to break a prejudice."

One day, Clinton's son Donald who was just turning six years old, came to Clifton's to celebrate his birthday. A cake was presented, Julius Johnson played "Happy Birthday" on the organ, and a new idea suddenly clicked with Clifford. As he watched his son bask in the attention, he thought, why not offer birthday parties for his guests? Clifton's could set the table, provide the cake and decorations, and families could celebrate. This idea stuck and became a favorite among a half-million celebrants over the years. To Clinton, this feature was biblical and "blessed him who gives and him who receives."

As he looked out into the new crowds coming to Clifton's, Clinton realized that his associates and many customers were young people living alone in rooming houses and nearby hotels. It occurred to him that these people needed better housing and that he could help. In 1934, he met with the head of the Hotelmen's Association, Ray Langer. The pair partnered to form "The Hotel Company." Two downtown hotels, the Clifton and the Figueroa, were selected since they were well constructed and within walking distance of the cafeteria. Associates and guests could rent rooms for three dollars a week, and they also received a card entitling them to a twenty-five-percent discount at Clifton's. Soon, bus service from the hotels to the cafeteria was provided mornings and evenings, leaving every thirty minutes. All six hundred available rooms were quickly occupied, and there was a waiting list. The arrangement proved extremely lucrative for the owners.

Official records from Langer's estate showed that in 1944 Nelda and Clinton earned twenty-six thousand dollars for one year's net profit from the partnership. They made sufficient profit from these hotels to invest in cafeteria refurbishing and investments in buildings and securities.

Clinton tried to help a wide variety of downtown residents, many of whom were retired. An elderly woman who was a Clifton's regular, gradually stopped coming. "I loved Clifton's," she wrote, "but I am growing so blind that I cannot cross the street." Clinton arranged for an associate to escort the woman from her hotel twice daily. When her eyesight failed completely, he delivered meals to her room.

There were also young, single people who found it difficult to meet others. Clinton instituted an exchange board at the front of the building. For a small fee, guests could place a typed card listing items for sale or exchange. But the most talked-about heading was, of course, Lonely Hearts, where a person could place a code number and a message. Replies led to friendship and sometimes to marriage. Clinton also instituted a barbershop, a sightseeing bus, and a daylong trip to Switzer's Camp at the foot of Mt. Wilson, so city dwellers could see more of the beauty of Southern California.

> These ventures *were* Clifton's. We were trying to be a *service* to our community. The
> bus, the barber shop, and Switzer's camp were not great earners, nor were earnings

intended. Our aim was to have them be self-supporting and bring added services to our patrons. The prices, were kept in relation to the "Repression" period, which followed the Depression.

Clinton had never been interested either in drinking alcohol nor in serving it. Prohibition was in force, and although many establishments chose to ignore it, he felt an obligation to the ministers who encouraged their congregations to visit Clifton's after Sunday services because it was a wholesome place. When Prohibition was repealed in 1933, Clinton's associates suggested that beer might attract more customers, but he refused. When Clinton was quoted from the pulpit of local churches around town, parishioners came to support him and his no-alcohol policy. His Sunday business boomed:

> We cannot reject the basic principles of our Christian training. This decision has been made for us.

In 1935, the Clintons moved to a home on Wilton Place in a prestigious neighborhood in Los Angeles, and the Pattersons were living with them. Clinton severed the last ties with his Bay Area life when he sold his share in the Clinton Company to Paul Mills, who by then had divorced Evangeline. Aunt Mabel and Uncle Burton had both died. Clinton's own family was cohesive and cheerful, a contrast to his childhood.

Charles Plummer was still a partner and a stalwart, but his architectural firm needed him, so he suggested Clinton hire Ransom "Calli" Callicott, a Boos Bros. Cafeteria manager. Calli mortgaged his Highland Park home and bought Plummer's one-fourth interest in Clifton's. Clinton was grateful to share the load:

> I had always felt the need of a partner—one who could handle operations. I knew enough of my own personality. When a project was launched and running smoothly, I was not the one to oversee it. By nature I was a radical, driven to analyze, to make changes, to improve. Such a temperament does not accept routine.

With Callicott running the business, Clinton was free to concentrate on those many complex projects that really engaged him.

> I had never wanted to build a one-man business, as is so easy to do in the food service line. A popular personality can so build himself into his enterprise, that the survival of the enterprise is dependent on his personal presence. My true aim was to build a worthy service that could survive and prosper without any one member.

Though he had added many features to Clifton's, his prices stayed the same, and on that point, a competitor attempted to overtake him. The Childs Company had its main Boos Bros.

Cafeteria at 720 South Hill St. One day Clinton was startled to see a banner stretched across its façade. ALL YOU CAN EAT FOR 45 CENTS! Putting aside his distaste at its implied gluttony, Clinton contemplated its economics. He could not see how this company could make such an offer. Boos Bros. had been struggling for survival. He knew this because its employees were coming into Clifton's to "case the house." They would become chummy with management, all the while clocking the number of patrons. While Clinton's competitors were sizing up his establishment, calling it a circus, his customers were multiplying. Theirs were vanishing. First Leighton's closed and then the Edison.

Suddenly the tables turned. "All You Can Eat" became a catchphrase. Customers were no longer interested in the quality and service they could receive at Clifton's—only in how much food they could get for a fixed price. Boos Bros. was mobbed, its lines stretching down the street. Even after reports that people had literally eaten themselves to death, customers kept coming. Month by month, Clifton's grew quieter. Its earnings turned to losses. Many of Clinton's employees left to work at Boos.

In desperation, Clinton authorized his remaining staff to spy on the place.

> We made studies of hundreds of their guests' trays. On the basis of known costs, their average check was costing them a dollar, sometimes four or five, as guests could return an unlimited number of times. We checked our calculations again and again to see where we were missing the secret, but always arrived at the conclusion that they must be losing their shirts.

Clinton was certainly losing his. He was more than thirty days behind on his bills, and vendors were losing patience. Though Clifton's was in crisis, Clinton believed there was no problem that couldn't be solved.

> There is an answer. It can be found by seeking the advice of experts, by assembling the available knowledge, by listing the different approaches, and then leaving the answer to Divine guidance. Release your mind from the problem. Cut the thread of thought. Go off somewhere. Take a trip. Play. Sooner or later the answer will come. Often it will appear too simple, too different from our conception. The challenge is to be sensitive enough to hear it. To know it for what it is, and to be courageous enough to follow it. God is Master of All and He works in mysterious ways.

Clinton's conundrum continued for weeks. How could he improve this situation in which Clifton's was losing customers to a cafeteria that seemed oblivious to the increased cost of "All You Can Eat" without plunging his own business into the same losing spiral? Part of the answer came from his analysis of the Boos Bros. system. The cafeteria was packing in the customers, but its service was declining. The quality of the food was low, the counters were unsightly, and the tables were stacked with dirty dishes. The staff was indifferent to their patrons. There was confusion and noise.

Clinton saw the answer to his problems when he thought about the consequences of customer indifference. What if Clifton's offered an "All You Can Eat" plan but kept its commitment to service and quality standards? Finally, a workable solution. He decided to try "All You Can Eat," but on his own terms, without cheapening his business, without sacrificing the touches that made Clifton's unique—the spotless settings, the singing, the attentive hostesses and associates. And of course, the moral lesson was always there:

> A hungry person who receives food from an understanding heart receives far more than bodily nourishment. His spirit has been touched by something intangible.

Up went the banners. The Boos Bros. staff chortled, but their scorn was short lived. Up went the attendance. Clifton's daily headcount rose from the hundreds to the thousands, leveling off at ten thousand. Landlord James Warren could hardly find a seat in the dining room when he came to lunch. Paul Mills and Robb Crist journeyed to Los Angeles to observe the phenomenon. In a few months, Boos Bros. was empty. In a few more months, it closed.

Clinton's creative response to "All You Can Eat" kept Olive Street Clifton's afloat. His breakfast business was still too scant, but at least the number of lunch and dinner patrons increased substantially. Further attempts to increase the number of breakfast patrons included music, which wasn't the answer, and handing out newspapers to each breakfast guest, which was. Providing an egg cooker and a fast double-tray counter helped to increase volume for busy morning customers. Olive Street business improved, and Clinton realized that his various strategies had paid off.

The Penny Cafeteria was still in operation in 1934 but was serving fewer meals as economic conditions improved. The Works Project Administration (WPA), Civilian Conservation Corps (CCC), and general welfare programs were reducing the number of unemployed, so there were fewer indigents to serve.

That year, Clinton noticed two well-dressed visitors in the Penny asking those in line if they needed meal tickets. These men had purchased rolls of tickets to hand out to those in need. One of the men mentioned his employer, a Mr. Carr, would be interested in meeting and talking with Clinton. Somewhat surprised, Clinton agreed to meet with Carr at his private home where Clinton recognized him as someone who had been a frequent visitor to the Penny. Owner of the vacant property that had been occupied by one of the now defunct Boos cafeterias at 648 South Broadway, Carr proposed that Clinton take over the lease.

"I like the way you do business," Carr said, noting that he was particularly impressed with Clinton's concern for the needy. From a purely business standpoint, Carr liked Clinton's ability to feed two million people at the Penny for twenty thousand dollars.

The new location was prime, situated in the center of the theater district, which meant that people going to the moving pictures at the Los Angeles, the State, or the Orpheum, could eat at Clifton's first. Clinton felt an instant bond with Carr and after consulting with his own management team, agreed to pay three thousand dollars for the lease. Carr's attorney drew up a forty-page contract. Clinton did not read it. Neither did Carr.

"Is it alright with you, Mr. Clinton?"

"If it's alright with you, Mr. Carr."

The deal was struck, and Clinton felt justified. The bread he cast on the water with the Penny Cafeteria had come back to him in the form of a ninety-nine-year lease to this desirable real estate. He had no idea how desirable it was until a realtor approached him and offered him fifty thousand dollars for the property.

Ideas do reward, even in terms of the hardboiled businessman.

By 1935, Clifton's was open for business at 648 South Broadway. The Penny Cafeteria had closed, and some of the equipment was moved to South Broadway. A version of the Penny meal was instituted in the basement of "648" where individuals without funds could still receive meals free and those who could afford it, paid a nickel. They called the new meal, the Subsistence Meal.

This five-cent meal, assembled on a tray and transported on gravity rollers, provided no individual selection. A complete meal from soup to sherbet, it could be assembled in seconds, picked up by the guests who then sat at dining tables. No questions were asked if the guest lacked funds. As many as 1,500 nickel meals were served daily. (Ten years later when Clinton worked as a military-food consultant, he adapted the basics of this meal for countries plagued with postwar starvation.)

The 648 location was propitious, but the interior of the property was uninviting, an expanse of sterile, white tile. Clinton fondly remembered the Brookdale Lodge near Mount Hermon in the Santa Cruz Mountains where he spent much time in his early days. The lodge had a real brook laden with trout flowing through its dining room. He commissioned Plummer to turn the new cafeteria into a lodge, so Plummer and his team went to work. The columns supporting the dining room were covered with redwood tree bark, trucked from the mountains. Artist Einar Petersen painted murals of redwood forests. Sculptor Francois Scotti fashioned a life-size brook (minus the trout) and a towering waterfall. The remodeling took eight months, with the cafeteria remaining open for business. The result was Clifton's Brookdale Cafeteria.

Although they came for the food, customers inevitably talked about the ambience at Brookdale. How could they not? There were three levels of dining: the main floor, the mezzanine, and the second floor. A musical trio serenaded guests from the Melody Ledge mezzanine with an Einar Petersen forest mural as its backdrop. Associates and other amateurs often added to the entertainment. Another Petersen mural of a redwood grove was painted to cover the two-story back wall in the main dining room, so guests had the sensation of dining in the middle of a forest. On shelves around the room were forest animals including a grizzly bear, a raccoon, and a deer. In one corner was a cross section of a 1,400-year-old redwood tree trunk, with its rings labeled to show historic events, including the signing of the Magna Carta in 1215. Surrounding the second floor were backlit photographs of forests, streams, and mountains.

To select their food, guests walked through a tunnel on the left of the entry that took them past backlit photographs of sequoia trees to a stainless steel tray line. As guests moved along the line, they encountered individual food items arranged on beds of ice. Different flavors of Jell-O were displayed near salads of cottage cheese, lettuce and carrot, and coleslaw. Baked apples were next, then fruit cocktails and desserts. Choices of pie included apple, custard, and lemon meringue, and, when in season, strawberry. Guests then turned the corner to the hot food aisle where they found baked halibut, prime rib, and turkey carved to order. Chicken Parmesan was a favorite dish, but by far the most beloved was Clifton's Macaroni and Cheese. Stuffed bell peppers, green vegetables, and potatoes were kept hot with special heat lamps. At the beverage station, cherry sodas, lemonade, and iced tea were arranged by color, with chocolate and regular milk, tea, and coffee nearby. Not far away was a selection of ice cream, each serving packaged in a square box.

The third floor was later made into group meeting rooms, including the larger "Red Room" which contained the framed oil painting of the founders of Clifton's. One of the notable regular diners was Ray Bradbury.

Soon after Brookdale's opened, Clinton installed a small chapel of simulated rock on the edge of the mezzanine overlooking the main dining room. Inside the chapel was a forest diorama that included a recording by radio actor Gayne Whitman reading Patience Strong's poem, *The Groves, God's First Temple*:

> If you stand very still in the heart of a wood, you will hear many wonderful things—the snap of a twig and the wind in the trees and the whir of invisible wings.
>
> If you stand very still in the turmoil of life, and you wait for the voice within—you'll be led down the quiet way of Wisdom and Peace in a mad world of chaos and din.
>
> If you stand very still and you hold to your faith, you will get all the help that you ask—you will draw from the Silence the things that you need—Hope and Courage and Strength for your task.

One day in October 1935, shortly after leasing and refurbishing the Broadway cafeteria location, Clinton was standing near the cafeteria entrance when a man he recognized approached him. John Anson Ford was a regular guest, and Clinton knew that he was on the Los Angeles County Board of Supervisors. Ford introduced himself to Clinton and said that he had come to Clifton's because his advertising firm was only a block away. Ford paused and then made his appeal. "Mr. Clinton, the Board is hearing complaints about the food service at the County General," Ford explained. "As chairman of the committee which directs the hospital, I would like to call upon you to make a survey and investigation of that institution and report your findings to the Board."

Clinton was taken aback.

> Of politics I knew nothing. But I knew the County General Hospital.

County General dominated the landscape of East Los Angeles. It was a honeycomb of concrete that held nearly two thousand beds for low-income patients of the city. Ford explained that there were rumors of extravagance and waste in food preparation and delivery to indigent patients. A committee was needed to investigate. Would Mr. Clinton be interested in heading such a committee? It was clear that Mr. Ford wanted a "yes."

Clinton discussed it with his family and told Ford that he was willing. Other committee members included Mrs. Edna Davis, a caterer at Pomona College; Mrs. Harry A. Ford, a caterer at the Ebell Club; and Ransom Callicott, who was now Clifton's vice president. The members made four visits to the hospital, on different days at various meal times, undertaking a thorough inspection and review.

> This hospital was the largest institution of its kind in the world. It was also a huge, cumbersome institution. It had a kitchen of enormous proportions situated a great distance from food services. There was mismanagement, favoritism, and waste.

After due research and consideration, on April 11, 1936, Clinton submitted his "Report on Food Services at the General Hospital" to Supervisor Ford and the board. The report covered facilities, costs, food, and employees. It stated that the hospital's food service was inefficient, with facilities, equipment, and space enough for four times the patients and employees it was serving. Employees, including physicians and nurses, would be more efficiently served if some of the dining areas were closed and a rotating meal service instituted. Patient meals were excessively starchy. Patients were receiving cold food that should have been hot. Many items were unpopular, such as raw apple desserts, raw cabbage salads, and undercooked vegetables. The committee found a scandalous amount of waste. Unsliced bread served in chunks was left untouched. Only twenty percent of the milk served in large containers had been consumed. Patients left great quantities of food on their trays. Service was very poor. Food was served in the men's ward by an old man in overalls who was unshaven and discourteous. The food service favored hospital staff over patients, serving prime cuts to doctors and nurses, while patients got stew.

Clinton and his committee offered a course of change. There should be more varieties of food and smaller quantities prepared. Food should not be slopped onto plates, but prepared and served with precision. Both food and the plates should be warmed before service. The group felt meals should be better balanced and seasoned to taste. Ice cream and Jell-O would make more appetizing desserts than raw apples. Attendants who served the patients should be hired for efficiency, as if they were in a private food establishment.

The most controversial report dealt with the kitchen staff. Food preparation areas were overstaffed with careless employees. Forty dishwashers did the work of twenty-seven stations. Workers stood idle in every area. Supervision was lax. Attitude was poor. The committee recommended cutting staff from twenty-five to fifty percent.

The report was filed April 11, 1936, and on April 28, Ford wrote a letter to Clinton and Callicott. He stated:

> I want to take this opportunity to thank you and the other members of your committee most sincerely for the very valuable piece of work which you have done with respect to the Hospital. The data which you have placed before us is going to be of very great benefit to us in preparing our budget and in working toward a better Hospital administration.

Ford sent another letter on July 9 that stated:

> I think there is significance in the fact that recent personnel changes at the Hospital followed closely on the work of your committee.

Supervisor Ford's July follow-up letter to Clinton informed him of the consequences of the report. Ford was using the report to shuffle positions at the hospital. Because of the committee's report, the board was able to shave $120,000 from the hospital budget in the next fiscal year. What did this mean? It meant that someone would not be happy about it. But who? According to Ford, there was a "political playground" at the hospital that had been established by a former board member, Supervisor Frank L. Shaw. Shaw had come from food merchandising and was using hospital contracts to repay industry friends for support of his campaign.

With acceptance of the critical report by the board, Clinton felt he and his committee had performed an unselfish and valuable service that would save thousands of taxpayer dollars.

> Our eyes had been opened to the sorry conditions and the poor reputation of the Local Civic Affairs and the general unawareness and the resulting indifference of the average citizen. Such apathy is the perfect soil for the growth of corruption and the failure of

local government. We determined to become informed and to take a keener interest in Civic Affairs.

Clinton's report drew wrath from the garbage collectors who sold uneaten hospital food to hog farms. Then came a series of negative newspaper articles. "Restaurateur Meddles in Hospital Report," one headline blasted. The accompanying article made a point of misinterpreting Clinton's suggestion that pre-sliced bread was more economical than having eleven workers standing around slicing bread and sending unappetizing chunks to the patients, and thence to the garbage. The article pounced on this item chuckling that the "committee recommends such savings as slicing the patients' bread thinner!"

> We were very confused by this strange attack, but when we inquired we were told, you have stepped on a lot of toes, bigger than you realize. Just keep quiet, and your "nose clean" and it will blow over.

8

POLITICAL FIRESTORM

STUNNED BY THE FINDINGS IN HIS REPORT, CLIFFORD CLINTON BEGAN THINKING LIKE A TRUE POLITICAL REFORMER. He became obsessed with the pervasive graft that was built into the hospital food budget. It meant city and county officials were benefitting at the patients' and taxpayers' expense. Clinton was convinced that the only solution was to replace the elected officials who were involved. Upcoming elections for county in 1936 and city offices in 1937 were approaching, and Clinton saw an opportunity to educate the citizens of Los Angeles.

He was responding as a reform-minded Protestant who grew up in an America where Christian citizenship was measured by direct action for good rather than by inactive piety. Both of Clinton's parents had demonstrated Christian faith through action when they had left their homes and livelihoods behind to preach the Gospel in China, and the sermons in the churches he attended as a young man preached active involvement in the life of the here and now as a way to live a Christian life. Clinton was raised to believe when he found unchristian behavior in life, it was his Christian duty to act to fix it. To Clinton, his moral principles applied to everything—including politics. *Especially* politics. The more he learned about corruption, the more determined Clinton became—he wanted to cleanup the city.

But unfortunately for Clinton, Frank Shaw, the former county supervisor, had been elected mayor of Los Angeles in 1933.

Money and power interests were controlling the focus of local and state government. Instead of government providing for the wellbeing of its people, corporations were profiting and a handful of already wealthy men were getting richer and richer, while working people's wages decreased, and slums increased. In California, the railroad corporations were doing much the same thing to the common folk. Reformers developed strategies to change these trends and cleanse governments.

Progressivism in Los Angeles began in 1890 when the city's chamber of commerce fought to keep the Southern Pacific Railroad from taking over governance of the city. The transcontinental railroad had opened California to the rest of the country in 1869. The Big Four—Leland Stanford, Collis Huntington, Mark Hopkins, and Charles Crocker—were behind this amazing transportation revolution, but they wanted control over the state, and they bribed and intimidated politicians to obtain favored routes and rates.

By 1902, the Municipal League was formed and tried to pass charter reform as a first step to cleaning up and reorganizing the city. This time the group was able to get enough votes to pass the 1903 city charter which produced a modern civil service system, expanded executive authority for the mayor, beginnings of a social welfare program, and with the help of Christian socialist, Dr. John Randolph Haynes, a package of direct legislation including initiative, referendum, and recall provisions. The intent of the direct legislation package was to provide the public with more influence on the state of city government. The recall provision would eventually benefit Clinton in his campaign to clean up city government.

In 1907, a group of the reformists coalesced into the Lincoln-Roosevelt League to counteract the continued power of the railroads. The group was made up of California journalists and Republican activists who worked tirelessly at both the grassroots and electoral level to replace individuals who worked at the behest of the Southern Pacific. The railroad's puppet governor, James Gillett, was replaced in 1910 by the first reform candidate Hiram Johnson, and a national Progressive Party was formed in 1912. The group supported regulation of public utilities, outlawing of child labor, and a minimum wage for working women.

Reformers uncovered evidence of local government officials' involvement in vice and rackets. Elected in 1906, Los Angeles Mayor Arthur Harper resigned in 1909 when evidence revealed his connection to underworld individuals. Mayor George Alexander took office in March 1909, elected on a reform platform, and set to work cleaning up the red light districts in and around Chinatown. The progressive movement had by this time accomplished much but seemed to lose its motivation to pursue further reforms.

Prohibition shifted the reformers' focus from the structure of government to eliminating the pervasive corruption inherent to vice and gambling. With the passage of the 18th Amendment to the Constitution in 1920, the Volstead Act, national prohibition became law. Almost immediately, Los Angeles became a port of entry for bootleg hooch, and a criminal class was born.

Gangsters operated smuggling rings and speakeasies, gambling halls and houses of prostitution, all with the tacit blessing of Mayor George Cryer, who had been elected in 1921 on a platform of clean government. Cryer may have looked like the *American Gothic* farmer in Grant Wood's painting, but he was a crafty attorney. His key strategist Kent Kane Parrot, was a big, personable man who preferred the backroom to the limelight. A master of coalition politics, Parrot became the unofficial boss of City Hall. Cryer and Parrot had their detractors, and, in 1923, two churchmen launched a reform movement to expose the machinations that threatened the sanctity of city government.

The Reverend Gustav Briegleb, a pastor of the Westlake Presbyterian Church, was also president of the Ministerial Union and vocal advocate of police reform. Working with him was Robert "Fighting Bob" Shuler, a Trinity Methodist minister who used the radio as a pulpit. Shuler believed in a literal interpretation of scripture. His sermons were moralistic, and he had a large, devoted following. However, he was also anti-Semitic and anti-Catholic, which reduced his appeal. Lizzie Glide, one of his congregation members, donated twenty-five thousand dollars to buy him a radio station, KGEF (parodied as "Keep God Ever First"). Shuler's nightly tirades pilloried African Americans, alcohol imbibers, and William Randolph Hearst. He would lead his flock into Mayor Cryer's office, complain about vice, and then denounce him in church.

As the 1925 mayoral election approached, Cryer lost the support of Harry Chandler, the powerful publisher of the *Los Angeles Times*. Cryer had disregarded Chandler's wishes in a number of instances, so the publisher wanted him replaced, as did Briegleb and Shuler. Despite their efforts, Cryer was reelected. Still, he had to placate Chandler. To do this, he appointed James "Two-Gun" Davis as police chief. Reporter Harold Story remembered Davis as a "burly, dictatorial, somewhat sadistic, bitterly anti-labor man who saw Communist influence behind every telephone pole." Born in Texas in 1889, Davis joined the Los Angeles force in 1912 and fought vice on the so-called Purity Squad in the late teens. It was during this stint he served with Guy "String Bean" McAfee, a former Southern Pacific fireman. One of McAfee's other nicknames was "The Whistler." He would warn gambling dens of an impending raid by whistling into a telephone receiver.

Prior to Cryer's administration, bootlegging, gambling, and prostitution had been controlled by private businessmen and madams. Cryer consolidated three rackets into one and gave the underworld a pipeline to city officials and police. The Cryer-Parrot machine operated with necessary policies: in exchange for money or services, major criminal interests were protected, regardless of promises to eliminate vice; middle-class progressives received support for public ownership of water and power; and the Central Avenue "Negro vote" was purchased with both money and protection of its red-light district. Reformers were pacified with periodic raids on black honky-tonk operations, "pansy clubs," and opium dens. Administering all of this was

Charlie Crawford, who, unlike the immigrant East Coast gangsters, was American-grown.

Charles Henry Crawford was born in Ohio in 1879 and moved to Seattle as a young man, where he operated a casino whose silent partners were the mayor and chief of police. After he had learned criminal organization and political fixing, a reform city council forced him to leave the city. He found a greener pasture at Fifth and Maple streets in Los Angeles, where he turned a former rooming house into the Maple Bar, a combination casino and brothel. Crawford was known as the "Gray Wolf of Spring Street," even though he had an oddly effeminate voice. The popularity of the establishment was exceeded only by its influence, and it brought him a lucrative acquaintance with the Cryer-Parrot machine. Parrot lived at the opulent Biltmore Hotel and provided "Good Time Charlie" with tips on upcoming raids. Crawford, in turn, began to divert funds to Cryer's government. In time, Crawford was in charge of all organized crime in Los Angeles County. Under him were Guy McAfee, who made sure gambling ran smoothly; the Gans brothers (Bob and Joe), who oversaw slot machines; Ezekiel "Zeke" Caress, who handled bookmaking; Augusto Sasso, who was the master of prostitution; and Jack Dragna, a member of the Italian Protective Association, who took care of bootlegging operations.

After a falling out with Parrot, Cryer opted not to run for mayor in 1929. John Clinton Porter stepped in, promising to clean up city government. Shuler approved of Porter, who had the distinguished good looks of the late Warren Harding. Better yet, Porter was a teetotaler, a former president of the United Church Brotherhood (UCB), and a former member of the Ku Klux Klan (KKK). Porter had been chairman of the very effective 1928 Grand Jury, which indicted District Attorney Asa Keyes for accepting bribes from the Julian Petroleum Company. This helped him win the mayor's office with help from Shuler and UCB member John Anson Ford who would eventually become a Los Angeles County Supervisor.

Frank Leslie Shaw was born in Canada in 1877, raised in Missouri, and, after a bout with polio, worked in the grocery business. He moved to Los Angeles for the Cudahy Meat Packing Company in 1909. In 1925, his friends in South Los Angeles helped elect him to the city council representing the Eighth District. He served his district without notoriety, a liberal in favor of parks, the harbor, municipal ownership of electricity, lower taxes, and efficient government. In 1928, he ran for a seat on the County Board of Supervisors. Incumbent Jack Bean ridiculed him as the "grocery boy who made good." Shaw was anything but a boy. He was corpulent, had a toothbrush mustache, and limped. He also had the backing of the American Federation of Labor (AFL). But he had ties to Kent Parrot. Because of this connection, the reformers were wary of Shaw. Shuler didn't trust him, nor did Harry Chandler, who determined that Shaw's affiliations were unfriendly to business interests. Nonetheless Shaw won a spot on the board of supervisors.

The construction of the county hospital took place in Supervisor Shaw's district. It opened years late and millions of dollars over budget; indeed, a couple of million could not be accounted for. The Hall of Justice had worse accounting problems, somewhere in the neighborhood of five million dollars were missing. There were scandals involving Southern California Gas, and Supervisor Sidney Graves was sent to prison for accepting bribes during the San Gabriel Dam project. On the positive side, Shaw gained a reputation as an energetic problem solver. He introduced a share-the-work plan which encouraged businesses to avoid layoffs. He initiated projects to spur employment, created an Employment Stability Bureau to register the unemployed, and applied for Reconstruction Finance Corporation loans to reduce the county welfare burden.

Supervisor Shaw gave the impression he was an engaged official and began to marshal his supporters into a coalition. Mayor Porter, on the other hand, did little and sat on the sidelines while the Depression solved itself. The 1933 mayoral election found Shaw with support of labor, public utilities, Protestants, and the press. The KKK and John Anson Ford were also behind him. Shaw promised federal relief for Depression victims and reform of the police department which had become known for its specialized undercover surveillance unit called the Red Squad that had evolved as a result of the Red Scare following the end of World War I in 1918. Porter had the right in his back pocket: the *L.A. Times* supported him as did the conservative Protestants who weren't backing Shaw.

The Red Squad was so named not just because American citizens dreaded the thought of a communist takeover after the Russian Revolution, but because the police sought to intensify the depth of their fear. This secret organization was designed to root out threats against the established order by the Industrial Workers of the World (IWW). The so-called "Wobblies" advocated militant takeover of the state for the benefit of workers. In 1920, then-mayor Meredith "Pinky" Snyder had authorized the Los Angeles Police Department to form a spy squad to ferret out anarchists and prevent bombings. Functioning outside of the police department, it had its secret headquarters in the chamber of commerce building and spied on meetings, demonstrations, and members of unions and radical groups. In the mid-1920s, the perceived communist threat had diminished, but the Red Squad was quietly maintained. As Clinton would find out, it could be used against political enemies.

Once in office, Mayor Shaw curried favor with special interest groups by giving their political managers important positions in his administration. As Porter had done, he gained the support of the *Times*. He brought back James Davis to serve a second term as police chief, reporting directly to the mayor instead of the police commission. Together they created a Special Intelligence Unit in the Metropolitan Division—a political spy bureau. Shaw appointed his brother Joe as executive secretary, with an office next to his at City Hall. From this "corner pocket," Joe Shaw, a retired

Navy man, ran Los Angeles for his brother.

Joe Shaw filled requests for city jobs and appointed campaign contributors to city commissions. He made civil service a source of revenue by selling promotion examinations. He charged one thousand dollars for police captain exams and $250 for patrolman exams. He held clandestine meetings with syndicate members, collecting contributions and reciprocating with city appointments. He also maintained contact with bookies and Chinatown lottery operators.

To bolster the economy, Mayor Shaw began construction of a municipal airport, and the new Union Station. To his credit, these projects had a beneficial effect. In order to focus on federal aid, Shaw left local matters to the corrupt District Attorney Buron Fitts, who ignored gambling and vice. After Frank Shaw began to show his hand, letting his brother become another Kent Parrot, his supporters banded against him. In 1934, they formed a coalition to recall him. And who should be leading it but Bob Shuler, who was firm in his stand:

> There is more vice, more crime, more debauchery, more graft in this city than there ever was before in its history.

The recall coalition included *Daily News* publisher Manchester Boddy, bookie Jack Dymond, and the "Secret Six," a clandestine group that privately investigated vice during the term of the 1934 Grand Jury. One of the more distinguished members of the coalition was the Hollywood otolaryngologist Dr. A.M. Wilkinson who was a former county welfare commissioner, a member of the American Temperance Federation, and the president of the Federated Church Brotherhood.

Frank Shaw began to attack the credibility of Shuler's coalition. Shuler fought back with radio broadcasts, but he had a basic problem: he could not raise enough money to launch a recall campaign. His coalition addressed real issues, though, and it attracted disgruntled Shaw supporters like John Anson Ford, whose plan was to run against Shaw, Reverend Roy Smith, president of the Anti-Saloon League, and Fletcher Bowron, a superior court judge who believed the only way to fight corruption was with an honest grand jury. Shuler was unable to hold his coalition together, but he marshaled the forces that would continue the reform movement.

In 1936, the Shaw machine looked invincible—that is, until the publication of Clifford Clinton's "Report on Food Services." Because of the report, the Board of Supervisors was successful in cutting the 1935/36 hospital food budget by $120,000. Frank Shaw was suddenly aware of Clinton, and his impression wasn't positive, since the cuts that resulted from the report implied inefficiencies and wasteful spending under Shaw's leadership. Acting a bit naive, Clinton said he was trying to understand the hostile reactions to his well-intended investigation. Why had the press ridiculed him? Why were some usually friendly policemen giving him the evil eye? Whose toes had he stepped on? Maybe there was something unsavory under the surface. At least from the way he spoke, Clinton was beginning to understand that he was making some very powerful enemies. But he said his goal was to clean up gross overspending, and the people behind it. The implication was that there was graft behind the dollars.

> The more we saw and heard, the more convinced we became that certain city and county officials needed replacing.

City and county elections were being held in September 1936. Clinton knew one of the candidates. Judge Harlan Guyant Palmer, whom *Time* magazine described as a "pious progressive from Minnesota," was publisher of the *Hollywood Citizen News*, the fourth-largest daily in Los Angeles. Palmer had for years been waging a campaign against Hollywood vice from his office at Wilcox and Selma. He was running for district attorney against incumbent Buron Fitts. Clinton promoted Palmer as an ideal candidate. If anyone could make a clean sweep, he told anyone who would listen, Palmer could.

As the elections approached, Clinton had an idea. He had for some time been presenting entertainment on Saturday night in his restaurant. Guests could take their trays of food to the mezzanine and see a homespun variety show emceed by Jerry Coleman, a popular Clifton's regular who often chatted with fellow diners. Following the entertainment, an attorney hosted a discussion club where civic issues were informally debated. Because these sessions were so well attended, Clinton decided to launch a morning discussion group devoted exclusively to local issues. These morning programs were broadcast from the mezzanine on radio station KNX at seven o'clock. The program presented issues and interviewed candidates who supported graft-free government. Palmer appeared on several broadcasts to explain his concept of civic reform. Clinton's show eventually endorsed candidates—Palmer was the first. Fitts was offered equal time but never condescended to appear.

Not long after these broadcasts started, he noticed changes in his business. Professional "floppers" began to invade his restaurants, taking fake falls on the dining room stairways and subsequently filing injury claims. Clinton started receiving anonymous telephone calls with unidentified voices telling him to stay out of civic affairs.

There was formal harassment, too. Dr. George Parrish, a city health officer, ordered an investigation of the sanitation conditions at the Broadway Clifton's; they were looking for code violations in food preparation. The results of this probe were issued on November 5, 1936. The health department's report stated, "Food was stacked in trays filthy with refuse. Salads were exposed to the drippings of evaporation from ceilings and pipes. Rubbish was strewn on the floors, and eggs and icing was smeared on walls and doors."

Clinton responded that this report was obviously punishment for his County Hospital report. Nonetheless, he had to spend ten thousand dollars for "improvements" to his cafeteria. After fifteen individuals sued him for food poisoning, Clinton installed first-aid stations and posted signs, "The management cannot be responsible for accidents and disturbances beyond their control." At one point, the City Health Department sent Clinton an order to close the "unsanitary" Olive Street cafeteria; he refused.

The harassment caused Clinton to suffer both stomach trouble and depression, or what was then called "spiritual malaise." Once again, he felt that he was losing control of his environment. Although he remained steadfast in his religious beliefs, he was not affiliated with any particular church. As the pressures mounted, he began to feel the need of solace, of a supportive religious influence. He found it in Dr. Stewart P. MacLennan and the Hollywood Presbyterian Church, which claimed the largest Protestant congregation in North America. "The doors of this church are as wide as the gates of Heaven," said the minister each Sunday as he welcomed his flock. Like Clinton, "Dr. Mac" was interested in civic affairs and concerned about corruption. Dr. MacLennan encouraged Clinton to persevere in his campaign and supported him when it grew more difficult.

> We each confessed a lack of political knowledge, but we could not evade the responsibility that Christians and businessmen bear for their community.

It was obvious that Clinton had angered Shaw. And Davis. And Fitts. And Chandler. He continued his broadcasts, but Fitts defeated Palmer. Now it was Clinton's turn to be angry. As he saw it, evil had triumphed over good. Thanks to John Anson Ford, he would soon have a chance to right this tremendous wrong.

9

GUARDING THE RIGHTS
OF EVERY CITIZEN

ARLY 1937 PROVIDED A RESPITE FOR CLIFFORD CLINTON. Clifton's Cafeteria was doing
well, and he felt his day-to-day presence was less necessary since the company's vice president, Ransom Callicott had a good handle on operations, and Clinton could trust his
longtime family friend and buyer, Charles Gowanlock. Nelda was still very involved as well. Clinton had installed an office in his home; it afforded him time with his family and time for himself.

> My day started with forty refreshing laps in the pool but only after I had skimmed the
> leaves from its surface. This was my time to meditate on the coming day's activities. Each
> day needs its reflective moments, its white space, its communion time. This was mine.
> Then I joined my family for breakfast, the children were sent to school, and I repaired
> to my home office to lay out plans and programs.

On January 29, 1937, there was an unexpected knock at the door. Clinton's heart sank when
he saw a process server. At first, he thought this was another instance of harassment. He had been
served numerous times as a result of nuisance suits. This, however, was something new.

In November 1936, unbeknownst to Clinton, John Anson Ford had submitted his name to
Superior Court Judge Fletcher Bowron, asserting that Clinton was highly qualified to sit on the
upcoming Los Angeles County Grand Jury. Bowron placed Clinton's name in a pool of citizens
recommended for their work in the community. Clinton received a subpoena ordering him to
appear before Judge William Tell Aggeler. When Clinton read the document more closely, he

realized that this was no ordinary jury summons. He asked his attorney to explain the function of a grand jury. As he was informed, cases that come to trial before the Superior Court must be supported with sufficient evidence to convince of guilt, and this evidence must be presented to the grand jury. This elite jury only hears cases that involve criminal offenses punishable by a year or more in prison.

Clinton's name had been picked at random from the pool and added to a smaller list. From this list, nineteen men and women would be chosen to serve for one year on the grand jury.

> I felt that it was a citizen's duty to accept this responsibility. When my name was drawn, I gladly joined.

Clinton was grateful to the community that had made him prosperous. He needed to do something in return. During Harlan Palmer's campaign, Clinton had glimpsed the underbelly of Los Angeles. He saw "hopheads," "hook shops," and gambling dens—all the vice, perversion, and turpitude that were flourishing under Buron Fitts and Frank Shaw.

> I knew that payoffs on pinball and marble games, one-arm bandits, bookmaking, and prostitution were illegal, but I saw with my own eyes that this corruption existed. I witnessed decent young men on city streets receiving flagrant invitations to houses of ill-fame. And I saw members of our fine police force walk blindly past.

Clinton began to present this information in his ongoing 618 Clifton's mezzanine radio broadcasts. Because he felt it his duty to improve Los Angeles, he was pleased to be chosen for the 1937 Los Angeles County Grand Jury. His first duty as a jurist was to join his fellow jurors in an orientation meeting with Judge Aggeler, the impaneling advisory judge. On February 16, 1937, the members of the new grand jury were given a bound booklet that explained its history and their responsibilities as members. Clinton absorbed its message:

> In a free and popular government, it is of the utmost importance to the peace and harmony of society not only that the administration of justice and the punishment of crimes should in fact be impartial. To accomplish this nothing could be better contrived than a selection of a body from amongst those who without regard to time, person or occasion, have been selected from among their fellow citizens as persons deemed worthy of this high trust by their moral worth and general respectability of character.

Clinton paid particular attention to Judge Aggeler's next statement:

> If you have reason to believe that any public official is guilty of corruption or willful misconduct in office, if you have reason to believe that graft or corruption exist—wherever they may be found and regardless of who may be involved—in such a situation, I charge you to act diligently, faithfully, and courageously.

CLIFTON'S CLIFFORD CLINTON

The nineteen jury members seated in the jury box took their solemn oath, after which Judge Aggeler named the foreman, a painting contractor named John Bauer. Each juror was given a small gold star as a badge, to be used when entering county institutions. Clinton left the courthouse immersed in thought.

> This serious and rather awesome occasion left me deeply impressed. Only now did I realize the power of this body, and its importance in guarding the rights of every citizen.

Clinton diligently studied the handbook. Section 922 of the Penal Code states:

> If a member of a grand jury knows or has reason to believe that a public offense, triable [sic] within the county, has been committed, he must declare the same to his fellow jurors, who must thereupon investigate the same.

On February 23, the foreman of the previous year's grand jury came in to offer advice to the new jurors. "Be a mill, and grind up what they bring you," he told them. This cynical counsel flew in the face of everything Clinton had heard and read.

Clinton's first sessions were purely formalities. Buron Fitts visited and promised to assign a deputy to present cases for attention. Ugene U. Blalock, deputy district attorney, explained procedures. The first order of business was for the foreman to set up committees and their chairmen. These committees could make recommendations, and, after investigation of their cases, the grand jury could take action. Only action taken by the grand jury as a whole was legal. Committees included: Criminal Complaints, Finance, Audit, and Schools and Jails.

> It was immediately obvious that the Criminal Complaints Committee was the one with the power and importance." Any criminal matter would have to be presented first to this group. The foreman was himself a member of this committee. I found my name on the Schools and Jails Committee.

At the meeting Clinton was surprised to see Fitts and Blalock treating the jurors "like irresponsible children." Blalock attended this and subsequent meetings, offering to fix traffic tickets and to set up lighthearted excursions on jurors' lunch breaks.

Irresponsible was an appropriate description. Soon Clinton was aware that only a few of his fellow jurors cared about what the law required of them.

> Of the nineteen jurors, only four wanted the facts uncovered—John Bogue, a Baptist minister; Harry L. Ferguson, a retired architect; Earl Kelly, a businessman; and myself. For an indictment, however, twelve were necessary. We four became known as the Minority.

Motions by the Minority to investigate civic corruption were sidetracked, sent to the Criminal

Complaints Committee, or simply voted down, usually in the ratio of seven to twelve.

> One of these motions sought to determine why half a million dollars was spent to put a candidate into public office when he could earn no more than one tenth of that during his entire term of office. Who contributed this campaign funding? What did they expect in return? Did they get it?

Eager for answers, Clinton got a private appointment with the judge:

> I asked Judge Aggeler for his advice on how to pursue an investigation of vice and gambling in Los Angeles. He told me that similar investigations had been attempted many times, and that nothing could be done about the situation. Then the judge turned in his chair, pointed through the window toward City Hall, and said, "But if you can get at the real people behind this, I will be for you one hundred percent."

On February 24, 1937, Clinton submitted a motion to the grand jury that read in part:

> That a study be made by this grand jury in a manner deemed expedient and proper to determine if there is existing in the City or County wholesale and wanton permission of violation of certain laws or ordinances in respect to gambling, operation of places of prostitution or permission of the operation of prostitutes . . . [because] inference is being consistently made that our officers in charge of the enforcement of these laws are either in collusion with these illegal agencies or are lax in their interpretation or enforcement of the law in these cases.

Clinton was following the example of Thomas Dewey's "runaway" grand jury in New York, which had indicted and convicted mobster Lucky Luciano. Clinton's proposal was voted down. He soon deduced that no investigation of protected rackets could proceed because the grand jury was under Fitts's thumb. The only way to go around him was to have an independent investigator appointed. This was highly unlikely. The Minority approached Judge Aggeler and told him that they were being ridiculed by other jurors who accused them of "keyhole peeping." The judge was in poor health and not able to pursue their complaints. He was also aware that several of the jurors were doing business with City Hall and consequently afraid of an honest investigation.

In March 1937, the grand jury heard testimony from A.M. Wilkinson, the Hollywood ear-nose-and-throat specialist and erstwhile member of the County Public Welfare Commission who was conducting his own private investigation of gambling and vice syndicates in the Sunset Strip area. Clinton sought out Dr. Wilkinson after the doctor's grand jury testimony gave explicit information on vice, and they held a meeting at a local church to alert the public to the problems facing the grand jury. Clinton quoted Courtney Riley Cooper's book *Here's to Crime*. "Look about your town," wrote Cooper. "If there are slot machines, if there is a numbers racket, if there is concerted gambling—then someone in your administration is crooked."

John Anson Ford was challenging Frank Shaw who was running for a second term as mayor. Clinton gave three radio speeches in support of Ford, promising that Ford would appoint an independent prosecutor to investigate the connection between the vice syndicate and "certain officials of the city and county governments." In response, Shaw printed a brochure entitled "Frank Shaw: The Man, the Executive." It emphasized the fifty-one million dollars in federally funded work projects he had brought to Los Angeles.

The *Los Angeles Times* disliked Shaw's support of the New Deal, but he had appointed James Davis police chief, so Harry Chandler endorsed him. Ford was outmatched. His only support came from Harlan Palmer's *Hollywood Citizen News*. Ford attacked Shaw for creating a "political patronage trough out of unemployment relief," claiming that the mayor awarded WPA funds only to those who supported him.

Voters, however, could not see graft, but they could easily see increased construction, which they translated to mean more jobs, which translated to prosperity. On May 24, they gave Shaw a second term.

On June 29, at a grand jury session, panelist John Bogue reported the results of the investigation that he, Clinton, and the other Minority members had been conducting. Los Angeles was home to 1,800 bookies, two hundred gambling spots, and six hundred brothels. Bogue provided addresses and details of operation in locations he had personally visited. Clinton immediately requested a formal grand jury investigation. A resolution passed, but it was quietly shuffled to the Criminal Complaints Committee, where it was left to expire.

On July 15, 1937, Judge Aggeler died, creating a momentary vacuum in the court.

The *Los Angeles Times* and Hearst's *Examiner* and *Herald* scoffed at Clinton's claims of corruption, calling him a "one-man grand jury," a "crackpot reformer," and a "would-be political boss." When Palmer's *Hollywood Citizen News* offered to publish names and addresses of the establishments, Clinton's campaign began to gain traction. Palmer also published editorials against Fitts and other officials linked to protecting vice operations. Yet to Clinton's chagrin and frustration, the grand jury had accomplished little more in its first few months than an indictment of 342 sit-down strikers at Douglas Aircraft. Louise Blatherwick of the Civic Betterment Division of the Federation of Churches then demanded that Shaw explain the statistics contained in Bogue's report. Shaw denied that there was any protected vice in Los Angeles and vowed to support any unbiased investigation.

Urged on by Wilkinson, Clinton began his own investigation, going where other officials in the City of Angels feared to tread.

GIRDING FOR BATTLE

CLIFFORD CLINTON'S INVESTIGATION BEGAN IN THE SUMMER OF 1937, WHEN HE ENTERED A JAIL AND INTERVIEWED JAMES UTLEY, A FAT, BABY-FACED CRIMINAL. Utley had a history of arrests for liquor law violations at transvestite clubs in West Hollywood. At the time, the area was an unincorporated part of Los Angeles County and a nest of unconventional entertainments. Utley explained the hierarchy of protection to Clinton and arranged for high-ranking police officers to bring evidence of payoffs to his home. Nelda asked her husband why he was consorting with people she called "perverts" like Utley.

The kind of information I need doesn't come from Sunday school teachers.

Notebooks in hand, Clinton and his colleagues took their investigation to the streets. There was much to record. They found widespread installations of pinball machines. They saw bookies taking bets on street corners, witnessed petty crooks soliciting innocent citizens to enter gambling dens with police cars parked nonchalantly outside, and found brothels functioning with no attempt at concealment. Clinton, whose attitude toward sexual license matched his aversion to waste, set his formidable jaw and marched in.

....120;.As a rule, there was a lounge where girls were selected by the waiting men. Sometimes the girls were "hard," sometimes cooperative. Some were very pretty, and some very young. The couple would repair to a small room for about fifteen minutes. In the open houses, the going scale for a "trick" was three dollars. For "daisy chains" or for catering to patrons who desired longer time, special favors, or abnormal acts, the charge was set on the spot by the girl. Girls told me that they could sometimes handle twenty-five patrons a night. Some houses were open twenty-four hours a day.

A few girls and even a few madams quietly slipped us cards with their names and addresses and said they would help if called upon, but privately, and not to press them
inside the establishment.

When Clinton saw police officers going in and out of these places, blithely conversing with
patrons and employees, and dawdling in their cars for hours, he was convinced that criminals
were paying bribes.

Clinton kept up a running commentary in *Food for Thot*.

I had taken an oath to serve the interests of all the citizens by searching out dishonesty
in public office. Inasmuch as there was an apparent effort on the part of the grand jury
and of the District Attorney's office not to let all the facts be told, I felt it my duty to tell
the citizens as much as I could without violating secrecy.

Because the grand jury ignored the results of the Minority Group investigation, Reverend
Bogue published them in a local newspaper. The Civic Betterment division of the Federation of
Churches, a powerful women's group, were astounded and shocked by these revelations. Louise
Blatherwick, the group's president, met with Los Angeles Mayor Frank Shaw to demand an explanation. Shaw denied the existence of protected vice and said the Los Angeles Police Department
was one of the best in the nation. He agreed to any fair and unbiased citizen organization who
wanted to investigate vice in the city.

Startled and pleased that Shaw agreed to her demand for an investigation, Louise Blatherwick quickly called a meeting of Los Angeles religious leaders to discuss the formation of an
investigating committee. Determined to pressure the mayor to keep his word, they met on July
19 at the German Methodist Church. They formed a committee, which included Robert Shuler, Reverend Wendell Miller, Dr. Wilkinson, and Louise Blatherwick, and four days later asked
Clinton to join it as chairman.

In July, Clinton began to write a political column entitled "The Truth Can Set You Free" for
the *Shopping News*, a weekly publication distributed to homes. Before long, the publishers told him
that they were feeling some heat. His column was canceled.

On July 24, Clinton wrote a letter to Mayor Shaw asking for a meeting. It began "Dear
Friend Frank Shaw," which was his way of proposing a collegial relationship. He requested that
Shaw meet with the new committee and signed it, "Yours for a fine L.A., Respectfully."

Soon after, the as-yet-unnamed committee met with Mayor Shaw, Chief Davis, and Joe
Shaw. As Clinton recalled:

I, as chairman, made a clear statement, as previously approved, laying out our aims and
intentions, and stating we wanted the Mayor's authority to act.

Clinton was more than surprised, then, by the mayor's response. Shaw angrily pointed his finger at each member (except Clinton) and accused them of being "snoopers, busy-bodies, and self-seekers" who were trying to smear his administration. Shaw then accused Dr. Wilkinson of taking four thousand dollars from gambler Guy McAfee. In fact, McAfee had made a donation to "The Last Days of Pompeii," a pageant staged to benefit underprivileged boys, but his was only one of hundreds of donations collected by Wilkinson. Shaw also charged Reverend Miller with telling his barber that officials in the city were corrupt and deserved to be ousted from office. Clinton had to speak up:

> Mr. Mayor, all this is beside the point. This committee pledges itself on two things. First, to act as a body, not as individuals; second, we promise you if we find your statements to be true, we shall be your best supporters. We plan to deal in facts only, and if your administration's actions are as you claim and if you wish to silence the critics, this is a certain and sure method.

Then Chief Davis announced that "This whole thing is against the true public interest. It is bad. It undermines morale. I still say your motives are insincere. I know what you are contemplating. You are making this effort as a basis for instituting recall proceedings in January."

Clinton expressed surprise at this statement and asked for an explanation of a "recall" election. He then denied any such intention. Although the concept of using a recall to remove an official from office was unfamiliar to Clinton, and a rarely invoked clause, it had in fact been incorporated into the city charter in 1903. Three amendments to that charter—initiative, referendum, and recall—were progressive reforms designed to allow greater public say in how local government was run. Clinton never identified with the progressives. They preceded his entry into local politics, in fact, but he benefited from the foundation they laid encouraging direct public participation.

After the meeting adjourned, Clinton had a warm visit with Chief Davis, of whom he was a little in awe. In view of reporters and photographers, Davis ceremoniously pinned badge No. 4010 on Clinton's lapel and deputized him as a private vice investigator. Clinton beamed, thought himself as "one of the boys," and could use the badge to gain entrée to places he wished to investigate. (He later learned from a police officer that eight thousand of these meaningless badges had been given out to placate critics.)

On August 5, the committee met at Clinton's home, and Clinton offered to hire an independent investigator to work for his new committee. The investigator, appropriately named "X," was hired to provide Clinton with regular reports of underworld activities. (The identity of this person was never revealed.) At the meeting, Clinton proposed a name for the committee, the Citizens' Independent Vice Investigating Committee (CIVIC). The name was ratified, and, on August 19, CIVIC became its official name. Its first order of business was to produce a working document listing various criminal activities that needed investigation:

1. A local crime syndicate controlled local operations of pinball operations, protected gambling, bookmaking, and prostitution and, after payoffs to local law-enforcement officers, pocketed millions of dollars in profits.
2. Press employees, reporters, and editors received money from the rackets.
3. The grand jury had been stacked with people who had connections with the syndicate or public officials.
4. Citizens who attacked the syndicate or its component businesses were being silenced.
5. Public officials who cooperated—even with silence—were receiving campaign contributions.
6. Public officials who didn't play ball had their election campaigns sabotaged.
7. Out-of-town gangsters who tried to "muscle in" on this homegrown syndicate were severely dealt with by the police, the district attorney's office, or the syndicate itself.

The governing board then discussed tactics the new organization would employ. Clinton summarized its approach:

> Keep the spotlight on the gamblers and bawdy houses. Keep them "hot" and partially closed. Deplete the enemy's sources of income, the payoff. Advertise in the papers. Go on radio. Hold meetings. Interview all sides of every question. Be constructive.

One morning shortly after this meeting, Clinton awoke to a startling headline in a local newspaper. "Mayor Shaw Repudiates CIVIC Committee." Shaw's about-face came as a surprise to Clinton, who had naïvely assumed that they had a gentleman's agreement. Shaw was quoted in the accompanying article, calling the members of the committee "malcontents and snoopers intent on besmirching the name of the fair city of Los Angeles." Shaw's apparent treachery reinforced Clinton's resolve to proceed with an investigation.

Press coverage was politically slanted and nasty, calling Clinton's colleagues "a lunatic fringe" stirred up by "defeated candidates." Palmer's *Hollywood Citizen News* was the only metropolitan paper reporting on the allegations CIVIC was making. "If there is nothing to fear," Palmer asked City Hall, "why try to muzzle them?" Yet the attacks intensified.

Clifton's was facing another warning from Health Department Commissioner George Parrish, a not-so-subtle message to lay off the Shaw administration. Clinton was understandably outraged.

> Clifton's was still abused by the Health Department claiming its attempts to enforce sanitary laws within our establishments was the motivation for revenge against City Officials. From Main Street, long the domain of the depressed, indigent men and women of the city, came a long stream of these unkempt folk who sat in our lobbies, congregated around our entrances and in our dining rooms, seating themselves with our better dressed guests, causing annoyance. Fortunately, some of these who would as soon serve

our side, when approached, told us what was happening: "Someone" unknown to them would approach them daily and pay them to frequent Clifton's. The exposure of this in our table leaflets, "Food For Thot" and over our People's Voice Program was an effective answer. We actually found that the man who was engaged in paying these people to annoy us, and bring discredit upon our dining places, was on the payroll of the Health Department. This man, eventually told his story to us, on the Air, to the dismay and increased rage of the city administration.

This only further incensed those behind these tactics. Clinton assumed that city employees told gangs to swamp Clifton's free-meal service for the needy. First-time diners, under city direction, claimed they were poisoned. Altercations were staged and disturbances created. More stink bombs were planted. The health department made new accusations. All this was accompanied by a smear campaign conducted with pamphlets, community newspapers, and stickers. These attacks, instead of deterring Clinton, strengthened his resolve.

Once CIVIC was formed, Clinton started realizing how many individuals had laid their lives on the line. Dr. Wilkinson had undertaken an independent investigation to identify vice lords. Palmer had used his paper to alert the public to corruption. Shuler had broadcast criticism of political featherbedding. Dr. John Buckley, chairman of the 1934 grand jury, had also investigated vice connections. Journalist C.H. Garrigues had provided Buckley with hard evidence of political graft and corruption.

Soon after CIVIC was incorporated, Harry Raymond, a former San Diego police chief who became a private investigator, visited Clinton. Raymond confided to the restaurateur that there existed a treasure trove of evidence that could tie City Hall to the local crime syndicate. An attorney friend of Raymond, A. Brigham Rose, compiled and was in possession of this damning material. Clinton contacted Rose, who confirmed Raymond's story. Rose had a plan to present this evidence to the grand jury. He would also represent Clinton, the Minority group of the grand jurors, and CIVIC, and help them clean up the corrupt government.

Clinton gave Rose a five-thousand-dollar retainer and girded his loins for battle.

11

DEN OF THIEVES

CLIFFORD CLINTON ENDED THE SUMMER OF 1937 WITH A MASS OF EVIDENCE AGAINST THE SHAW ADMINISTRATION. As he began organizing it, he saw the need for a second assistant. His secretary Laurel Ewing was having a hard time keeping up with both his correspondence and CIVIC paperwork. A man named Hanson Hathaway offered to help. Clinton did not interview him very thoroughly. He often hired people purely on instinct—he either liked them or he didn't. He saw no need to do background checks. He trusted his own judgment, and that trust would come back to haunt him.

After hiring Hathaway, Clinton noticed that his work ethic was odd. Not that the new publicist was unmotivated; on the contrary, he worked a little too hard.

> From the beginning, I noticed that Hathaway was inclined to stretch the facts. If we witnessed one policeman making a bet with an illegal bookie, Hathaway would write "a number of policemen."

Clinton cautioned him that details in his accounts had to be accurate. Hathaway did not agree. "This is the way to make it interesting," he told Clinton. "You have to be dramatic. Actually, what we need is a good bombing or something." What he got was a visit to the demimondaine.

A regular listener to Clinton's daily radio broadcast called in a tip. A suspicious-looking establishment had just opened near her home on Santa Monica Boulevard. Would Mr. Clinton look into this? He lost no time. While Minority members John Bogue, Harry L. Ferguson, and Earl Kelly waited on the sidewalk, Clinton entered the lobby of Rose's Sunset Shading Company.

A nice-looking young woman, wearing a nurse's uniform, came through a draped entrance. I said I had been sent by a "Friend," and was taken into a room divided by others only by white cotton curtains. In this cubicle there was a massage table.

"What do you want tonight, Deary," she inquired.

"The works," I answered. "What do you charge?"

"We do a good job, honey, and the charge is ten dollars."

I gave her the ten. Slipping out of her front-opening nurses uniform, she stood before me nude, except for her stockings and bra, ready to deliver the works. I sat on the edge of the table, and produced my Grand Jury badge. She turned as white as a piece of paper, and her eyes stared.

"O," she said at last, "we just opened tonight, and I was waiting for the officers to pay them. We've spent so much getting started," and she raised pleading eyes to mine. I assured her, that we meant her no harm, and she could proceed in whatever she thought wise. I wanted information. She gave me some quickly.

"I have worked freelance, and been pushed around," she said. "So my friend and I thought that we would open our own small place, and establish our own contacts."

Further information I did not get, for in at the door came several of our party saying that a police car had just passed, stopped, then gone on, and the girl slipping into her uniform said, "Scram, will you? Give me a chance. I'll talk to you later."

Clinton and the other men moved their car to a side street. Sure enough, an officer of the Los Angeles Police Department went into Rose's. Then he ran out and drove off, but not before Clinton could copy down his license plate number. When Clinton gave the information to Hathaway, he expanded it into a story entitled: "CIVIC Chases Cops," embellished with a madam, girls, and numerous rogue policemen. The material Clinton was getting did not need to be embellished. There was a lot of it, and it was dynamite.

It was unlikely that Clinton's activities would go unnoticed, especially since he was publicizing them. The question was: would he be allowed to continue? The LAPD surveillance unit, a sanitized term for what was more accurately known as the spy squad, maintained a case morgue. In it were dossiers on hundreds of citizens and voluminous reports of harmless activities that could be distorted into trumped-up charges. More significantly, there were recordings of conversations made with hidden microphones or from tapped phone lines, and memorialized using Dictograph recorders in sound trucks parked nearby or in adjacent buildings. The individuals being subjected to this illegal surveillance were not criminals; they were law-abiding citizens whose only crime was decrying corruption.

The spy squad headquarters was in an abandoned warehouse at 311 East First St. Its front door was chained and its windows were painted gray. The squad had eighteen members. To

CLIFTON'S AND CLIFFORD CLINTON

enter the building they passed through an alley, went down a flight of stairs, followed a dark passageway, and then went back up to street level, where a cubbyhole housed a machine that could transcribe recordings made from remote sources. There was also a machine to transfer recorded conversations from wax Dictaphone cylinders to large sixteen-inch acetate discs that could hold more transcriptions. This growing collection of licorice-black platters contained hundreds of hours of conversations. Clinton's recognizable voice would soon be one of those recorded.

Burly, balding Harry Raymond lived in a one-story house at 955 Orme Avenue, just across the river from downtown. Someone had learned that he was snooping for Clinton, because on September 17, Captain Earle Kynette of the Special Intelligence Unit rented a house across the street and installed recording equipment. Not long afterward, spy squad members entered Clinton's home, which was widely known to be left unlocked, and hid microphones in his office.

In late September, Clinton requested an audience with the grand jury. He and the other Minority members had prepared a report to prove that corruption did exist. Not surprisingly, Deputy District Attorneys George Stahlman and Ugene Blalock, jury foreman John Bauer, and several jurors told Clinton that before he could present his findings, he had to give them a preview. He wanted to know why. He was told that they needed names of witnesses and a summary of their testimony. Clinton saw where this was leading—a blind alley for him and the witnesses. He refused. Then he quoted statutes guaranteeing his right to a formal hearing. Clinton said he endured several pointless meetings with Buron Fitts, and then the grand jury took a vote. It was thirteen to six against Clinton's right to present his findings.

Until this point, Harlan Palmer's *Hollywood Citizen News* was the only newspaper that had supported Clinton and would print names and addresses of illegal activities that Clinton and the Minority identified. Arrayed against him were the Hearst papers and the *Los Angeles Times*, which featured a blast from Bauer. "The grand jury has never refused to hear Clinton's evidence," said the jury foreman, "and it is not going to be led around by the nose and be made the laughing stock of the entire country by one man."

In an editorial, Palmer wrote a rebuttal to Bauer in his paper on September 30: "It is regrettable that the foreman of the grand jury should be leading the attack upon the one man who is doing effective work against the underworld." Apparently as many people were reading Palmer's paper as were reading the other dailies. Both the Criminal Complaints Committee and the grand jury began receiving letters from irate citizens, urging them to let Clinton present his findings. Palmer published an open letter to the grand jury by Reverend Roy Smith, pastor of the First Methodist Episcopal Church of Los Angeles.

> This is much more than a matter of closing houses of prostitution or banning slot machines. It is a matter of confidence in our municipal government. . . . The appeal I am making is that Mr. Clinton be allowed to bring his evidence to the Jury in whatever

way he pleases, so long as he presents the facts. Get the facts whether you save your procedure or not. If his evidence warrants indictments, then vote them. If it does not, then notify the public that you have heard the evidence and found nothing to warrant a prosecution.

Harry Chapman of the Criminal Complaints Committee ignored these letters. Minority juror Ferguson then brought a resolution before the jury, stating that the Criminal Complaints Committee had no standing in law, and that if it did not cease its illegal conduct, it would be reported to Judge Fricke, the judge assigned to the jury, and to Judge Fletcher Bowron, the presiding judge.

Clinton tried to present his evidence three times. After his third unsuccessful attempt, he was attacked as a "man with a criminal record" in a letter from J.E. Lambert of the Municipal Improvement Association. Clinton's "criminal record" was a reference to the 1929 incident on the mothballed Navy ship in the Oakland Estuary. Buron Fitts declared the charges without substance, but only after giving the press sufficient time to label Clinton a jailbird. Clinton was too busy investigating to notice.

On October 3, Clinton met with Dave Hutton, the ex-husband of Aimee Semple McPherson, the famed evangelist. Hutton was in touch with a defector from McPherson's legendary Angelus Temple. Rheba Crawford Splivalo had won fame as the "Angel of Broadway" in New York's Salvation Army and then become a Los Angeles radio evangelist before joining forces with McPherson. After a number of harmonious years at the Angelus Temple, Crawford had been ousted for trying to unseat McPherson. Crawford had her own seamy milieu. "I kick them in the shins until they come across with a donation," she boasted, and there were plenty of bruises to prove it. Her donations were nothing more than money extorted from the syndicate in exchange for silence. Clinton wanted to subpoena Crawford as a witness. Hutton said he could arrange it.

When Clinton and Hutton met at the Los Feliz office, they did not realize that a microphone was relaying their conversation to a recording machine in a nearby truck. Spy squad technicians rubbed their hands together when they heard Clinton describe—for the first time to anyone—the evidence linking the Shaw office to the Los Angeles underworld.

Unaware that he was being spied on, Clinton continued with his campaign. Brigham Rose advised him not to confront the grand jury again. Instead they tried a new strategy. On October 13, they presented a writ of mandamus to the Special Remedies Department of the Superior Court, Judge Emmet Wilson presiding. The writ directed charges against five members of the Criminal Complaints Committee, demanding they be disqualified because of conflict of interest:

· Myron Carr Jr. was a Los Angeles Department of Water and Power executive.

· Fred McClung, a broom manufacturer, was doing business with the city and county.

- Harry Chapman, secretary of the Criminal Complaints Committee, had ties to the pinball machine racket. His brother Abe was one of the incorporators of the California Amusement Machine Operators Association (CAMOA) as well as the son-in-law of Bob Gans, the "Slot-Machine Czar."

- Mrs. Rosanna F. Tondreau was the wife of Harry Tondreau, one of Gans's auditors.

- W. Arthur Taylor had accepted $2,300 from George Duncan, a gambler in the red-light district of Central Avenue, as a "contribution" for John Porter's mayoral campaign.

In addition, Clinton submitted an affidavit that grand jury foreman John Bauer be disqualified and removed. Paint contractor Leo Flowers had testified that Bauer won a "traffic zone" paint contract because of his association with Shaw, even though Flowers was a low bidder.

"Judge Wilson asked for answers from those charged," said Clinton. "But none answered." Wilson ruled that this case was unprecedented because the grand jury was a sacred body and could not be ordered by a superior court to hear evidence. "Even so," Clinton recalled, "Judge Wilson was astounded that the grand jurors would not answer the charges."

Facing another stonewall, Clinton backed up and continued to seek the specifics of payoffs. In the last week of October, with another showdown looming, Clinton told Nelda to take the three associates who were convalescing in their home and drive to Lake Arrowhead for a few days of vacation.

On Friday, October 29, Bauer and nine other jurors issued a resolution:

> The grand jury demands of Clifford E. Clinton that he forthwith conform with the law and declare such evidence as he asserts is in his possession of the commission of a public offense in order that this jury may conform with the law and proceed with an investigation thereof."

The resolution gave Clinton a deadline of Tuesday, November 2. The resolution further charged Clinton with violation of his oath and creating "a misleading impression as to the integrity of this grand jury." The resolution passed by a vote of fifteen to one. This group then became known as the "we-won't-hear-the-evidence bloc" of the grand jury.

Clinton immediately prepared a press release:

> My position is adamant and unequivocal. I have established as a matter of law that the grand jury is contaminated by insidious influences and that the Criminal Complaints Committee has no standing. I will not permit this smokescreen to be foisted on an unsuspecting public.

That evening Clinton went to the home of a young married woman who had agreed to an anonymous interview about her work as a prostitute. She gave him an earful:

I've been in the racket only a few years, just enough to earn some extra money. Tricks are just business with me, you know. My emotions aren't involved. My husband doesn't object. He'll tell you so. In fact, we think prostitution should be legalized.

This struck Clinton as a startling concept, but the woman spoke on behalf of the single men, the lonely men, the displaced men who had no recourse but to visit a prostitute:

What are they to do? If there is to be a lessening of sex crimes, killings, and so on, this urge must be satisfied. Why doesn't the government legalize what everyone recognizes as the "Facts of Life?" I consider what I do a service. These men don't come to me for love or lust. They come for physical relief. And they leave assuaged. Any tendency they may have to force themselves upon some good woman or to commit some crime in the sex category has been dissipated.

"What about the crime factor?" Clinton asked, diverting the conversation to political payoffs. Again, the young woman answered him directly, and he took notes right after the conversation:

"I know it exists. I have a friend working singly who pays her officer herself. I will see if she will talk to you if you promise not to let her get hurt. In the house where she worked, the landlady rents the Place for big money and pays the local officer ten to twenty-five dollars a week per girl. She has contacts also with the higher-ups, who take care of the 'brass.' I don't dare ask her, but I'm sure that half her take goes to the Big Boys. And those leeches! I'd like to see them get theirs. If prostitution was legalized, they'd lose their hold on City Hall and the District Attorney's office."

After Clinton concluded his interview with the prostitute—and her husband—he drove home. It was shortly after midnight when he arrived. Something was wrong. He was aware of a terrific disturbance at the front of his home: a large hole in front, right under the kitchen. His children were in turmoil and police sirens could be heard in the distance.

The official report declared that a tin can pineapple-type bomb had been detonated at 12:10 A.M. on Friday October 29 at 5470 Los Feliz Blvd. Clinton recalled the night:

The unbelievable had occurred. Our home had been bombed. In the subsequent smoke and panic and confusion, I raced up the stairs, through the smoke-filled hallway, to find my sleepy-eyed, pajama-clad youngsters dashing downstairs. They were unhurt. Firemen and police were soon swarming over the grounds.

Clinton and the authorities found a large hole in the outside wall of the house directly under the kitchen. The bomb had wrecked tile, torn plaster, damaged plumbing, smashed dishes, and spilled food. Detectives determined that the perpetrators had pulled loose a wire screen, entered the basement, crawled toward the front of the house, and attached the bomb to one of the joists under the kitchen. Gordon Hammond, a neighbor, described a muffled explosion and reported seeing a green car racing away from their home.

Clinton had in fact received five death threats since beginning his investigation. Luckily his three children, his in-laws, and a maid had been sleeping in back bedrooms. Police immediately placed the family under protective guard. Two hours after the explosion, the telephone rang.

> Well, how did you like the little puff we gave you? That was just a little puff to scare you. If you don't lay off, that will prove to be as nothing!"

Clinton recognized the voice with an Italian accent from a previous call in which a man threatened to dump his body in a ditch if he continued his vice probe. "There was little sleep for any of us in that Los Feliz home that night," remembered Clinton. Worse, he was unable to reach Nelda, so she learned about the attack from a newspaper she encountered on her way back from Lake Arrowhead. "Clinton Home Bombed," said the headlines.

Police Chief Davis hinted that Clinton had set the bomb himself in order to buttress his case against the Shaw administration. Clinton brushed aside the insult and pointed to the gang that had killed gambling czar George "Les" Bruneman the previous week. "It evidently is the work of politico-underworld enemies," he told the press. "But they are not going to stop me. They can blow up the entire house, but I will keep on."

Despite his bravado, Clinton realized that his crusade was becoming costly in ways he could not have foreseen. The bombing of his house and many verbal threats indicated that all the publicity was creating fear among his enemies. In early November 1937, a customer approached Clinton in the cafeteria. "I work in the Den of Thieves," the customer said in a low voice. "You'd better lay off." Was it a whistleblower's warning, or was it a direct threat? The biblical allusion troubled Clinton.

Not long afterward, a police officer, who was a regular guest, offered still more advice:

> You don't know what you're doing. Those birds will finish you before they're through—and Clifton's, too. Believe me, Clinton—they can do it. They have the power and the dough. When they finish with you, you won't be able to operate a peanut stand.

12

THE WHOLE SORDID, STINKING MESS

FLETCHER BOWRON WAS THE PRESIDING JUDGE OF THE SUPERIOR COURT, AND IT WAS HE WHO HAD RECOMMENDED CLINTON FOR THE GRAND JURY. "Judge Bowron was a square-jawed, determined, yet soft-spoken man," recalled Clinton. Bowron had been fighting his own battle with Fitts and the city hall mob. Bowron warned Clinton:

> They've had this county tied up for twenty-five years. There is no way you can break that. You will only destroy yourself if you try. I know. I have fought Buron, and I have paid an awful price. I advise you to go about your business. Do your jury duty as best you can. Don't try to clean the Aegean Stables. It's impossible.

Bowron had handpicked the nineteen members of the 1934 Grand Jury. He had seen previous grand juries hamstrung by a selection process that stacked the juries in favor of the administration. He instructed the 1934 jurors to investigate Shaw's finances for a fifteen thousand dollar contribution from underworld forces. Then-foreman John Buckley authored a report that showed bank account evidence that Shaw had taken bribes from a street-paving firm. Buckley also came out against the district attorney, accusing Fitts of trying to "bulldoze, bluff, and intimidate the grand jury almost from the time it was impaneled." Although the jury indicted Fitts and he went to trial, it ended in acquittal. The grand jury may have gotten some attention, but it accomplished nothing, and, in the end, Buckley was financially ruined by banks friendly to Fitts.

"Those men will stop at nothing," Bowron warned Clinton.

"Your Honor," said Clinton, "I believe what you say, but we feel so strongly that we are under oath, and we must do all in our power to break the stranglehold of the racket."

Thursday, November 4, was the next grand jury meeting, and Clinton hoped the deadlock would be broken. Instead, Foreman Bauer and other majority members stopped him from presenting his affidavits and witnesses. Clinton and his supporters wondered why. His evidence was "probably worthless and based on hearsay," he was told. Then, in a startling turnabout, Buron Fitts brought contempt charges against Clinton, demanding release of the evidence. Clinton, supported by the Minority Group, refused. This would jeopardize their case and intimidate witnesses. He was going to present his evidence to the entire body or not at all.

On Friday, Fitts went after the contractor who had testified against Bauer about the paint contract. He indicted Leo Flowers for perjury and hauled him into jail. That night, Fitts, Ugene Blalock, Bauer, and three officers visited the Eagle Rock home of notary Frank Angelillo, who worked in Brigham Rose's office and had witnessed Flowers' affidavit. A scuffle ensued. Fitts struck Frank's brother Tony with a pistol. Their mother Giovannina was also pushed around, but she defended herself. She grabbed a stick of firewood and struck Blalock on the head, opening his scalp. The next day newspaper pictures showed with graphic clarity the puffy face and discolored flesh resulting from the pistol whipping given to Mr. Angelillo and his aged mother.

Other significant events followed in short progression. Arthur Sims, the former police investigator who had fingered W.A. Taylor as the "bag man" for the Central Avenue vice district, disappeared. CIVIC investigators found Sims sequestered in county jail on a trumped-up vagrancy charge.

On November 10, Clinton's assistant Hanson Hathaway resigned from Clinton's employ, giving an extremely damaging interview in the process. "I am no longer convinced of Mr. Clinton's altruism," said Hathaway. "He told me he wants to make Page One every day." Some others who worked with Clinton remembered that Hathaway had actually suggested a bombing as a great way to get publicity.

> There was a question in many minds concerning Hathaway's statement and switch, especially among the members of CIVIC, because some of them had warned us that there was certain to be an attempt to place a "plant" in our camp. It had come true. Actually we had two resignations of members who, though, they still had faith in the Cause and in our integrity, became rather fearful of our boldness and naivety. My only answer was that if Hathaway had been a planted spy, we could not suffer, we were doing nothing dishonorable, nothing that the opposition group could not know. In fact, almost daily, I invited any of that group who would to speak on our Radio Voice, and answer, explain or denounce what we were saying or doing. They never appeared. We did what we knew to be right, honest, and "above board" . . . but I knew there was much concern. . . . Lest our campaign for decency fall victim to the opposition as had every other attempt to unseat the vice-lords from their powerful seats of control.

Taylor was summoned to appear at the trial of Sims, which meant that he would have to explain his connection with Central Avenue. On the morning of November 12, he was at the gasoline station he owned at Country Club Drive and Crenshaw Boulevard, talking with the pastor of a local Christian church. Taylor, who was on his way to testify in court, suddenly took ill and had to be helped to his Crenshaw Boulevard home. He died before inhalator equipment arrived.

The unproven suspicion by the other grand jurors was that he died of a heart attack from the stress of Clinton's accusations of his connection to vice in South Central Los Angeles. Following this event, and unfortunately for Clinton, the jurors who were impartial and conscientious began to believe the charges of those who were not, that Clinton was out to get all of them in a bid for his own fame and power. A number of jurors turned on Clinton and blamed him for Taylor's death. But Clinton dug in his heels, convinced that his decision not to divulge evidence was a good one.

> When "little people" such as Mr. Sims and Mr. Flowers are subjected to the pressures of a whole city and county, they often quail and wish to avoid the dangerous, though righteous, defense of their liberties, their jobs, and their safety. . . . We felt certain that if the jury heard the evidence as a body, they would act as honorable citizens, which was their sworn duty. A grand juror is supposed to act impartially and is adjured to have no interest in the matters that come before him or her.

Superior Court Judge Emmet Wilson dismissed the contempt charges against Clinton on November 14. "The district attorney," said Judge Wilson, "has no authority to compel Mr. Clinton to submit his evidence to him or his office." The struggle between the two factions had brought the grand jury to a halt. The contempt charges did have one constructive effect. They enabled Clinton to get his charges into open court records. Clinton beseeched the judge:

> If you will give me an unattached deputy district attorney and permit me to bring in witnesses, I shall unfold in competent, unimpeachable sworn testimony the whole sordid, stinking mess.

Eight days later, Judge Charles Fricke, who had succeeded Judge Aggeler, ordered the jurors to hear Clinton's evidence and had Fitts assign a deputy named D.L. DiVecchio to administer the hearing. On November 25, the grand jury assembled.

> The air was thick with animosity, emotions were taut. My inner feelings are best compared to quivering Jell-O ready to slide down the drain. Mr. O., one of those who had been named, came to me first, trembling as with rage and red of face. [He] pulled aside his coat, showing his revolver in a holster, and said, "Clinton, if you go on with this, I'll kill you." I assure you I had already been scared before that!

The first witness was Wilbur LeGette, a former associate of the notorious syndicate boss Charlie Crawford. Until he was assassinated in 1931, Crawford had controlled all gambling, bootlegging, and prostitution in Los Angeles County. LeGette testified that while working for Rheba Crawford Splivalo, the associate of Amy Semple McPherson, he saw her extort money from both the police department and the syndicate.

Blalock halted the proceedings, charging that the testimony of a liar and criminal was worthless and inadmissible as evidence. Clinton produced as evidence bank statements showing payoff deposits to Splivalo's bank account. Bauer interrupted the presentation, charging that Clinton was only trying to smear public officials. Bauer then called as witnesses two former CIVIC investigators. One was Hanson Hathaway, who characterized Clinton as insincere. To the press these charges confirmed the image of Clinton as a "publicity monger and political charlatan." Bauer and Fitts had accomplished what they planned, most likely by paying the Clinton's investigators to betray him. Stung by these charges and seeing the hopelessness of his position, Clinton declined to continue.

On November 29, Bauer and the Majority group again filed charges of contempt of court against Clinton, as well as A. Brigham Rose and Harry Ferguson. "It is a great pleasure to be held in contempt," said Rose. "The grand jury has no idea of the immensity of the contempt I have for it."

The three quickly filed countercharges of contempt against Bauer. In a fit of pique, Ugene Blalock said Clinton and his fellow jurors should be thrown in jail and see how easy it would be to get out. The next day, Judge Wilson dismissed the charges against Clinton and Ferguson, saying that Bauer had exceeded his authority in filing them. The charges against Bauer, however, were not dismissed.

By December 1937, the grand jury's term was about to end, and the body, despite all the wrangling and disagreements, was determined to present some accomplishment to the public. It indicted realtor William Coyne for extortion. Coyne had used the cover of the A.M. Wilkinson vice campaign to threaten houses of prostitution in neighborhoods where he was selling homes. The indictment implicated Dr. Wilkinson, but the grand jury was unable to prove any connection between the two. The term "reform racket" stuck, however.

By this time, Clinton informed Bauer that although the Majority's tactics had prevented him from revealing evidence, he had every intention of pursuing his goals as the leader of CIVIC. DiVecchio stated that Clinton's evidence was insufficient. Clinton responded that it appeared insufficient because not all of it was presented.

> Not by any means was all our information given, nor will it be given until we can bring
> it before an impartial body. The jury has wasted three months of its session in needless
> litigation.

On the last day of the term, Bauer was convicted of contempt and fined one hundred dollars, a small vindication for Clinton and Rose.

In late December, Clinton and Rheba Crawford engaged in a spirited debate in an open forum format at the Central Congregationalist Church in Los Angeles. As the grand jury was about to disband, its members exchanged gifts. Clinton gave a big white cake to Buron Fitts.

On December 31, the 1937 Grand Jury released the *Grand Jury Report of 1937*, which was authored by Bauer. The report lauded the indictment of William Coyne, and it condemned Clinton and the other Minority members for their "cannibalistic delight in tearing to shreds" the mayor, the district attorney, and numerous others. Bauer's words were pointedly brutal:

> Public Enemy No. 1 in this county is not the gun-toting racketeer, nor the oily-tongued confidence man, nor the Shylock of business. Public Enemy No. 1 is malicious, unbridled, reputation-smearing gossip!

The report was praised in the *Los Angeles Times* and published without editorial comment in the Hearst papers. The *Hollywood Citizen-News* called it a whitewash of corruption. The report infuriated Clinton, and he was not going to let it go unanswered. He sat down with Bogue, Ferguson, and Kelly to write the *Grand Jury Minority Report of 1937*. When they presented the document to Judge Fricke, he refused to file it, stating that there was no mechanism in the rules for an unofficial report. The group then took its report to Judge Bowron. He, too, was unable to endorse the report; he did suggest that Clinton distribute the report to key individuals and agencies. Clinton followed his advice, sending copies to political organizations, labor unions, and church and civic groups. Three hundred copies of the *Grand Jury Minority Report of 1937* were disseminated in early 1938. Part of the report read:

> Upon disbanding the 1937 Grand Jury, Judge Fricke received and filed for public record a report signed by the foreman. Immediately upon that report being filed, Mr. Clifford E. Clinton, on behalf of the minority presented a report. This the judge refused to file as a public document, ordering it kept secret. Protest was made by juror Harry L. Ferguson but the judge ruled that, until reversed by the Supreme Court, the document would be kept secret. We print it because the same document was made in duplicate, and one copy filed with the presiding judge with the Superior Court. Below is the report of the minority.

> TO THE SUPERIOR COURT OF THE COUNTY OF LOS ANGELES

> Pursuant to our oath of office and to the instructions of the late Honorable William Tell Aggeler, then in charge of the Grand Jury on behalf of this court, we have "diligently inquired into . . . public offenses against the people," and exerted the "greatest and most conscientious efforts towards the securing for the people of this county, clean, decent and honest government," and have searched out "graft and corruption." Our conclusions follow:

1. In the County of Los Angeles a deplorably bad influence is being exerted over local government by a powerful, greedy, cruel, ruthless underworld political machine supplied with an abundance of funds from the growing profits from illicit operations.

2. A portion of the underworld profits have been used in financing campaigns for the election of District Attorney, Mayors of various cities, some Councilmen, some Supervisors, and some other officials in vital positions, and the crime clique frequently designate the personnel for important commission and key spots in our local government.

3. It is through this medium and modus operandi that these official Molochs and Raffles succeed in avoiding the searchlight of official scrutiny and investigation into their iniquitous activities. Numerous public officials and their apologists and defenders have pronounced: "There are no racketeers in Los Angeles City and County. . . . Los Angeles City and County are free from vice and racketeers." We therefore propose to name some of the *dramatis personae* of the Los Angeles racket drama, and we ask pointedly of the Los Angeles City and County officials if they deny that these persons exist and whether they disclaim these persons have operated joints and rackets because of the protection afforded by the political racketeers who direct this crime coalition. Guy McAfee, Bob Gans, Wade Buckwald, Sam Temple, Chuck Addison, Nola Hahn, George Goldie, Eddie Nealius, Joe Botch Davis, Andy Foley, the Curland brothers, the Page boys, Homer "Slim" Gordon, Dennie Chapman, Doc Keboe, Doc Daugherty, Joe Hall, Tudor Sherer, Theodore "Teddy" Crawford, Richard "Dick" Elgin, Louie Bardeson, Floyd Odin, Rich Baker, EXBAILBOND Murray, High Goldbaum, Dick Considine, Lucius Lomax.

4. The public in large part has been kept in ignorance of deplorable conditions through:
   A. Clever propaganda in radio broadcasts and the sinister control of news sources.
   B. Seemingly vigorous prosecution of various offenders, thugs and mobsters who are not members of the protected crime syndicate, prosecuted as an example of those who are not in on the payoff.
   C. Campaigns to discredit or terrorize every sincere citizen who, learning the truth, raises his voice in warning to the public.
   D. Gifts, campaign employment with generous compensation, the subsidizing of certain newspaper attaches with emoluments from secret service funds, the cajoling of prominent citizens, civic and religious leads by the conferring of honorary police and sheriff officer's courtesy cards and shields and promises of special favors or protection.

5. The tremendous profits from large gambling establishments, bookmaking, slot machines, marble games, punch boards, and other rackets are made possible by the monopoly maintained by the few organized as a "syndicate" for the maintenance of their kind of government.

6. Influence is also exerted over government by a large group comprising those who seek business favors from governmental agencies, those who fear that they may need protection in questionable acts or protection against injury that might result from a scandal connected with individuals prominent in their businesses.

7. The Crime Coalition seldom resorts to the crude machination of bribery as a base of their operations. The control is acquired through prearranged provisos upon which

campaign contributions will be made and frequently two contestants for important public office are supported by the combination. Campaign deficits are cleared for agreed considerations and allegiance and fealty on the part of the candidate seeking contributions is procured in advance and sometimes takes the form of a resignation signed in advance. The most significant fact is the amount of these campaign contributions in the key offices. The sums which are contributed by the czars of the crime incubus frequently exceed by tenfold the salary for the full term for which such officials are elected.

HIGH PLACE HARMONY

8. The principal law enforcement agencies of the County, the District Attorney, the Sheriff and the Chief of Police of Los Angeles, work in complete harmony and never interfere with the activities of the important figures in the underworld. Although the District Attorney has a crew of sixty investigators and the Police Department its so denominated "Metropolitan Squad," used primarily to terrorize citizens opposing the administration, together with stupendous so-called "secret service funds," these agencies have never attempted to lay facts before the Grand Jury pertaining to the system under which the underworld carries on its activities.

9. Control of the Grand Jury is sought by those to whom immunity from law enforcement is important. The following testimony appears on the records of the Grand Jury: "It is a matter of common knowledge by everyone on Spring Street that this jury is controlled twelve to seven by the combination." It has also been legally established by failure on the part of those charged to deny the same in open court, that certain of the personnel of the present Grand Jury have a close connection with Bob Gans, slot machine racketeer, and affiliations with the present political machine through business and other connections.

10. Service of the public interests by the Grand Jury is prevented by membership in that body of:
   A. Politically ambitious persons who will accept the aid of the "syndicate" in the furtherance of their selfish ends.
   B. Persons connected with institutions that seek business or favors from public officials, associations and friends of those in public office whose operations should have the scrutiny of the Grand Jury.
   C. Persons over whom can be held a club in the form of a threat of exposure or embarrassment or promise of special favors.

11. Complete control of the Grand Jury by the District Attorney and by stacked committees can prevent the Grand Jury from even starting to perform the duty which it is commanded by law to perform.

The report stated that it was "common knowledge along Spring Street that the 1937 Grand Jury was controlled by gambling syndicates" and reiterated the charge that John Bauer and Harry Chapman should have been disqualified. The report ended with specific recommendations:

1. Make improvements in the method of selecting members of the Grand Jury so as to exclude all who would be subject to ulterior influence.
2. Make provisions for the grand jury to select its own legal advisor and to issue subpoenas without first obtaining the approval of the District Attorney.
3. The State Attorney General should accept his responsibility and exercise his authority by conducting a thorough investigation of the political operations of special interests in Los Angeles County and by prosecuting those involved.
4. Make changes in the law governing campaign contributions to the end that underworld earnings, racketeering profits, and all special interest funds may be either excluded from campaigns or made public.

Response to the Minority Report was predictably vehement. The *Los Angeles Times* called it an irresponsible smear meant to further Clinton's political ambitions. Harry Chandler, the publisher and editor-in-chief of the *Times*, was a conservative partisan and, beyond that, the most powerful man in Los Angeles. He was not going to let Clinton destroy his hold on Los Angeles. Mayor Shaw called Clinton a "ruthless, self-seeking muckraker bent on character assassination" but did not sue him for libel. He had other means of reprisal.

The Minority didn't stop. They released a subsequent document to bolster the arguments in the Minority Report. This document entitled "Addendum and Appendix to Minority Report 1937 Grand Jury" reads as follows:

TO THE SUPERIOR COURT OF LOS ANGELES COUNTY

The general public should be aware by this time that the probe the Minority of the Grand Jury so arduously endeavored to initiate was hampered at every turn by the powerful forces that were being affected by it.

Even the uninitiated would not believe that thousands of gambling joints, houses of prostitution, tango games, slot machines, bookmaking establishments and other devices through which millions of dollars are taken, could operate outside the knowledge of those paid by the public to prevent such operations.

Surely this being the case, there could not have been any good and valid objection interposed to our erstwhile efforts to investigate the persons who were then and now are conducting illegal operations in this area.

Public officials and their apologists and defenders are even now denying that joints and dens of iniquity have operated because of the protection afforded by the politico-racketeers and are accusing those of us who have opposed graft, racketeering and corruption, with playing politics.

We wonder if these defenders and apologists of the gambling and vice incubus will claim these are figments of political imagining.

Gambling joints, houses, and bookies have been operating for months. Numerous reports have been turned in by private citizens only to be ignored. One place operated within a few yards of one of the Sheriff's sub-stations, but why argue about that?

Law enforcement officials have declared seemingly in response to our first report, that they have no evidence of such activities. Despite these declarations, several of this minority declare without equivocation that as late as last night such joints were operated, and unless tipped off, will be operating when the shades of night fall this evening, and for the edification of officialdom we refer the gentry to the following establishments: (Addresses were here listed of many illegally operating establishments with the number of patrons visiting them on the day before this report.)

These sundry institutions are an infinitesimal portion of the joints operating and are particularly specified because some of the undersigned personally were able to check these operations only yesterday, and we respectfully submit, if the law enforcement officials do not know of these activities, how in the name of common sense would it be possible for several of this minority to know and so easily ascertain the facts pertaining to their operations up to the typing of this document.

For the sake of brevity we will only mention a few other facts:
1. Marble games throughout the city ceased to pay off a few weeks before the last mayoralty campaign.
2. They resumed payment a few weeks after, according to a prearranged schedule thousands began simultaneously to pay off.
3. They continued until the activities of a certain citizens' committee brought about a drought when it appeared that a real investigation might actually break through.

We desire to go on record as declaring that:
1. We have no personal animosity toward any public official.
2. That the heads of the leading departments have royally entertained the undersigned along with other members of the Grand Jury, and that there is no lack of appreciation.
3. We are, however, in a quandary to ascertain an answer to the question why certain illegal, law violating places are allowed to operate continuously.
4. And what part do the huge campaign funds play in this stage production?
5. And why an honest investigation cannot be initiated.

With these minor, but most significant items abbreviated, let us pass to a situation that will make it all very plain:

We now address ourselves to a consideration of a few of the aspects reverberating around the so-called Clinton case, and we feel that these will in some measure lift the veil and remove some of the camouflage engendered by propaganda of the last three months:
1. It should be known that the investigation requested by Juror Clifford E. Clinton was authorized by the jury.
2. The presentation of the case started in apparently good faith.
3. The proceedings were tolerated and testimony heard up to the point when certain public officials appeared upon the horizon, whereupon the proceedings were, with unusual ceremony, abruptly halted by a majority of this body.

4. It has never been revealed what particular agencies determined that this investigation should not go on.
5. It was claimed by the District Attorney and certain favored members of the majority of this body that one of the witnesses produced was incompetent.
6. Thereupon in replication, Mr. Clinton advised the Jury that he would establish every statement of fact made and testified to by this alleged incompetent witness by other witnesses whose competency and qualifications could not be impugned.
7. This proffer was rejected and three months of bitter court litigation and consternation, with attending acrimony, ensued. We ask respectfully whether this was a result of any act of the taxpayers in this community or the general public. Can there be any doubt as to the source of the obstruction and activities aforesaid?
8. The court and the public are entitled to know that:
    A. Mr. Clinton did not have a monopoly upon corruption in high places.
    B. Anyone seriously impelled to do so could and can procure evidence to support an indictment and conviction.
    C. It should be generally known that the Grand Jury can investigate any matter it chooses where the objective is the bringing to justice of persons engaged in criminal practices, and the corruption and pollution of our government.
    D. This jury had in the past actually investigated numerous matters and causes without this form of procedure. The fact cannot be disregarded that an inquiry of the character proposed by Clifford E. Clinton necessarily entails the consideration of the jury as a body. And it is this character of case that justifies the existence of, and is the most outstanding and pronounced function of a Grand Jury.
    E. Why should this particular case have been turned over to a deputy district attorney after months of wrangling, for the purpose of inquiring into the matter which was primarily the Grand Jury's business and most important function?
    F. The salient point is that the Grand Jury could have determined in several hours the matters that it determined not to inquire into and shun for a period of three months.
    G. It is unfairly claimed that these conditions were provoked by reason of the asserted wide publicity given to the Clinton matter, whereas it is most manifest that no publicity would have ensued save for the antics of the obstructionists and the artifices employed in the endeavor to kill the inquiry in its incipient stages.

Be it said that the activities of this minority have been directed against this underworld influence and we call upon all law-abiding citizens and officials to aid and not to discredit or minimize, our humble efforts in this direction.

Before we return to our places as citizens, we desire to call attention, in passing, to the now familiar antics and the obstruction tactics employed to prevent an uninterrupted inquiry into matters of grave public concern.

Respectfully,

Harry L. Ferguson
Earl H. Kelly
John L. Bogue
Clifford E. Clinton

The Los Angeles press publicized the "no-holds-barred" *Grand Jury Minority Report of 1937* in an unexpurgated form. In contrast to the majority report, which created little interest, the inflammatory statements by Clinton and his group were definitive in their accusations and conclusions and caused a strong public reaction. The *Hollywood Citizen News,* which had provided favorable press coverage for Clinton and CIVIC during the struggle to present evidence to the grand jury connecting the underworld to the Shaw administration, labeled the report courageous and shockingly accurate. Without expressing editorial opinion on the matter, the *Daily News, Examiner,* and *Herald & Express,* published much of the contents of the document. The *Times* portrayed the report as a pathetic attempt to smear public officials as a way for Clinton to attain his own political ambitions. But as Clinton recalled it:

> Attacks were made on Clifton's Cafeteria by the health department and other city licensing boards. We were struck a real blow when the property taxes on our Broadway location were suddenly reassessed to the tune of $6,700, a huge increase, and totally out of line with assessments of adjacent properties. We tried to appeal but to no avail. Anonymous threats were common during this time, some written and some by telephone.

Because of the hostile *Times* coverage, Clinton's patrons were aware of his campaign. And Clinton was frustrated:

> Scandal sheets were circulated against us. They charged that our motive was revenge against county officials for enforcing health statutes. According to these publications, we had been enjoined to clean up a filthy establishment.

Although Clinton strongly denied the charges of filth and unsanitary conditions in his restaurant, once these charges were made public by the health department, there was little he could do to refute them. There was a series of food poisoning cases in which an alleged patron would go to the city emergency hospital and claim to have eaten at Clifton's, thereby ensuring that a file at the Board of Health grew larger and larger. Other patrons would create a disturbance after finding a foreign object in their meal. Still others would take a noisy spill down the stairs and then demand a settlement from Clinton's insurance company.

> Our carriers necessarily raised our premiums—over 400 percent—and we eventually canceled the prohibitive policies. We met this challenge by placing a large sign at each entrance and by handing a small printed slip to each guest. It said: "Enter at your own

risk." We explained that Clifton's was taking special precautions to guard against all hazards to guests. If despite our diligence they should experience the unavoidable, it would be at their own risk.

As might be expected, the volume of business was affected. Clinton wrote promises and warnings to his guests through the table brochure *Food for Thot*. He promised to do everything possible to assure his customers' safety and to strive to serve wholesome, nutritious food. He also warned them not to believe everything they were reading in the papers about him. This helped his business, but not his public image.

As 1937 ended, his crusade was becoming expensive. Shaw, Fitts, Chandler, and Davis were stronger than ever. Clinton was the one who had stuck his neck out, and, while he had escaped physical harm, he looked pretty foolish. His political enemies had planted the seeds of doubt, causing many to believe that Clinton was nothing more than a malcontent attacking an honest administration. But he wasn't about to give up.

The Clifton Tray...of
FOOD 4 THOT

"A TRA-FUL FOR A TRI-FUL"   Sept. 29, 1938.   Issue No. 342

"We pray our humble service be measured, not by Gold, but by the Golden Rule," Clifton's: 618 So. Olive St. and 648 So. Broadway, L. A., TR-1673. Suggestions and criticisms appreciated—Drop in Bowl at Cash Desk. Happy to be at your service.—Clifford E. Clinton.

THESE SERVICES at "618" South Olive St.—"Free Meals to Deserving," "Meal Credits," "How to Find a Friend,". "Free Advisory Service," "Guests' Exchange," "Travel Service," "Clifton Chaplain, Your Friend," "CIVIC Information," "Phone, Mail and Notary Service," "Food 4 Thot Mailing," "Gold, Silver and Diamonds Bought," "Barber Shop," "Beauty Salon," "Free Tourists and Residents Official Information, Maps, etc." "Complete Hotel and Housing Accommodations," "Daily Free and Paid Sightseeing Trips," "Gerry's Get-Together Club"—For fuller information—See:

'About Cliftons'—An informative folder available at front desk answers questions.

HEAR CLIFFORD E. CLINTON
KEHE — Four Times Daily — Monday through Friday — 9:30 A. M., 12:30 Noon, 7 P. M., 11 P. M.

A CHALLENGE — LOS ANGELES
"HOLD HIGH THE TORCH"

Hold high the torch! Do not forget its glow;
It was given you from other hands, you know.
'Tis only yours to keep it burning bright,
Yours to pass on to those who need its light.
I guess the world is movin' on;
  A lot of good old things are gone.
But why be sad and why be glum?
  A lot of good new things have come!
　　　　　　　　—*Douglas Malloch.*
　　　Copyright, McClure Syndicate.

MEN OF EARTH - *Edwin Markham*

We men of the earth have here the stuff
Of Paradise. We have enough.
We need no other stones to build
The stairs into the unfulfilled
No other marble for the floors
No other ivory for the doors
No other cedar for the beams
And dome of men's immortal dream.

Here on the path of everyday
Here on the common human way
Is ALL the stuff the gods would take
To build new heavens. To mould
And make New Edens
Out of the stuff sublime
To build Eternity in Time.

The gates of yesterday are closed behind us and the fields of the other years we shall till no more. We gather no harvests from the acres of Tomorrow. But Today is ours to use and to enjoy. Are there heights to be climbed, are there wrongs to be righted, are there deeds to be accomplished. Then let us attempt to do them now.

This is our hour for labor, for liberality, for service. Today is our day for worship, for friendship, and for love. Let us make the most of it while it is ours.—Rev. Willsie Martin.
　　　　　　　—Compliments of Elihu W. Sargent.

FORWARD MARCH
My idea is this: Ever onward. If God had intended that man should go backward, He would have given him an eye in the back of his head.—*Victor Hugo.*

THE WAYS - *John Oxenham*

To every man there openeth
Full many a different way,
And the high soul climbs the high way,
And the low soul gropes the low,
And in between on the misty flats,
The rest drift to and fro,
But to every man there openeth
A high way and a low,
And every man decideth
The way his soul shall go.

WANTED

God give us men. The time demands
  Strong minds, great hearts, true faith, and willing hands;
Men whom the lust of office does not kill;
  Men whom the spoils of office cannot buy;
Men who possess opinions and a will;
  Men who have honor; men who will not lie;
Men who stand before a demagogue
  And damn his treacherous flatteries without winking;
Tall men, sun-crowned, who live above the fog
  In public duty and in private thinking.

WE CAN BUILD THE WORLD'S GREATEST CITY

We bargained with Life for a Penny,
We worked for menial's hire,
Only to learn dismayed,
That any wage we had asked of Life,
Life would have paid.
I want the folks at home to say,
  Whatever others say about me,
That here or there or far away
  There is no need for them to doubt me.
However separations grieve,
Or slanders hurt, if they believe
  A fellow still can do his best
  And not much care about the rest.
　　　　　　　—*Douglas Malloch.*
　　　Copyright, McClure Syndicate.

THE GUESTS' VOICE
Letters, criticisms, suggestions welcome.

ACCUSED

"You are accused of being a KKK; that the recall was an attempt to seize control of the city; . . . Of figuring on nepotism, by controlling New Mayor Bowron, to have your father, brothers and other relatives and yourself appointed on various commissions or city jobs at fat salaries; of threatening your help, if any of them were found not working and voting for Bowron, they would be fired; that if Bowron was not elected—they would all be fired—and you would close up and leave the city."
—*B. C. C.*

Dear Friend—You miss so many other things of which I have within the last few months been accused—Communist—Ultra Conservative—Open Shopper—Labor Hater—Food Poisoner—Degenerate—Thief—Convict—Blue Nose—Advocate of licensed vice—Hash Slinger—Dictator—Politician—Disgruntled bigot—Malcontent—Subversive Influence—The greatest enemy to the city, etc.

AND BLESS YOU—*These charges are not mere whispers—They have been showered upon this city in newspapers—thrown from airplanes—distributed on every doorstep—printed in scandal sheets by the millions of copies.*

And most of you know that our business has been falsely branded—As unutterably filthy, working our Associates under unspeakable conditions—paying them little or nothing, and other terrible charges.

As to our business—What I might say—might be considered biased—But any guest may ask our Associates themselves—And feel perfectly free at any time to ask our managers to take you through the cafeterias. See for yourselves—We feel the need to put up no further defense.

Here are the simple facts about the Health Department treatment of our business—

I served in late 1935—as chairman of Citizens Committee—under appointment of Board of Supervisors—through which the Management of the General Hospital was changed.

After this we suffered some unfavorable attention from our Administration.

We felt if a citizen and a business could not assist his city without reprisal we should oppose that type administration—We did in the 1936 Election.

About this time we took over "648" which had many years operated under permit from the Health Department—We immediately instituted a complete rehabilitation program as we found the premises—worse than the scandal sheets charged—During this the Health Commission took most unusual steps to harass us—Even though they had long permitted without molestation the vile premises which we took over. Its operators were not openly active in securing a more honest administration—

In 1937—Judge Bowron placed my name in the Grand Jury—It was drawn—The Health Department worked constantly to oppose me in an effort to bring the truth to light—As well as the police department and other departments—my home of times were attacked and bombed—Our taxes on "648" were raised after "We" took it—$6500 a year—a raise 30% out of proportion with city or neighborhood increase.

We desired nothing and do not now—more than an honest—efficient—honorable local government—And the privilege to work in its behalf without thought of recognition—reward—jobs—favors or anything—We feel it a privilege to be able to give our service in this cause—Our guests and loyal Associates have made whatever progress is and will be made possible—A debt of gratitude will be long owed to you—by this great city.

I urge all of you—not to ask me to assist you, or anyone to get city jobs—I am fighting for a city free from spoils system—and patronage policies—I therefore must not break this principle—If you desire to assist this city—and want a job—make your application through the proper process—If you desire to give service without reward or remuneration—Give of your help—your information—your true understanding and devotion—and together we can continue to build a still finer Los Angeles.

CIVIC

Many would like to assist financially — Keep CIVIC fact-finding bureau and the Radio programs—so these peoples can know the truth—

You will be issued a "Good Government Bond"—if you contribute a dollar or more a year—Citizens united—contributing their small bit—can outbid selfish and corrupting influences—and keep their city government that they so recently and grandly regained.

CIVIC Headquarters and Clearing House—618 S. Olive St., Front Mezz. Phone TRinity 1673.

SIX EVENINGS with noted lecturers, musical artists and the screen — Temple Baptist Church, Burdette Hall, Second Floor, the Philharmonic Auditorium Building, Fifth and Olive Streets, Los Angeles — Wednesday Evenings, October 5th - November 9th, 1938; 7 to 8 o'clock. Tickets, six events, 50 cents.

TO MAKE A TOWN - Douglas Malloch
Copyright, McClure Syndicate.

One tree will never make a wood,
A thousand others make it good,
Create a leafy neighborhood.

When you behold a certain town
Whose huts are gray and lawns are brown,
'Twas not the houses that fell down.

It was the people, it was these
Who did not grow as grow the trees
That make the forest harmonies.

Oaks do not leave it to the pine,
Pines to the oaks—they intertwine

To make this woodland word of Mine.

Green cannot leave the work to Gray,
Or Gray to Green. Each his own way
Must build a city day by day.

Beside the maple stands the beach,
While all around the others reach,
In purpose one, what race or speech.

And so profession links with trade,
And business comes to labor's aid,
For so it is a town is made.

"I AM ONLY ONE, BUT I AM ONE"

I am only one
But I am one.
I cannot do everythng,
But I can do something.
What I can do
I ought to do.
What I ought to do
By the Grace of God
I will do.

NO TASK is too trivial to be well done. Progress lives not in the nature of the work we do, but in the manner in which we do it. Any job offers possibilities far beyond the most distant dreams of the worker. Why? Because every man places the trademark of his hand and brain upon the result of his work, and the searchlight of business is constantly seeking out those who are reliable, sincere and loyal.

DANGER! KEEP MOVING! - Capt. Arthur W. Beer

One summer day I paused to view
Some workmen on a building new,
When, "Hike! you loafer," someone cried—
From nervous shock I nearly died—
A rock that weighed a tone or more
Just missed me by some inches four;
Then, as I jumped, this sign I saw:
        Danger! Keep Moving!

These were my thoughts, as on I fled:
It seems 'tis best to forge ahead;
Quite evident it is to me,
Side shows I must not stop to see:
As thru this earthly vale I speed
My new-taught lesson I will heed,
And in the skies this signal read:
        Danger! Keep Moving!

Then hearken kindly one and all,
While words of wisdom from me fall:
If you would scale the heights of fame,
Or win fair Fortune—fickle dame!—
Whatever be the game you play—
From politics to making hay—
This be your slogan every day:
        Danger! Keep Moving!

13

ENGINE IN THE STREET

JANUARY 1938 WAS A CHEERLESS PERIOD FOR CIVIC AND FOR CLIFFORD CLINTON. The organization slowed down. Four of its members had been actively involved with the controversy, so there was no full committee to administer projects. The other members tried to keep busy. They tried to study city government, but it was hard to concentrate when morale was low. CIVIC needed a focus, a rallying point. It would soon have one.

Private detective Harry Raymond was still working behind the scenes to link the Frank Shaw administration with the syndicate. In addition to sleuthing for CIVIC, Raymond was working for a former Shaw employee, Ralph Gray. Gray had been on the Shaw campaign in 1933, and he wanted to collect the $2,900 owed him since then by a campaign manager named Harry Munson. Ironically, Raymond saw a connection between his two unrelated cases. The Gray-Munson case and the Clinton investigation shared one element: Frank Shaw.

Gray had seen Munson accept a twenty-thousand-dollar campaign contribution from the slot-machine boss Bob Gans. Gray had also seen gambling kingpin Guy McAfee negotiate with Shaw to appoint Munson police commissioner. This information could galvanize the CIVIC crusade. As Raymond got closer to completing the Gray investigation, he sensed that he was being watched. He was. Captain Earl Kynette, the head of the spy squad, and his assistant, Lieutenant Roy Allen, had rented a vacant house on Orme Street in Boyle Heights directly across from Raymond's home. Beginning in September 1937, they began a rotating surveillance routine involving members of the spy squad who monitored Raymond's phone calls and visitors.

Kynette was another policeman who had come up through the ranks. In the 1920s, the Los

Angeles Police Department was well known for its rough-and-tumble police tactics. If a witness or suspect grew difficult, an officer could kill him without fear of prosecution. Kynette joined the department in 1925 on the advice of Albert Marco, the head of the syndicate's prostitution ring. When Marco was deported, Kynette's image was tarnished, but only temporarily. Chief Davis hired him back and rewarded him with a position on the infamous spy squad. By 1938, he was overseeing seventeen operatives.

On the nippy morning of Friday January 14, Raymond said goodbye to his wife and walked to his garage. His wife, who was visiting with her neighbor, had barely said good morning when she heard—and felt—a shattering blast. It came from the garage. When she got to it, it was a smoking ruin. The engine of the family car was lying in the street. Raymond was inside the mangled chassis of the car, torn and bleeding.

An ambulance rushed Raymond to the Georgia Street Receiving Hospital. He was in shock, but conscious. He asked to see Jim Richardson, the city editor of the *Los Angeles Examiner*. Raymond was in serious condition. He had suffered a broken ankle, compound fractures in one arm, and a severed artery. His body was riddled with more than 180 fragments of metal, glass, and wood. His car had been rigged with an iron pipe bomb that was packed with dynamite and wired to the starter. When he pressed the starter button, the bomb detonated. He was lucky to be alive.

Clinton and Brigham Rose entered Raymond's hospital room. He recognized them.

> Harry lay bleeding when we arrived, but he was still tough, flint-eyed, and hard as a rock.

Clinton recalled that Richardson rushed in and went to Raymond's side, and beseeched the patient: "Who did it, Harry?" Clinton heard the answer:

> That sonofabitch Kynette. They told me they would get me. They put Kynette on me. He and his boys were shadowing me. I've known for weeks. They had my phone tapped. Somewhere in the neighborhood you'll find where they had their listening devices. Kynette takes his orders from City Hall. He's the one who rigged the bomb. I want you to promise you'll get him for me.

"I'll get him for you, Harry," said Richardson.

Gray also came to see Raymond, who was by this time receiving the first of a hundred stitches. Gray started to talk to him, but was called to the phone. He told Clinton that when he answered, he heard an unfamiliar voice that threatened: "You're next. Maybe tomorrow. Maybe next week. We'll do a better job on you." Before Gray could speak, the anonymous caller hung up.

Another visitor entered Raymond's hospital room.

> I was bending over Harry's bed. I looked up—into the angry eyes of District Attorney Buron Fitts.

If Clinton was surprised to see Fitts, he was even more surprised to hear what he said. "Clinton, they've gone too far," Fitts whispered. "I'll convict them if it's the last thing I do."

Clinton could only wonder what was causing this abrupt change of direction. Was Fitts having an attack of conscience after seeing one of his former associates near death? While Raymond underwent further treatment, Clinton and Fitts adjourned to a secluded area of the hospital and worked out a truce. Hours later, a reporter from the national magazine *The Forum* saw them leave the hospital together, talking earnestly. Fitts returned to his office and went after Kynette.

On January 19, Fitts, along with his chief investigator Eugene Williams, Chief of Detectives Joseph Taylor, homicide detective Bert Wallis, and investigator John Klein, interrogated Acting Captain of Detectives Earle Kynette in the district attorney's offices. Accompanying Kynette was his attorney Joshua T. Oliver. The transcript of this interview was released in the *Examiner* on January 21, 1938.

The following is the interview between Kynette and his superior:

WILLIAMS: Your name is Earle Kynette?
A: Right
WILLIAMS: Are you an officer in the Los Angeles police department?
A: I am.
WILLIAMS: What is your official title?
A: Acting Captain of Detectives.
WILLIAMS: Are you assigned to any particular squad?
A: Intelligence Unit.
WILLIAMS: Under whom do you work in the intelligence unit?
A: My immediate superior is Warren Justin, captain of Metropolitan Unit.
WILLIAMS: How many men are in this intelligence squad?
A: About nineteen, I believe.
WILLIAMS: Including yourself?
A: Yes.
WILLIAMS: You have immediate charge of that squad?
A: Yes.
WILLIAMS: Where are your headquarters?
A: 311 West First St.
WILLIAMS: How long have you had charge of that squad?
A: About two years.
WILLIAMS: Do you take orders from anybody except Captain Justin?
A: Just what is the purpose of this questioning?
WILLIAMS: The purpose is to find out what, if any, connection you had with the bombing of Harry Raymond.
A: Then I refuse to make any further statements.
WILLIAMS: You decline on what grounds?
A: My Constitutional rights.
WILLIAMS: What rights?

CLIFTON'S AND CLIFFORD CLINTON

A: Constitutional rights on the grounds that it might tend to degrade or incriminate me or otherwise injure me.

WILLIAMS: You haven't any feeling of innocence in the matter?

OLIVER: I advised Mr. Kynette not to answer any question which in his opinion amounts to privileged communication or a violation of his Constitutional rights.

WILLIAMS: You understand Mr. Kynette is now being questioned in front of Joe Taylor, chief of detectives; the district attorney of this county, and you assert that it is a privileged communication in respect to any police work he has been doing?

OLIVER: I advised him so.

WILLIAMS: Chief Taylor, will you ask the questions as his superior?

TAYLOR: Have you done any work in connection with the Raymond case?

A: Section 202 of the city charter states that no superior officer can ask any question or force me to answer any question which may in any way be used to incriminate me or against me.

WILLIAMS: Have you the idea this questioning is to incriminate you?

A: I don't know what it is about; I have no idea.

WILLIAMS: You know that Raymond's garage was bombed?

A: It looks to me like a lot of politics—that like somebody is trying to pull a fast one.

WILLIAMS: I am not interested in politics. It is my job to investigate that explosion and try to get all the evidence we can in connection with it.

A: If I know any evidence that would tend to clear up any crime in this city, I would go and act on it myself.

WILLIAMS: Will you give that evidence to the superiors in the police department or the district attorney's office?

A: If it was on behalf of that idea, but where any idea—I have been brought up here with people apparently guarding me and have every reason to believe that I am under suspicion of something or that is not—

WILLIAMS: You are definitely accused of having participated in this crime of having bombed Harry Raymond on the fourteenth of January.

A: I had absolutely nothing to do with it.

WILLIAMS: Were you in the vicinity of his house on the fourteenth of January?

A: I will answer no more questions.

WILLIAMS: You refuse to answer that question?

A: I will answer no questions at all.

WILLIAMS: Do you refuse on the grounds that it might incriminate your?

A: I have no recollection of being in his vicinity. I may have been in his vicinity on police work.

WILLIAMS: Were you in his vicinity on the date of the bombing, the fourteenth of January of this year?

A. Yes, I was, in the afternoon after the bombing happened.

WILLIAMS: Were you in the vicinity of his place on the morning of the fourteenth of January 1938.

A. No.

WILLIAMS: Were you engaged in doing police work in the vicinity of his home at any time within two weeks prior to the fourteenth of January 1938?

A: There is no use asking me any more questions.

WILLIAMS: You decline to answer that question because your lawyer shook his head to you warning you not to answer?

A: That's it.

WILLIAMS: Is the reason you refuse to answer because you have a consciousness that you are guilty?

A: No.

WILLIAMS: Don't you regard it as a duty as a police officer to give any and all information you have in connection with the matter?

A: I do as in any case of crime.

WILLIAMS: You regard the bombing of Harry Raymond as a crime?

A: I do, and if I knew anything about it I would make arrests myself.

WILLIAMS: You wouldn't give any information you had to those in authority in the police department?

A: I would, but when there is any suspicion—I am under suspicion of this—the only thing I can do is not to make any further statement.

WILLIAMS: Were you working in the vicinity of Harry Raymond's place at any time during two weeks immediately preceding the fourteenth of January?

A: I decline to answer.

WILLIAMS: Were you there in the afternoon? What time?

A: I don't remember.

WILLIAMS: Why were you there?

A: I don't remember.

The rest of the interview was filled with "I don't remember" and "I decline to answer" as Kynette evaded the questions, and was eventually sent home by the district attorney.

Joseph Shaw and Police Chief James Davis were in Mexico on the day of the bombing, accompanying the police department's pistol team. Joseph Shaw, the mayor's brother and executive secretary, finally broke his silence by issuing a statement from City Hall, picked up by the *Examiner*. "I hope that the guilty persons in this affair will be promptly prosecuted and adequately punished, whoever they may be," he was quoted. He did, however, warn against any hasty judgments ("curbstone prosecution") about anyone until all evidence could be considered.

Mayor Frank Shaw was in Washington, D.C., obtaining federal assistance loans. He canceled the remainder of his trip and entrained for Los Angeles, arriving January 22. Davis returned the same day, and, before examining any evidence, proclaimed Kynette's innocence. Mayor Shaw denied any police involvement in the crime and blithely stated that if Raymond had been the target of a police stakeout, it was fully justified. Shaw went on to charge Clinton with perpetrating a publicity stunt that had gone awry. When Clinton was interviewed, he alleged that Raymond had had in his possession papers that would prove city officials had underworld connections.

The *Daily News*, the *Evening News*, the *Hollywood Citizen-News*, and the *Examiner* held that Shaw was behind the bombing. The general public who had been following the Clinton home bombing and the Raymond bombing were shocked by what they perceived as murderous attacks by Shaw. But the *Times* continued to criticize Clinton, as did various scandal sheets, including the *Herald of Decency*.

When unofficial polls were taken, though, they showed that opinion had shifted in Clinton's favor; the press coverage was convincing the public about duplicity within the administration. Many citizens now believed Clinton had been justified in fighting the administration. On January 31, the *Examiner* accused the Shaw administration of dealing with the underworld. The article identified Harry Munson as the courier between the syndicate and Joe Shaw's "Corner Pocket."

CIVIC wanted to make the most of the Raymond bombing. Even before the bombing, the membership of CIVIC had expanded, including two of the 1937 Grand Jury Minority members. After the bombing, CIVIC members were in demand to speak to church and neighborhood meetings throughout the city. Clinton began a letter-writing campaign in an appeal to the department of justice, the treasury, the governor, attorney general, and even the president of the United States for help in cleaning up the mess in Los Angeles. A deputy attorney general was assigned to assist Buron Fitts with the Raymond case. The state legislature named an Interim Vice Investigating Committee and a special Morals Committee. State House Speaker Moseley Jones, a member of the Interim Vice Investigating Committee, had several meetings with Clinton. Governor Frank Merriam stated he would support the Morals Committee. All of this outside interest turned out to be political posturing and did not add substantially to the CIVIC-Clinton investigation.

The *Times* limited its coverage of the Raymond case to statements by Mayor Shaw and Chief Davis, who averred that there was no connection between the bombing and the police department. Then the audacious Chief Davis assigned Captain Kynette to investigate the bombing. There was an outcry, so Davis began conducting the probe himself. On January 30, he announced that he was satisfied that neither Kynette nor any other member of the intelligence squad had any connection with the crime.

Kynette stated that Raymond had been responsible for the bombing. Raymond made no comment. He was undergoing a series of operations to remove debris from his body. District Attorney Fitts had heard enough. On February 6, he submitted evidence to the 1938 Grand Jury to indict Captain Kynette, Lieutenant Roy Allen, and Sergeant Fred Browne on four felony counts: conspiracy to commit murder, attempted murder, assault with intent to commit murder, and malicious use of explosives. Harry Raymond had suddenly, out of nowhere, become a central figure in the evolving story of the Clinton-Shaw fight.

In the 1920s, Raymond was a Los Angeles police officer working with Dick Lucas, a lieutenant described as "a racketeer with a police badge." Lucas was chief enforcer for syndicate boss Charlie Crawford, the "Gray Wolf of Spring Street." Raymond and Lucas were sent to kill a bootlegger who had hijacked illegal booze from syndicate member Albert Marco.

In 1927, Raymond was implicated in the frame-up of a local politician. City councilman Carl Jacobson had given the *Daily News* the addresses of some Sunset Boulevard brothels. Crawford's men offered Jacobson twenty-five thousand dollars to lay off. After Jacobson refused the bribe, Raymond and Lucas paid a flashy divorcee named Callie Grimes to entice Jacobson to her El Sereno home; she purportedly needed his help with an unfair property assessment. After offering Jacobson a drink, which he declined, Grimes gave the high sign to the police waiting outside. Someone bumped Jacobson over the head, stripped him to his red long johns, and photographed him lying next to the semi-clad woman. Jacobson and Raymond were both tried, and both trials resulted in hung juries, proving only that jurors could be intimidated. Two years later, Grimes admitted her part in the crime.

When Roy Steckel took over as chief of police under Mayor John Porter, his first order of business was to deprive Crawford of police protection. Steckel then fired Raymond and Lucas. In 1931, Crawford was assassinated by a politician he had demoted. Raymond left town and served as police chief in San Diego before returning to Los Angeles in 1934 to work for the Automobile Club of Southern California. In 1936, he became a private investigator. In June 1937, when he took on Gray's case, Kynette began watching him. In the process of investigating the case, Raymond had found enough information to "blow the lid off City Hall."

One day, Kynette stopped Raymond on the sidewalk in front of the Hall of Records. "This thing has got to stop," said Kynette. "You can't put the heat on this administration. And I hope you don't try to get tough. You remember what happened to Red Foster." Kynette was referring to a December 1935 incident in which a political publisher's home was bombed.

The Los Angeles press was having the proverbial field day with the Harry Raymond story. Manchester Boddy, the publisher of the *Daily News* and the *Evening News*, took the unprecedented step of congratulating his rival the *Examiner* for printing the whole story of the "invisible government mess," and for fingering Bob Gans, Guy McAfee, and Harry Munson. The *Times* was still holding back, but Boddy was delighted that the Hearst papers had joined the pack. "This means," wrote Boddy, "that four out of five Los Angeles newspapers are now facing the fact that an aroused public can compel the housecleaning necessary to reestablish confidence in local government."

A dramatic consequence of the Raymond bombing was the shift in the relationship between Fitts and the police. Considered a crooked do-nothing who had allowed police collusion with the underworld, Fitts was a changed man, railing and threatening:

> This is the most unspeakable outrage to occur in Los Angeles in years. I intend to place a full force of men on the case. We intend to get to the bottom of this matter and will leave no stone unturned to ascertain why an attempt was made to assassinate Raymond.

Fitts began by exhorting the 1938 Grand Jury to investigate "political higher-ups and under-world bosses." Then he continued to pursue charges against Kynette. Fitts appointed Detective Joe Taylor as his second in command in charge of the probe. Taylor had been a close friend of Raymond's since they served on the Purity Squad ten years earlier, and it was thought that Taylor could help break the case.

In the days and weeks that followed, Clinton wondered why Fitts would change so suddenly. After all it was Fitts who had blocked Clinton at every turn in the grand jury chambers, calling his evidence worthless. Perhaps he had an ulterior motive. Rumors circulated that in December Joe Shaw had extended his tentacles to a new racket, the shakedown, and had encroached on territory earmarked for Gans and McAfee. If so, Fitts could throw in his lot with the more powerful faction, the syndicate, and let the greedy Shaws fall off the limb. Or perhaps Fitts could tell that the groundswell of support for Clinton and CIVIC would be more powerful than anyone expected. For whatever reason, Clinton had an ally. He was also adding a new weapon to his arsenal.

Late in the afternoon of January 27, Captain Kynette surrendered to authorities to face charges and was taken into custody before being released on bail pending a trial date.

On February 1, 1938, sensing the public shock and horror at the bombing and attempted murder of Harry Raymond, Clinton and his seventeen-year-old son Edmond began a series of radio broadcasts on Los Angeles station KEHE (AM 790). *The People's Voice* was meant to make the connection between the Raymond bombing and the administration, and to educate the public about corruption. Revenues from Clifton's underwrote these broadcasts, fulfilling its early mission of supporting local community involvement as part of the Golden Rule.

Clinton, whose own home had been bombed just six weeks earlier, seized the opportunity to dramatize the attack. The radio program was broadcast six days weekly, up to four times each day, but the evening program at seven o'clock was the most popular. Each program began with a "theme song"—a chilling one-minute reenactment of the Raymond bombing complete with bomb blast, sounds of twisting metal and breaking glass, and agonized screams. The gritty reality that this dramatization brought home to the audience created great public sympathy for Harry Raymond who, after recovering from multiple wounds, was interviewed on the program and proclaimed "people will be able to leave their door unlocked at night when Frank Shaw is recalled." Charles Hanson, the city hall editor for the *Los Angeles Times,* stated he felt Clinton had skillfully made Raymond into a symbol of a "broken, bleeding Los Angeles, prostrate under the heel of the Shaw Administration."

The colorful radio coverage of this crime—which proved to be tied to the secret LAPD Spy Squad—was the turning point in an otherwise sluggish attempt by CIVIC to obtain signatures for the Mayor Shaw recall in September 1938. These broadcasts convinced the public, who eagerly tuned-in nightly, that the Shaw administration was responsible for the attempted murder and of forming illicit liaisons with gangsters and criminals.

Clinton, Edmond, and CIVIC members repeatedly accused three officials—Mayor Shaw, his brother Joe Shaw, and Chief of Police James Davis—of corruption and collusion. CIVIC told the public of a secret intelligence unit run by Chief Davis whose aim was to intimidate, threaten, and even murder opponents of the administration. Joe Shaw was charged with running a cabal made up of underworld figures whose illicit gains were funneled into campaign coffers of high-ranking city officials in exchange for appointments to city commissions.

Clinton and Edmond had a "just plain folks" style that appealed to a wide range of listeners, and sat well with voters, so they included on-air discussions and short talks on the show. One example of such a talk is taken from the broadcast of June 7, 1938:

> Members of the CIVIC Committee, friends of Good Government, and prospective members of future Los Angeles County Grand Juries. It is my contention that the most powerful body in the county government is the Grand Jury. . . . In the City and County of Los Angeles at the present the Grand Jury faces an unparalleled challenge to assert its power to investigate and punish corruption in high government circles. . . . A Grand Jury represents the people in exercising this high phase of its office: investigation of corruption at the head of our government—it is not to be under the thumb or control of any official, judge, governor or political clique. . . . Thru skillful manipulation by heads of governmental departments at the instigation of those who in turn control them, Grand Juries are restrained from using the "dynamite" which has been placed by tradition and law in their hands. May I say with emphasis, nothing can throw a well-greased political machine or a corrupting influence in fields of government completely out of kilter so quickly as a grand jury that knows its field of operation and its strength.

CIVIC members were presented once a week to discuss their personal attitudes toward the recall election, a strategy designed to acquaint the public with individuals who made up CIVIC. Clinton invited officials such as Judge Harlan Palmer, Supervisor John Anson Ford, and Judge Fletcher Bowron to appear, but most of his on-air guests were average citizens who told of their experiences with graft, bribery, and vice.

Public interest in *The People's Voice* rose to a peak when the program covered the Kynette-Allen trial where accused high-level LAPD officers were prosecuted for the Raymond bombing. Clinton presented former police officers with inside experience with the secret spy squad implicated in the bombing, and these officers characterized the squad as a "terrorist organization," whose mission was to silence individuals who were suspected of proving a link between Frank Shaw's administration and organized vice. Captain Kynette's attorney petitioned Superior Judge Ambrose to stop Clinton from commenting publicly during the trial but the judge refused to issue an injunction. So Clinton kept speaking out:

> Pressure was applied to the station owners. The city tried to make them cancel this

controversial program, but they held firm because they believed our accusations were true. Several axioms affirmed our theme. My son Ed closed each broadcast with "The Cause is Right, I Know" or "Eternal Vigilance is the Price of Liberty."

The Roper Poll estimated an audience of three hundred thousand listeners for each broadcast; on nights when broadcasts were particularly sensational, as many as five hundred thousand tuned in. After a trying year, it looked like Clinton was finally having an effect on Los Angeles. As Manchester Boddy wrote in the *Evening News*: "One thing is certain, Clinton's 'one-man crusade' on the 1937 Grand Jury was not in vain."

TURMOIL

CLIFFORD CLINTON WAS AN IDEALIST. He believed that public servants should deal only in truth, fair play, and honesty. He could not believe that Frank Shaw and his associates were evil. Clinton hoped to find good in them and bring them around to his way of thinking:

> These were most personable people to meet and even to know. They lived by a code so different from mine, but according to their standards they lived exemplary lives.

> Guy McAfee had a charming personality and Bob Gans was a wonderful man. Frank and Joe Shaw, Buron Fitts, and Chief Davis were all delightful people, personable, and social, all of whom it was easy to like. I never felt personal animosity or hatred toward them.

> Yet we stood on opposite sides of a pitched battle. Even so, when I used names and made charges, I never did so with viciousness or anger. I used the advantage of the underdog. I played up humor. When I called my opponents by name, I offered them time on our radio program to answer my charges. When it was necessary to meet them, we were civil, even friendly. In many instances, persons we had attacked later helped us overthrow other dominos.

In early 1938, Clinton was unhappy about the names that were being used to describe him. Peeping Tom. Power seeker. Crackpot. There was a flyer that showed the mug shot from his 1929 arrest. He decided to make one last effort to reach out to his opponents:

> If I could convince them that our motives were sincere, they would see that civic corruption was not the way to build our City of the Future.

He first called on Mayor Shaw:

> Frank Shaw was cordial and glad to talk, but I could not get past his claim that all was well, and when I expressed the hope that we might unite all factions to create not just a big city, but a better city, he said he was already doing this.

Clinton next met with Chief Davis, whom he had gotten to know outside official circles when Davis let Clinton and his daughter Jean visit the police training facility.

> James E. Davis, who had formerly shown me the excellent training center for his police department and who had let my little daughter, Jean, try her ability in the pistol range (a crack shot she was on this her first try), was a handsome, solid man impressive in appearance for this position, or for any organization. When I called upon him, I asked this simple, perhaps naïve question, after stating the reason for my call. "Chief," I said, "I need not tell you what goes on in this city? Do you feel there is any possible way that the connections can be cut, so that your fine department can bring the law enforcement back to a high standard of all law enforcement and integrity." He said nothing for several minutes, and when he spoke there was moisture in his eyes, as he said, "Clinton, I'm doing the best I can."

Clinton's third big interview was with Harry Chandler, the publisher of the *Los Angeles Times*, the most widely read newspaper in Southern California and the most prosperous in the country. He was also a real estate baron and a tireless booster of Los Angeles, the growth of which he had aided immeasurably. He was a powerful man, the most powerful in Southern California, and he was not terribly interested in meeting Clinton:

> Mr. Chandler received me in his paneled office, at first rather warily, I thought. He sat there, his patrician face crowned by snow-white hair, quietly composed, and waited for me to state my case. I aimed for a basis of understanding. My approach was that of a fellow businessman, even if my business was only a small one. I told him we were not Reds or Radicals trying to take control of the city as his paper charged. Our hope was to unite with the *Times* and better a great city. As he listened, his eyes clouded over, as though his thoughts were far away. His answers, though not unkind, were brief, perfunctory, and non-committal. He said nothing to which I might tie my hopes.

Clinton had tried to reason with his opponents. He had failed. There was no alternative but to fight them.

On January 17, 1938, three days after the Raymond bombing, the governing board of CIVIC voted to seek a recall election of Mayor Frank L. Shaw. Clinton had been opposed to such a drastic measure, but the bombing showed him that the Shaw administration would stop at nothing. There was no alternative. Shaw had to be removed. This was a momentous step for both Clinton and Los Angeles.

The turmoil following the Raymond bombing showed that CIVIC was not strong enough to meet the demands of a recall campaign; it needed an auxiliary organization. On January 27, there was a mass meeting of church and civic groups, hosted by Reverend Leonard Oeschli and the First Methodist Church in Alhambra. Clinton took the occasion to call for a united front in the battle against Shaw. The following Sunday, religious and political leaders who had attended the meeting brought Clinton's message to their respective constituencies. The Southern California Presbytery, which represented 115 churches, publicly expressed its support. In the weeks that followed, a grassroots movement rose to answer Clinton's call.

On February 5, the Federation for Civic Betterment (FCB) was founded to organize the recall of Mayor Frank Shaw. It comprised a committee of fourteen (later expanded to twenty-five) and was organized by Clinton and Dr. Roy Smith, with Reverend Oeschli acting as chairman. Members included the colorful radio evangelist Bob Shuler, as well as distinguished churchmen like Reverend Wendell Miller, Dr. Willsie Martin, and Clinton's pastor Dr. Stewart P. MacLennan. The Federation represented political, civic, and religious organizations, and even Clinton's bugaboo, organized labor. Where CIVIC's political base was narrow, the FCB represented a range of political and economic philosophies, from conservative free enterprise to organized labor to radical socialist and even communist. Although this diversity might make it harder to reach a consensus, Clinton was aided by board member Reuben Borough, who was successful in uniting the conservative (and mostly Protestant) CIVIC and the more radical (complete with laborites and socialists) FCB, which represented more than three hundred thousand members.

The unions might not be as eager to help. The Culinary Workers Union—not aligned with the FCB—still supported the Shaw administration. Ransom Callicott, vice president of Clifton's, chanced upon a meeting of this union in a church. An aggressive union leader was leading a discussion of Clifton's policies. Callicott sat patiently as the leader claimed that Clifton's paid such low wages that its workers were forced into prostitution. Callicott rose and respectfully asked the leader if she was sure of her facts. The leader said she had personally examined the books and the physical plant. Callicott then identified himself and invited the members to come to Clifton's to interview the employees and examine the books. "You can see for yourselves," said Callicott.

A number of union representatives took Callicott up on his invitation. They reviewed the books and spoke with employees, who were obviously well compensated and had a fully paid medical plan. Clinton had contracted with a Dr. Seals in the Subway Terminal Building to provide coverage for Clifton's 150 employees, a rare and valuable thing at the time. The union committee took note of this and made a report. Happily for Clinton, it was truthful, describing his working conditions as unequalled in the foodservice industry.

What Clinton had begun as an investigation was expanding, with the addition of the FCB, to include institutional reform. Harold H. Story, who was Frank Shaw's field secretary, later described the leadership of the FCB as "eight labor leaders, seven ministers, six communists, and four crackpot reformers, all cleverly manipulated by Clifford Clinton." The manipulation consisted of paying bills and galvanizing the followers of this diverse group into a recall movement. Since neither CIVIC nor the FCB had expertise in the structural side of city governance, Clinton hired a University of Southern California political science professor, Russell Ewing, as a consultant. "These were civic soldiers, and we were marching around Jericho's Walls," observed Clinton.

On February 28, CIVIC voted to institute recall proceedings against Mayor Frank Shaw. The decision was formally announced on Clinton's nightly broadcast on KEHE. The resolution said in part:

> Los Angeles needs a mayor elected without the use of questionable campaign funds.
>
> Los Angeles needs a mayor who will sponsor the simplification of the antiquated, unwieldy system of government by eliminating the duplication of departments and services.
>
> Los Angeles needs to free its law enforcement and administrative departments from the bonds of political tyranny.
>
> Los Angeles city employees need relief from the spoils system. The installation of the merit system will encourage enthusiastic public service, and will bring forth a high quality of service in the performance of duty.

With that, CIVIC and the FCB began the recall movement. Recall petitions received on March 4 revealed that 66,326 signatures (twenty percent of the voters in the most recent city election) were needed to qualify for a recall election. Gathering them turned out to be tedious and difficult. Between March 8 and May 3, CIVIC collected forty-four thousand signatures—only 22,416 of which were deemed valid by City Hall. Something was wrong, so the FCB hired the Stennet Company, a professional petition-gathering company. Meanwhile, there was already a special election set for September 16, so it was their hope they could piggyback the recall election on it.

(The special election had originally been a creation of organized labor who voted to put two propositions to a vote of the people. The ballot propositions, number one [the anti-picketing] and number two [allow labor picketing] had surfaced out of a dispute between the fledgling Congress of Industrial Organization [CIO] and the Shaw administration. The recall election ballot, qualifying as it did at the last minute, had been tacked on to this ballot. In many ways, adding the recall to an already scheduled election was a positive for Clinton and CIVIC who had been concerned that if the recall election had been scheduled on its own, the added cost of such an election would have crippled the campaign.)

At the suggestion of CIVIC member E.H. Kelley, attractive young women were hired to stand on the streets of Los Angeles and obtain signatures. They were outfitted in blue-and-gold jackets and pink pillbox hats. Many found the job daunting. One girl was stuck with a hatpin and told to get off the street. Another was shown a gun and asked: "How would you like to have a bullet through your back?" Others were followed, heckled, or offered bribes. A gruff, ugly, imposing man took to standing behind one girl, scaring off potential signers. A tiny old lady walked up to the girl and decided to sign the petition. The man advanced on the lady, intent on terrorizing her. She looked up, saw what he was up to, and summarily jammed her high heel into the top of his foot. "Get away from me!" she shrieked. "No one is going to scare me out of my rights! I am going to sign!" The brute beat a hasty retreat. Bystanders were emboldened by the woman's performance and lined up to sign the petition. It read:

TO THE CITY COUNCIL OF LOS ANGELES CALIFORNIA

We the undersigned qualified electors of the City of Los Angeles, and resident voters residing therein, equal in number to more than twenty (20) per cent of the total number of votes cast for all candidates for Mayor at the last preceding general municipal election at which the Mayor of said City of Los Angeles was elected, hereby demand the submission to the electors of said City of Los Angeles of the question whether Frank L. Shaw, the Mayor of Los Angeles, duly elected to said position, and who has actually held his Office for more than three (3) months since his election hereto, shall be removed from said office by Vote of said electors, and, if so removed, the election of his successor.

A GENERAL STATEMENT OF THE GROUNDS FOR WHICH REMOVAL IS SOUGHT IS AS FOLLOWS:

That it is now generally known and manifest that the candidacy of Mayor Frank L. Shaw was sponsored and financed in great measure by racketeers and politico-underworld personalities desiring to carry on illegal activities with the consent of a deliberately lax and cooperative administration.

That under his administration, the Police Department has become demoralized and is actually sanctioned and sponsored with his acquiescence, at great expense to the taxpayers, a system of espionage and terrorism against citizens of this community attempting to assert their fundamental constitutional rights as American citizens.

That in numerous instances, appointments to important Commissions and Boards have been made with a total disregard to the best interest of our taxpayers—in fact such appointments have been made at the behest and direction of underworld campaign contributors.

That numerous governmental departments under his domination have been and are now operated on a racket basis.

Because our City needs a Mayor with moral and electoral courage with ability and vision to cooperate with citizens in directing our city to its proper place as leader in civic progress.

That the official conduct of said Mayor Frank L. Shaw is in contravention and in opposition to the wishes of the majority of his constituents and inimical and adverse to the best interests of our City of Los Angeles.

Following this statement were twenty-five lines for signatures and a space for a notary's stamp and signature.

In late May, the future of the recall campaign was beginning to look bleak. There were insufficient signatures to qualify for a recall election, and the costs of the campaign were not being covered by either the FCB, as had been promised, or by donations from the public. This left Clinton with a bill of $2,500 per month and a faltering project. Attendance at meetings dropped off, so fewer meetings were scheduled. None were scheduled for June. By June 3, Stennet had collected only twelve thousand additional signatures, one third of which were rejected. Clinton discovered that the Shaw organization had been sending out phony petition gatherers who obtained signatures and then destroyed the petitions. Then it was learned that legal petitions were being invalidated after they had been delivered to City Hall, and there was nothing that he could do about it. A feeling of despair began to afflict both CIVIC and the FCB.

By mid-June, Clinton found himself facing defeat.

15

SAN QUENTIN

ON APRIL 19, 1938, CLIFFORD CLINTON FOUND A SEAT IN THE SUPERIOR COURT OF LOS ANGELES AND WENT FROM BEING A CELEBRITY TO BEING A SPECTATOR. The Harry Raymond trial was in session, with Judge Thomas L. Ambrose presiding. From the time Earle Kynette appeared for trial, he was accompanied by his attorney, Joshua T. Oliver, who admonished his client not to talk to the court and advised him to assert his constitutional rights against self-incrimination. Fitts questioned other members of the Spy Squad, with equally frustrating results. No one was going to admit to any guilt in the matter.

Prosecutors Eugene Williams and Joseph Fainer wasted no time in identifying the Special Intelligence Unit as the likely source of the criminals. Fainer told the court that the unit was spying on citizens who had questioned the Shaw administration. He vigorously questioned three members of the unit about the wiretaps used to monitor Raymond's telephone. Witnesses had seen Carl Phegley, Donald Draper, and Tom McDonald climbing telephone poles, wearing earphones, and boring holes in walls, but the three officers refused to answer, citing their Fifth Amendment rights.

On April 26, Police Chief James Davis testified that these officers had indeed tapped Raymond's phone on Orme Avenue; he had ordered this surveillance to protect the police department and the mayor's office from the "criminal and subversive elements" with whom Raymond was associating. If that was so, asked Fainer, then why had the squad been collecting intelligence on Clinton, Harlan Palmer, John Buckley, and two county supervisors? Davis conceded that he had no evidence against them, but speculated that they must have been associating with criminals.

On April 29, Raymond was brought into court in a wheelchair. He was visibly weak and at various times had to accept pain medication from a nurse. As he gave his testimony, the evidence grew more unpleasant. Spy squad surveillance consisted not only of wiretapping but also of tailing. Thus, when Raymond passed Captain Kynette and a group of other men on the street in early January, it was no coincidence; they had been following him. "It won't be long until I take care of him," Kynette muttered to the men as Raymond passed them. Raymond recounted his experience of January 14. "I pressed the starter," he said calmly. "There was an explosion."

Other evidence showed that Kynette and Allen examined Raymond's car, looked at his garage door with a flashlight, and visited a foundry to ascertain which type of metal pipe was most likely to break in small pieces. On May 5, the prosecution called an eyewitness, one George Sakalis, a neighbor of Raymond's who earned his living by selling vegetables. Sakalis testified that he saw Kynette and Lieutenant Roy Allen prowling around Raymond's garage on the night of January 13. When the two policemen realized that he was watching them, they ordered him to leave. On January 17, they recognized him and followed his truck into a wooded area above Glendale. They pulled him out of his truck, robbed him, beat him, and threatened his life if he said anything about having seen them by the Raymond garage. During this episode Kynette suffered the forehead bruise noted in the January 19 interrogation. Counsel for the Defense George Oliver then tried to discredit Sakalis by citing a petty larceny conviction in Arizona, a charge Fitts dismissed as trumped up.

On May 11, Fitts called each of the three defendants to testify. Each refused, invoking his right not to give testimony that might incriminate him. Shaw's secretary Harold Story presented a brief to the court stating that a police officer was entitled to the same constitutional protection as a regular citizen. Fitts attacked this argument, stating that such an action would destroy the public trust the police needed to perform their duties. An additional seven members of the spy squad refused to testify. Their silence became a moot point when documents and recordings smuggled out of the squad's First Street headquarters by Raymond's pal, Detective Joe Taylor, were introduced as evidence by prosecutor Eugene Williams.

Because of the sensitive nature and confidentiality of the conversations on the recordings, they were played in the judge's chambers. The jury sat transfixed as the voices of Clinton, Dave Hutton, and others echoed through the room. Clinton listened to his own voice in amazement. Here was proof that tactics used in fascist countries were being applied by Los Angeles politicians to safeguard graft.

On May 17, Davis was recalled to the stand and asked why he deemed it necessary to spy on leading citizens such as Democratic Assemblyman Sam Yorty, John Anson Ford, Reuben Borough, and Fletcher Bowron. His halting reply was that because of the influx of radical organizations and movements, he had to keep track of potentially subversive interests. To find a kernel of information took a lot of surveillance; this was the chaff that Clinton and his crusaders were pointing to. Judge Ambrose dismissed Davis's testimony as "debris of words."

On June 7, shortly after defense attorneys Oliver and George Rochester had rested their case, the prosecution delivered the coup de grace. They called to the stand an agent of the Southern California Telephone Company, and he produced records of calls made by Kynette to Mexico City on January 14. Kynette had repeatedly tried to reach Joe Shaw at the Reforma Hotel. After an hour of trying, he had called Chief Davis at the Regis Hotel in Mexico City and had spoken with him for seventeen minutes. This contradicted Kynette's testimony that he had not called Shaw. There were also calls to Bear Valley, where Officer Allen had fled after the bombing.

On June 8, Fainer delivered his closing argument. "The police intelligence unit is nothing more than a spy squad clothed in police power," he told a jury of eight men and four women. "Talk about 'subversive interests.' This squad contains the very kernel and basis of communism! When these men learned that Harry Raymond was about to take the stand in the Munson case, that he was going to tell what he knew about vice and corruption in this city, that he was going to blow the lid off City Hall, they decided to blow him into eternity!"

On June 16, the jury delivered its verdict. Sergeant Fred Browne was acquitted of all charges. Lieutenant Roy Allen was found guilty on the charge of malicious use of explosives. Captain Earle E. Kynette was found guilty of attempted murder, assault with intent to murder, and malicious use of explosives. A request for a new trial was rejected by Judge Ambrose. Allen and Kynette were sentenced to San Quentin. (Allen died there in 1942. Kynette was paroled in 1952.)

The press was unanimous in its praise of the verdict. Even the *Los Angeles Times* recognized that justice had been served. The *Times* recommended that the spy squad be disbanded but still felt that Kynette's superiors were not to blame. Public sentiment had been aroused by the officers' refusal to testify. On his nightly KEHE radio broadcast, Clinton voiced the opinion of many when he urged the city to discharge those involved. Robert McCurdy, the foreman of the 1938 Grand Jury, sent a letter to Chief Davis demanding their removal. Nevertheless, Mayor Shaw took no action. A Police Board of Rights exonerated the officers and Davis reinstated them without demotion or pay cuts.

"This verdict of Not Guilty is a disgrace to the community," said Fitts. "The officers should have been summarily fired. My experience has been that the majority of police officers want to do honest work. This verdict casts a stigma on them." On his next broadcast, Clinton commended Fitts for "exposing the entrenched corruption which passes for an impartial Board of Rights."

There was some consolation. On June 22, Davis abolished the Special Intelligence Bureau. Harry Raymond was pleased that "undercover gunmen masquerading as police" would no longer harass the citizens of Los Angeles. Kynette was on his way to prison. And Clinton had won another battle.

Top: Shui Hing Mission School for Orphans and Blind Girls, in Southern China, in 1910. Clifford Clinton, second row, second from left; his mother Gertrude Clinton, second row, fifth from right holding child; his father E.J. Clinton, last row, third from right on their second trip to China.

Above left: E.J. Clinton, stands behind his father David Harrison Clinton, with E.J.'s four sisters, circa 1890.

Above right: E.J. Clinton and children from left to right: Catherine, Marguerite, Ann, Esther, Evangeline, and Clifford, 1908.

Right: Clinton Cafeteria was on the ground floor of the Flood Building at 18 Powell St. in San Francisco.

Below: Announcement for the opening of the Clinton Cafeteria, "where the Portola Cafe used to be," 1921.

"We Welcome You"

CLINTON CAFETERIA

San Francisco's Largest and Finest

Flood Building

Lady Orchestras

Clinton Cafeteria
136 O'FARRELL STREET
Opposite The Orpheum Theatre

18 POWELL Near **MARKET**
where the Portola Cafe used to be

BREAKFAST :: LUNCH :: DINNER

Original façade of the Clifton's Cafeteria at 618 S. Olive Street before the remodel that created the legendary Clifton's Pacific Seas in 1938. Much of the struggle between the city and Clifford Clinton occurred here.

Clifton's Brookdale at 648 S. Broadway, after the former Boos Brothers Cafeteria was remodeled in 1935.

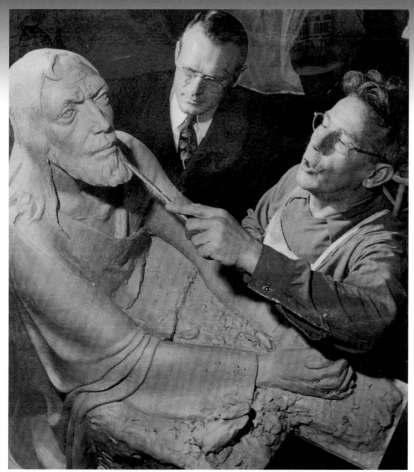

Left: Jesus in prayer the night before his crucifixion was the centerpiece of the Clifton's Pacific Seas Garden of Gethsemane, and was sculpted by Marshall Lakey. Clifford Clinton looks on as the artist works. By 1960, more than 2 million people visited the garden, 1943.

Below: Clifton's associates, dressed in period clothing, recreated a first-century home in the Holy Land, enacted in the Pacific Seas Garden of Gethsemane, 1943.

Right: The Spanish Fiesta was one of the Clifton's Cafeteria Olive Street activities for associates and their families; Clifford Clinton stands in the third row, at right of center, wearing a fake mustache, October 1932.

Below: The walls in the main dining room at Brookdale were covered with a redwood forest painted by renowned muralist Einar Petersen, 1935–36.

Left and below: After the remodel of Clifton's Cafeteria on Olive Street, it became known as Clifton's Pacific Seas. Its exotic neon palms and a tiki hut interior remained until the restaurant was demolished in 1960; 1938.

Above: Organist Julius Johnson led a trio who performed on the Aloha Stage.

Top: Los Angeles County General Hospital towered above its neighborhood, and inside, sheltered graft; circa 1930.

Above left: Modern hospital equipment included the B4 food cart which kept meals hot as they were delivered, 1934.

Above right: John Anson Ford, a member of the Los Angeles County Board of Supervisors, whose region included County General Hospital, recruited Clifford Clinton and a committee to investigate cost overruns in the hospital's food delivery system. The report was released to the public through newspapers in April 1936.

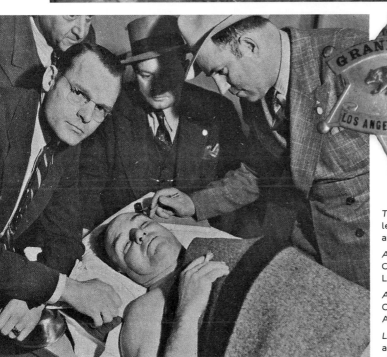

Top: Clifford Clinton peers out from hole left after the bombing of his Los Feliz home at 12:10 a.m., October 29, 1937.

Above left: Grand Jury badge given to Clinton after his appointment to the 1937 Los Angeles County Grand Jury

Above right: LAPD badge given to Clinton by Police Chief James Davis, August 3, 1937.

Left: Clinton consoles Harry Raymond at the Georgia Street Receiving Hospital after his car was bombed, January 14, 1938.

Above left: Clifford Clinton enters the 1937 Los Angeles County Grand Jury room, January 1937.

Above: Mayor Frank Shaw and his brother Joe deny the presence of vice in Los Angeles, but agree to a nonpolitical investigation by Clinton and his CIVIC team, 1937.

Left: A banner at Clifton's Brookdale shouts Clinton's support for Judge Fletcher Bowron in the recall campaign against Mayor Frank Shaw, 1938.

Below: Clinton presents evidence of malfeasance in City and County governments to the Board of Supervisors on August 11, 1937.

Top left: Judge Fletcher Bowron reluctantly agreed to run in the recall election against Mayor Frank Shaw.

Above right: After CIVIC instituted recall proceedings against Mayor Shaw, girls were hired to collect signatures on petitions to get the recall on the ballot.

Left: Clifford Clinton, at center in the white suit, watched the count of Shaw recall petitions in the office of City Clerk Robert Dominguez, who reviewed and disqualified many for fraudulent signatures. Because of this, two CIVIC members were assigned to the City Clerk's Office to supervise the validation of the signatures.

Right: Clifford Clinton, on leave from the U.S. Army, surveys his Pacific Seas cafeteria, 1943.

Below right: Second Lieutenant Clinton requested a transfer from Fort Benning in Georgia, to Washington, D.C., to serve on the United Nations Relief and Rehabilitation Administration (UNRRA). On December 28, 1942, Clinton met with Mayor Bowron, asked for a letter of recommendation for this new post, and received the appointment.

Left: Clifford Clinton cooks a sample of Multi-Purpose Food to demonstrate how easy it was to prepare nutritious food supplements for the hungry in post-war Europe and the United States, 1945.

Below: Fred Patterson, Nelda Clinton's father, mans a booth at the California State Fair in Sacramento to demonstrate and sell Multi-Purpose Food, 1948.

Top left: Always the gracious hostess, Nelda Clinton, left, entertains friends at tea time.

Top right: With her watchful eye, Nelda, left, supervises the serving counter at the Olive Street restaurant, circa 1940.

Above left: Clifford and Nelda enjoyed their Hawaiian vacation in 1937, and were inspired to create a Pacific Seas themed–Clifton's, so they shipped back samples of Hawaiiana to copy for the restaurant, circa 1935.

Right: Clifford and Nelda's three children Edmond Jackson Clinton II, left, Jean Marion Clinton, and Donald Harrison Clinton enjoy free time around the pool at their Los Feliz home.

CLIFTON'S AND CLIFFORD CLINTON

Top left: Clifton's Midtown; opened 1960, closed 1975.

Top right: Clifton's Lakewood; opened 1956, closed 1973.

Above left: Clifton's Century City; opened 1965, closed 1985.

Above right: Clifton's West Covina; opened 1958, closed 1980.

Left: Clifton's Lakewood interior; opened 1956, closed 1973.

Right: Clifton's Silver Spoon Downtown, opened 1973, closed 1981.

143

Above: The steam serving line at Clifton's Cafeteria Century City offered guests an array of hot entrees; circa 1950.

Far left: A waitress working in Clifton's Cafeteria Century City was not only anxious to make the guests feel welcome but wore a stylish bouffant hairdo of the day; circa 1965.

Left: At holiday time, Clifton's Cafeteria Pacific Seas offered a new concept: fully prepared turkey dinners to go. At its peak, Clifton's prepared as much as two tons of turkeys in one day; circa 1940.

16

RECALL

WITHIN DAYS OF THE RAYMOND TRIAL VERDICT, CLIFFORD CLINTON SAW HIS RECALL CAMPAIGN GAIN MOMENTUM. Before the conviction, sixty percent of individuals canvassed had signed petitions. After the conviction the percentage soared to ninety. Seventeen days after the conviction, the Stennet Company reported a total of 98,000 signatures, although only 55,000 of them were valid. The public was becoming aware of Mayor Frank Shaw's complicity in the Raymond bombing. At a joint meeting of CIVIC and FCB on July 6, 1938, it was resolved that Stennet should continue collecting petitions until the total reached 125,000. The goal was 66,326, but Clinton wanted to allow for the many who might be disqualified by City Clerk Robert Dominguez. Clinton suspected that the city clerk's office was tampering with petitions. For example, he saw the name Smith altered to Smithers. To prevent this, two CIVIC members were assigned to the city clerk's office to monitor the vetting of recall petitions.

Clinton was still underwriting the recall campaign. One day he received an anonymous call.

> We know you need money in your campaign. We are a group of businessmen who don't go for the runaround of the present administration. We would like to help. We will send you money if you will not divulge our names.

Clinton suggested that the caller send the money to CIVIC. He hung up and forgot about it until a few days later, when a Western Union messenger delivered an envelope containing the typed message: "For the Cause is right, we know." There was also a thousand dollar bill in the envelope. Clinton had learned from the Wilkinson scandal not to accept contributions from strangers. Western Union clerks described the person who had sent him the money as a bearded man with a monocle; he sounded like an underworld stooge. Brigham Rose suggested that Clinton place the money in a strong box in his bank safe deposit. The anonymous mystery donations kept coming in, eventually totaling $3,800.

Robert Noble, a former clergyman, was broadcasting on radio station KMTR. In 1934, he had been a supporter of Upton Sinclair's End Poverty in California (EPIC) and had come up with the idea of a "Ham 'n' Eggs" movement. This would be a pension plan through which the state would issue every unemployed individual over fifty a twenty-five dollar warrant. Noble encouraged his followers to sign the petition. Clinton credited Noble with helping to push signatures over the top.

On June 22, Mayor Frank Shaw sent an open letter to the 1938 Grand Jury.

> For several months, the citizens and the municipal administration of the City of Los Angeles have been harassed by a flood of criticisms and charges pertaining to police activities and the moral condition of the community. Our problem is greatly aggravated by broadcasting on the part of alleged reformers that Los Angeles is a "wide open town."

Shaw then proceeded to prove the efficiency of the police department by comparing its arrest and prosecution statistics to Cincinnati, Ohio, and to the nation at large. In regard to vice and gambling, Shaw said that nine percent more arrests for gambling and thirteen percent more arrests for prostitution were made in his administration than in the previous administration.

By July 25, a total of 69,816 signatures had been validated. Three days remained in which to have the recall signatures officially recognized, since the city charter stipulated that a special election should be held not less than fifty days after the date of certification by the city clerk. Clinton submitted the signatures. The recall election was officially certified and added to the September 16 special election ballot.

Then Clinton noticed a loophole. Under ballot conventions, the recall target candidate could also be listed on the ballot as a new candidate. If enough mayoral candidates split the votes, Shaw could be recalled and then, if he received a plurality, he would have enough votes to be re-elected, meaning the entire recall movement would have been for nothing. Clinton reasoned that there had to be a way to prevent this. (This provision has since been eliminated.).

On July 13, CIVIC and FCB held a joint meeting to nominate a candidate who could soundly defeat Shaw. The names that received the most votes were John Anson Ford, county supervisor; Lawrence Larrabee, a member of the board of education; and the superior court judge, Fletcher Bowron.

The selection process grew so contentious that it threatened to overshoot the filing deadline. A rift developed between conservative CIVIC members and left-wing laborites. Don Healy and

Roger Johnson represented the Congress of Industrial Organizations (CIO). Clinton was, of course, antagonistic to organized labor so he hired only non-union employees. The laborites favored Ford. The conservatives favored Bowron. Clinton was in the middle and it took a strong commitment to his goal to balance these politically disparate positions. As he came to realize, making the recall a success was most important to him. He also discovered that dealing with people of such varying beliefs and opinions was easier than he had thought. Once he sat down with a colleague and accepted his or her positions, but focused the discussion on the pertinent outcome, agreement was reached without rancor. He met privately with Ford and suggested that his recent loss to Shaw might be a handicap. Ford graciously agreed to withdraw.

Bowron made a stronger reform candidate. Born in 1887 in Poway, California, near San Diego, he put himself through law school by working for the Hearst papers as a reporter in the years before World War I. In 1926, he was appointed to the superior court. Known to be thick-skinned, realistic, and practical, Bowron had a pragmatic appraisal of what needed to be done and what kind of people he would be dealing with. This attitude made him the most likely candidate to succeed. He wanted to "replace crooks with honest men," but he felt he could accomplish more from a judge's chambers than from the mayor's office. Convincing him to run for mayor took carefully coordinated arguments. He was reluctant but listened when Clinton pitched the cause. Time was running out, and Bowron was still unsure. Only thirty-eight days remained until the recall election. He finally agreed after several appeals by Clinton and others who were supporting him. Also he saw he had a better chance against Shaw. "The selection of Bowron may have been hastily done," wrote an *Examiner* columnist, "but it was a brilliant political stroke."

One day Clinton received a call from a downtown businessman who was upset by the recall publicity. The Restaurant Association was worried that this crusade would reflect poorly on the environment and make tourists afraid to visit. "It's your methods we don't like!" they told him. Clinton answered with a quote from abolitionist William Lloyd Garrison.

> On this subject I do not wish to think, or to speak, or write, with moderation. No! No! Tell a man whose house is on fire to give a moderate alarm; tell him to moderately rescue his wife from the hands of the ravisher; tell the mother to gradually extricate her babe from the fire into which it has fallen; but urge me not to use moderation in a cause like the present. I am in earnest—I will not equivocate—I will not excuse—I will not retreat a single inch—AND I WILL BE HEARD.

The press liked Clinton's rhetoric and played an eleventh-hour role in the election. The *Examiner* and *Herald & Express*, the two Hearst papers, had supported CIVIC and Clinton since the Raymond bombing. The *Daily News* aggressively supported the recall campaign; Boddy wrote sixteen anti-Shaw editorials between August 1 and September 16. The *Times* was unhappy with Shaw's anti-picketing veto, his support of President Franklin Roosevelt's New Deal, and, of course, with the bombing scandal. Suddenly there was no mention of Shaw in the paper. Shaw, who had relied heavily on the *Times* for editorial support since his election in 1933, saw this as a betrayal. Even a *Times* election-day editorial was rather lukewarm. "The *Times* favors the re-election of Mayor Shaw," said the editorial but didn't go any further.

On September 16, 1938, forty-six percent of eligible voters went to the polls. 236,525 votes were cast in favor of recall. 129,245 votes were cast against recall. Bowron received 233,427 votes and Shaw 122,245. On one of the few recalls of a mayor in a major American city (mayors had been recalled in Seattle and Tacoma in 1911, Boise in 1915, and Detroit in 1930), Bowron drew the greatest plurality of votes ever given a mayoral candidate.

Frank Shaw, the soon-to-be-ex-mayor, expressed disbelief at the outcome and blamed himself for taking the challenge too lightly. Joe Shaw and Chief Davis had never expected CIVIC to muster enough signatures. In fact, they were surprised that Clinton's name never materialized on the ballot. "We weren't fighting Bowron," said Joe Shaw. "We were fighting Clinton."

On October 25, Bowron spoke to his supporters:

> I feel certain that I will prove an unpopular mayor, because I intend to do my duty. I fully expect to make bitter enemies. I know that I will appear ungrateful to many who expect rewards . . . and who will turn against me when they find I cannot and will not in good conscience give them appointments or employment at the expense of government.

The recall of Frank Shaw and election of Fletcher Bowron gave cynical Angelenos a new start toward a clean, honest government in which they could believe. Clinton could get back to business and family life and leave the governing of Los Angeles to the professionals.

17

BY STARTS AND FITTS

W HEN A PIECE OF PIPE USED IN THE RAYMOND BOMBING WAS FOUND TO HAVE BEEN PURCHASED BY CAPTAIN EARLE KYNETTE OF THE LOS ANGELES POLICE DEPARTMENT'S SPY SQUAD, MAYOR SHAW'S FATE WAS SEALED AND HIS RECALL WAS SECURED. The Kynette-Allen trial alerted the public and local press, at last, to the truth of the charges Clinton, who had now assumed the mantle of moral reformer, had been making against the administration.

With the election of Fletcher Bowron, both CIVIC and Clinton felt a sense of exhilaration, emotions brought out by a grueling, dangerous, expensive campaign, marked by vicious personal attacks. True to form, he did not dwell on his part in the historic recall, but worried that the employees of the movement would soon be out of a job. Bowron said that CIVIC need not disband, so Clinton's concern was momentarily allayed:

> My reaction was of tremendous relief. No more fighting for the privilege of staying in business. Relief from the harassments and intimidation of my family, my firm, and myself. The threats were finally over.

During his time in politics, with all it entailed—CIVIC affairs, radio broadcasts, bringing investigators and operatives into his home to share information and plot strategy—he had had little time to be with his family or run his business. Nelda and his vice president Ransom Callicott had taken over the day-to-day operations of Clifton's and consulted Clinton on issues that only he could decide. His eldest son Edmond, then seventeen years old and in high school, spent many hours with his dad in the home office on Los Feliz and in the radio studios rehearsing, polishing, and delivering four broadcasts daily.

Clinton had much more time now to get back to running his restaurants, and as he looked around, he saw the toll this campaign had taken on his business, especially as the flagship Clifton's Brookdale was pulling business away from 618 South Olive, and the older restaurant was looking a bit careworn:

> The 618 store was showing battle scars. It had stood up under pressure. It had endured accusations, vilifications, and harassments, but now that the spotlight was removed, it was wilting.

Clinton decided that an upgrade was in order, but he wisely chose to take a vacation first. He and Nelda boarded the Matson liner *Lurline*, spent five days on the Pacific, and then settled into a Hawaiian vacation. They were immediately taken with the aloha spirit that welcomed them to Honolulu. Clinton had not yet formulated a remodeling plan, fortunately because now he found Hawaii so enchanting that nothing but a South Seas motif would do.

The Clintons' vacation became a busman's holiday as the pair began making notes and sketches.

> We would have thatched roofs, bamboo, palm trees, giant ferns, tropical flowers, birds, fish, and, of course, a waterfall. We hoped that the physical properties and decorations would evoke this special place and that leis, music, and a warm, friendly welcome would capture the aloha spirit . . . woven palm screens, Tahitian swords and spears, Maori wai balls, colored glass, fishnet floats, baskets, *tapa* cloth, bamboo, and pictures of birds and flowers that artisans could duplicate.

When Clinton returned to Olive Street and announced his plans, there were mixed reactions. Some of his regular guests told him that he should leave 618 as it was. He explained that his plan was not an arbitrary redecoration. The fight with city hall had left a negative aura surrounding his restaurant and he wanted to bring a new lively happy spirit to the building. He admitted that remodeling would be both expensive and risky, but he thought customers would be attracted to a more welcoming place. Because of the expense involved, he would not be able to close 618 during the long months of remodeling. It would remain open for business, just as it had in 1931. His goal was to outdo anything ever seen in a modestly priced restaurant.

> I had conceived the Brookdale motif for 648. I started with nothing more than a mental conception. From there it became a sculpture, fashioned and changed moment by moment to match the picture in my mind's eye.

His concept would be executed by the same team: Ransom Callicott and manager Victor

Carlson, muralist Einar Petersen, rock-work sculptor François Scotti, and architect Charles Plummer, with the important addition of his partners, Walter Wurdeman and Welton Becket. The concept was novel, grafting South Sea elements onto an existing structure. Clinton rolled up his sleeves.

> Carlson and I worked nightly after the business closed, showing workmen how to tie six-inch bamboo, thirty to forty feet in length. . . . Each mold and indentation had to be sculpted over layers of tar roofing, wire frames, and cement. There were 180 feet of brook side, 300 feet of waterfalls, bubbling fountains, geysers, and a rain hut upon which rain fell every twenty minutes.

The palm trees were twenty-six feet tall and made of molded rubber over steel columns. Clinton showed workers how to set palm leaves so that they looked natural. Scotti laid rockwork over the original stainless steel walls.

Petersen covered the entire north wall with a tropical mural. As in a jungle, vegetation was everywhere. Fresh ferns were set into nooks of the rock. Artificial plants were used in the more inaccessible corners of the restaurant. Neon tubes designed to look like huge Hawaiian flowers climbed the walls and neon vines snaked along the ceiling. Colored stalactites illuminated by black light hung along the entrance route. Completing this explosion of color and texture were woven mats, baskets, leis, and fishnet-covered glass balls. At eye level, an aquarium was full of tropical fish, a grotto spouted limeade, and a volcano spewed a conveyor belt carrying individual dishes of various flavors of sherbet that guests could select as they glided by.

The exterior of the building was covered with concrete sculpted to look like a volcanic hillside, and finished with lush vegetation, terraces, and a waterfall. As the project neared completion, there were comments that it looked grotesque, and there were false rumors that the Los Angeles Architectural Commission was planning to bring an injunction. But the criticism that hurt Clinton most came from his father. E.J. predicted that the outlandish decor would destroy Clifton's. The hundred thousand dollar makeover had certainly cost enough; it couldn't fail.

Clinton renamed 648 Clifton's Brookdale and 618 reopened as Clifton's Pacific Seas. When its guests passed through its doors, they entered another world. Its walls were festooned with fresh plumeria and hibiscus leis. Associates wore authentic Hawaiian shirts and blouses. Primary colors were everywhere, except where black light created hues not seen in nature. This riot of color was softened by Julius Johnson's romantic music. Clinton had created a total environment.

Leis were spun from candy and cellophane in the curio shop. Guests were treated to so many special things—even more than at the previous restaurant: free birthday cakes, leis, and anniversary corsages. Huge neon signs read: "Dine Free Unless Delighted" and "Pay What You Wish." Clinton clocked incoming customers, which was a bit difficult, since they were bathed in pink and purple light.

There was color and there was warmth. And within a month, business had doubled.

The restaurant eventually hit a peak of twelve thousand guests a day. For decades both residents of and visitors to Los Angeles would remember the Pacific Seas as something almost otherworldly. There was simply nothing like it, either in Southern California or in the rest of the country.

Since CIVIC was still functioning, Clinton was able to watch the new mayor's progress. Mayor Fletcher Bowron was discovering that Frank and Joe Shaw had left city hall in worse shape than anyone could imagine. Cleaning up the city took more time than running it. There was evidence of misconduct in numerous departments: fire, police, civil service, utilities, and public works. Water and Power Commissioner Alfred Lushing was convicted of extortion in dry-cleaning rackets. Joe Shaw and Civil Service Commissioner William Cormack were convicted of sixty-three counts of job and promotion sales.

Bowron began a wholesale reorganization of the police department. He began by firing several officers. He then forced the retirement of a vice detective who was the reputed boss of the Central Avenue district, and then the head of the vice division, the chief of detectives, and, last but not least, Chief James Davis. In addition, twenty-three more officers, including Joseph Taylor, were forced to retire.

Next to be fired were one hundred city commissioners, and the entire police board. In their place, Bowron installed Van Griffith, John Buckley, Henry Bodkin, Raymond Haight, and Clyde Shoemaker as commissioners. The new team instituted policies that would weed out unfit officers. The rules prohibited publicity seeking, handing out special badges, loitering around pool halls, drinking liquor while on duty, and getting free food from merchants. Officers were required to report both the sum and sources of their income.

The shakeup at city hall sent shock waves through the underworld. Bereft of protection, the syndicate could no longer function with impunity. Many operators managed to pay off county law enforcement and continued their operations in outlying areas such as Hollywood's Sunset Strip area, which offered some legal immunity since it was outside the city limits. Gambling kingpins Tony Cornero and Farmer Page moved their dens to ships anchored off Santa Monica and Long Beach. They were outside county jurisdiction, so they flagrantly advertised casinos, gambling ships and other games of chance in newspapers, on the radio, and even with skywriting. In the end, though, Los Angeles was too risky for the syndicate. It was no longer an open town. Guy McAfee and others moved to Las Vegas, Nevada, which was still open territory.

Small operators continued to vex law enforcement. Bookies were difficult to regulate, and telephone betting was legal, so Pacific Telephone installed extra phones at racetracks and book-makers' offices; when this practice was outlawed, police forced bookies into the county. The police commission also went after small prostitution rings. Escort services were closely watched and massage parlors were prohibited from having masseuses for male clients.

Bowron and the commission started an initiative to ban all coin games in the city. In de-fiance, Kent Parrot, Charles Craddick, and the California Amusement Machine Operators Association (CAMOA) staged a five-night festival with chorus girls and free liquor. Clinton attended this event, a move that some interpreted as tacit approval of CAMOA, and certainly in contradiction to his anti-vice stance.

The 1939 municipal election was the first test of the reformers' ability to assist the new ad-ministration. During this race Clinton did not support specific candidates. He wanted to avoid any possible appearance of being a political boss. There had been negative articles here and there, so he hired two advisers to assist him in upcoming elections. Ernest R. Chamberlain, an Oklahoma journalist, became a publicist for CIVIC, a writer for *The People's Voice*, and researcher for Fact Finders. His friend Aldrich Blake had headed Western Democratic Party headquarters in Woodrow Wilson's second campaign. Blake became Clinton's political advisor and helped orga-nize precincts. Clinton did fund Fact Finders, a group run by Carlson, Blake, and Chamberlain. The group researched backgrounds of incumbents and candidates and published the informa-tion in a voters' guide. Seven of the ten new councilmen met the CIVIC criteria. Fact Finders conducted a governor's race poll and found that Clinton had enough recognition to be a candi-date. He was not interested. He was too busy with his crusade.

Clinton pleaded with the public to identify corruption. He was answered with a continuous flow of written reports and in-person testimony. Since Shaw supporters still occupied many city hall jobs, there were reports of police participation in vice. Despite the cleanup, it was obvious that protected vice still existed. Officers who had formerly helped Clinton were trying to set up their own vice rackets. When Clinton corroborated the reports of corruption in the police de-partment, he worried that Bowron's commitment to cleanup was cooling.

> We had no more qualms about exposing vice under Bowron than we had under Shaw.
> We were not seeking Bowron's favor.

Clinton's KEHE broadcasts had allowed many individuals to air their stories, but *The People's Voice* had been suspended by that station.

Clinton switched strategies. He began picketing gambling dens and brothels. His agents carried placards that said: "Unfair to Organized Police." The picketing worked; it closed es-tablishments. It also antagonized Bowron. When asked about Clinton by a reporter, Bowron responded: "That silly ass." This widened the rift between the mayor and the crusader. It also helped columnists brand Clinton as a publicity-hungry crackpot. In his *Los Angeles Times* column "What Goes On?" Chapin Hall summed up the attitude of many: "Clifford Clinton, the recognized power behind the Bowron throne, has over-touted himself. His public scoldings via the airwaves have ceased to have the effect of even third-rate entertainment. Nevertheless Mr. Clinton has a following. Some profess to believe that he is a latter-day Moses raised up to lead his Chosen People out of the wilderness."

Clinton was hurt by these jibes but not discouraged:

> We felt it our duty to act against evil.

The forces of evil felt likewise. On February 27, 1939, Clinton, driving his black Cadillac at Vermont and Franklin Avenues, allegedly skidded forty-seven feet and hit Joe Benoit, aged nineteen, a motorcycle courier, throwing him fifteen feet in the air. When he was arrested, Clinton, who could easily pay the twenty-five dollar bail, chose to spend the night in jail, just to see how someone who could not afford bail (or a Cadillac) would feel.

Benoit sued Clinton for fifty thousand dollars in damages. A subsequent trial and independent investigation revealed that pro-Clinton witnesses were being harassed and that, moreover, Benoit was a stunt driver. Clinton was acquitted in municipal court on April 14, but the case went to superior court where it was dismissed. It was clear that Clinton was unpopular in certain circles.

Clinton and CIVIC published a brochure instructing citizens how to fight crime. It featured Five Steps to be taken when an open violation of the law was reported.

1. List the report on an index card in a system.
2. Investigate to determine accuracy of report.
3. Report the possible crime to proper enforcement officials and send carbon copies to the District Attorney, the Grand Jury, the Attorney General, the City Council, the Board of Supervisors, and, if appropriate, to the Board of Equalization, the Liquor Control, or Federal Narcotics Bureau.
4. After two weeks, make a second investigation
5. Report it to the newspapers and commence an intensive campaign of citizens' action.

The brochure, which was distributed at Clifton's, also encouraged picketing, taking pictures of crimes, and copying license numbers, as well as mass opposition, legal action, and abatement proceedings.

Clinton next turned his attention to the most conspicuous holdover from the previous administration. Buron R. Fitts was still district attorney, and, from all reports, still a crook. Clinton, who received ongoing reports of the district attorney's failure to do his duty, wasn't deceived by Fitts's expedient—and temporary—conversion after the Raymond bombing.

> It gave D.A. Fitts the opportunity to appear as a knight in shining armor.

Reformers accused Fitts of prosecuting his enemies and accepting payoffs from Hollywood studios to suppress evidence that would convict personalities such as Busby Berkeley of vehicular homicide. Fitts also exercised undue influence over the grand jury system. Officials were safe as he quashed investigations of malfeasance. Grand jurors had nowhere to go for impartial advice when issues arose regarding public official misconduct. Fitts would be running for reelection in 1942, which was also an election year for city councilmen and governor. Clinton embarked on an anti-Fitts campaign.

The People's Voice had found a new home on station KMTR, and, in July 1940, Clinton and his son Edmond had begun broadcasting four times daily and five days a week. Ernest Chamberlain wrote scripts that satirized Fitts's personal life, with sidelights on his drinking and womanizing. Although Clinton described the tone as "cynical, hilarious, and heavily sarcastic," there was no laughter in the D.A.'s office. In August, the broadcasts recounted the findings of the 1934 Grand Jury, when Fitts had been indicted for perjury.

> In 1932, Fitts had a judge acquit George Gregory, president of the California Reserve Company, of criminal conspiracy and violation of the corporate securities act. Evidence showed that Gregory was guilty, but he happened to be Fitts's brother-in-law. In the so-called Love Mart Case, Fitts sequestered the sixteen-year-old plaintiff, Clarice Tauber, in a hotel so that she could not accuse the wealthy real estate mogul J.P. Mills of rape. Following the trial, a worthless orange grove owned by Fitts's mother was purchased for $18,500 by a Mills agent. Fitts eluded the grand jury's interrogation by pleading "temporary brain paralysis." He was acquitted.

Clinton and his son Edmond devoted several broadcasts to these proceedings. Clinton was not surprised to receive a phone call from the D.A.'s office. "Clinton," said a disembodied voice, "if you keep this up, I will kill you." Clinton kept it up, and even quoted the threat in his broadcast. This brought sneers from the *Los Angeles Times*: "Honestly, now, can the gentle reader by any stretch of his political imagination feature our very able District Attorney going about threatening to kill folks—even the Great Reformer Clifford Clinton? Phooey! The fur-lined bathing suit goes to Mr. Clinton."

On July 23, 1940, Clinton aired a poem sent to the station by a listener. Its title was: "Give Us Liberty or Give Us Fitts."

> When the father of his country
> Cut down the cherry tree
> He looked his father in the eye
> And said: "I cannot tell a lie."
> He didn't blame the preacher,
> He didn't blame the cook,
> Nor when his act was criticized

Contend his mind was paralyzed.
Pat Henry's "Liberty or Death!"
Inspired a nation's pride.
He did not cringe before a critic
And say: "My brain was paralytic."
But time moves on, by starts and Fitts,
And by the law's analysis,

A jury may purge perjury
If it's the mind's paralysis.
If Washington were young today
Perhaps he'd chop and wink
And boldly to his parent say:
"My mind was on the blink."
Or Patrick Henry might he say:
"I must have lost my wits,
I never wanted Liberty,
My mind was having fits."
Deliver us! The voters pray
As o'er life's road we journey,
From the paralytic hazards
Of a fistulite attorney.
Give us one whose gout is chronic
Or whose liver is bubonic
Or whose larynx is pneumonic,
But whose oath is not ironic.

Clinton tried another strategy to discredit Fitts. In 1938, Clinton had used Fitts to unseat Frank Shaw. Perhaps he could use a Shaw to unseat Fitts. By October of 1940, Navy Lieutenant Joe Shaw had been acquitted of all charges by the California State Supreme Court. He surprised everyone by accepting Clinton's standing invitation to anyone who was willing to provide information. Shaw was willing to talk, but only in his car, parked outside Clinton's home.

> Mr. Shaw was suspicious of me. He thought there might be a Dictaphone in my office. But he was hopeful of the defeat of Fitts. He said that no citizen could expect justice as long as Fitts was D.A.

This was amusing, coming from someone whose cohorts had recorded Clinton. But Clinton went along with it; Shaw had dirt. Shaw put Clinton in touch with Pedro Delgado, a former police officer, who had a tale to tell.

In 1938, Delgado had testified before the grand jury, implicating Glen Gravatt, the civil service commissioner, in an exam-selling scheme. At the insistence of Deputy D.A. Eugene Williams, Delgado denied selling exam questions and the grand jury indicted him for perjury. At this point, with a fifteen-thousand-dollar bond on his head, Delgado demanded that Williams drive him to Fitts's ranch in Monrovia to collect an envelope full of cash. The next stop was his bail bondsman. Then he hightailed it to Mexico.

Clinton was convinced that if he could interview Delgado for his program, it would prove that Fitts had colluded with corrupt officers. Shaw and Clinton traveled to Mexico and recorded Delgado's story, then announced that the recording would be played on *The People's Voice*. After several attempts to suppress the recording, the court gave Clinton permission to air it. The *Herald Express*, a Hearst paper, printed an article titled: "Clinton Interview a Hoax." The Hearst papers had been printing favorable stories about Fitts ever since he came out so strongly against the perpetrators of the Raymond bombing. The papers, which all followed the same editorial policy, believed the district attorney had done a courageous and exemplary job of finding, arresting, and convicting the Los Angeles detectives responsible for this crime. When Clinton threatened to air a recording that was critical of Fitts, they came to his support. On October 22, 1940, Clinton, who remained convinced of the district attorney's unsuitability for the job, aired the recording anyway.

> In spite of frantic protests by the District Attorney's office, both to us and to the station, we played the recording as we had promised. But we were forced by the station to delete the name of the Deputy District Attorney. In its place was the sound of a gong.

Clinton's choice to replace Fitts was John Dockweiler. A Catholic four-term House Democrat, Dockweiler belonged to an influential Los Angeles family that had a reputation for honesty. Fitts fought back. He accused Dockweiler of inexperience and of being too ill to combat corruption. He accused Clinton of "bossism" when he supported the removal of anti-Bowron city councilmen. He also claimed that Clinton was impeding justice:

"I state flatly," said Fitts, "that Clifford Clinton has attempted to impede, harass, overcome and intimidate, through motives best known to himself and his crowd, the prosecution of many major cases during the last two or three years." The *Los Angeles Times* backed up Fitts with headlines designed to discredit Clinton. "Fitts Charges Clinton with Meddling" and "Prosecutor Asserts Clinton Wants to Dominate Office" were only two of the many *Times* headlines on articles that smeared Clinton.

Clinton distrusted Chandler, at the *Los Angeles Times*, who he felt was interested only in maintaining his viselike grip on Los Angeles. The *Times* was partisan in its policy and lacked objectivity, throwing its considerable weight behind Fitts and enlisting anyone who was willing to impugn Clinton. Dr. Lewis Burger, a minister and former Clinton publicist, joined the chorus. "I was supposed to be a public relations man for CIVIC," said Burger. "But my real work was to build Clinton up. He evolved a five-year plan to control local and state politics. Bowron was to run for governor if he was successful as mayor."

Burger stated that when he had questioned Clinton's qualifications to be a political boss, Clinton had responded, "Hitler was once a paper-hanger and Mussolini, a blacksmith." Burger described Clinton's modus operandi as a sinister kind of ingratiation. Clinton decided to back Bowron because he could talk to him, as opposed to Municipal Judge Irving Taplin or Roger Jessup, chairman of the Board of Supervisors, who wouldn't give him the time of day. "That was his expression about candidates," said Burger. "He could talk to them or he couldn't."

Communism was again a hot topic. In his campaign to clean up City Hall, Clinton had fostered a coalition that included socialists and even communists. He needed the participation of disparate groups to achieve a common goal. His strategy worked, but it also provided grist for the mill of his detractors—and there was little he could do about their attacks. He was called more names: "Parlor Pink," "Community Dictator," and "Stormy Petrel." The *Times*'s Chapin Hall suggested that Clinton might be a dupe of communist infiltrators: "Whether these hysterical, publicity-seeking crusaders are innocent victims of red flag propagandists or whether they follow the dictates of their own conscience, it is apparent that their attack on the good name of Los Angeles is being prompted by means which are not entitled to the consideration of good, red-blooded Americans."

Clinton felt that Hall was libeling him, so he went to the *Times* to speak with him.

> This sharp-cutting columnist was as bitter and hard as his face proclaimed with its thin, deeply-etched lines. He sneered at my "naïve" request that he listen to my side. His cynicism froze me in the center of my being, and I have felt a distinct nausea ever since when I have seen his name at the head of a column in my morning *Times*.

On July 19, 1940, Stephen F. Chadwick, the past national commander of the American Legion, delivered a speech entitled "Stalin and Clinton over Los Angeles" at Patriotic Hall. "I have in my hand a list of nearly every communist in Los Angeles," claimed Chadwick. "Commissar Clinton is the hub of this vicious wheel of Communism."

District Attorney Fitts fought hard to defend himself and his record. He used *Times* articles to imply that Clinton had joined forces with the Shaw machine. Clinton responded by challenging Fitts to air his charges before an unbiased jury of seven judges, agreeing to pay ten thousand dollars to the American Legion if he were found guilty. Fitts did not accept the challenge. Former city councilman William Bonelli testified during a liquor license hearing that as Fitts's 1936 campaign financial manager he had seen three hundred thousand dollars collected from underworld sources. Fitts had attended meetings with Bob Gans, Guy McAfee, and Kent Parrot. In addition, George Stahlman, who was for eleven years a respected deputy, resigned. "Buron Fitts has often conspired to defeat justice," said Stahlman. As before, the *Times* printed numerous endorsements of Fitts. It was a wasted effort.

18

DICTAPHONE AND LIBEL

IN 1941, MAYOR FLETCHER BOWRON'S TERM OF OFFICE WAS RUNNING OUT, BUT THERE WAS STILL MUCH THAT HE WANTED TO ACCOMPLISH, SO HE MOUNTED A REELECTION CAMPAIGN. His support in 1938 had come from the reform groups that Clifford Clinton had sponsored, CIVIC and FCB. These groups had joined some unlikely allies in a common quest. Evangelist Bob Shuler stood shoulder to shoulder with Communist Don Healey because they wanted better government, and Clinton was underwriting their solidarity, an unlikely coalition of disparate types. Once they were rid of Frank Shaw and Buron Fitts, their accord began to evaporate.

Clinton had resigned from the FCB in late 1938 to concentrate on the more conservative CIVIC. Without his money, FCB lasted only one year. CIVIC, meanwhile, began to see more dissension. In 1939, seven clergymen resigned, saying that the organization was becoming too left wing. More changes came to CIVIC in 1941. Socialist Reuben Borough and Communists Healey and Roger Johnson resigned, citing the organization's lack of commitment to social and economic issues. John Bogue called Shuler and Robert Noble "dangerous opportunists" and "political faddists," and then resigned.

Clinton was still smarting from Bowron's criticism of both the CAMOA incident and the recruitment of Joe Shaw. Clinton, in turn, labeled the mayor belligerent and incapable of leadership. Clinton's habit of shooting from the hip did not go unnoticed. Communist Rena Vale accused Clinton of becoming the new boss of Los Angeles and claimed that he exerted undue influence over Bowron and John Dockweiler. Vale also accused Clinton of indoctrinating the public with opprobrious pamphlets and broadcasts. She characterized his recall election as a vendetta against the health department. "I am simply a small food merchant," replied Clinton. He added that he doubted that he had as much influence on city government as people were crediting him with, but if he did, he reasoned, it was needed.

In early 1941, Clinton had to deal with more repercussions of his anti-vice crusade:

> Many lawsuits were brought against us. These million-dollar claims were frightening, but we answered them with countersuits. Legal action is really a time-consuming, expensive, and dangerous way to settle a disagreement.

The first of these suits was a libel action brought by the former Deputy District Attorney Eugene D. Williams. He was suing Clinton for libel, accusing Clinton of implying in the Pedro Delgado broadcast that Williams had bribed Delgado and engineered his flight from justice. Williams was asking for three hundred thousand dollars in damages.

In a deposition made to Byron Hanna, Williams's attorney, Clinton confirmed the details of his trip to Mexico and how he had investigated Shaw's allegations about Fitts and Williams. His deposition was direct:

> A: We intended to give the public what we believed to be true. We believed the deputy district attorney had done these things.
> Q: But you knew you would do Mr. Williams great personal damage.
> A: I knew these were serious charges.
> Q: You knew they would do tremendous damage.
> A: Well . . . I didn't speculate on that. I was more concerned with the duties of public office than with an individual.
> Q: What is your personal worth?
> A: I have never calculated it.
> Q: Do you think it would be half a million?
> A: I think it would not.
> Q: A quarter of a million?
> A: I would say not.
> Q: Could you give us any estimate, Mr. Clinton?
> A: No, sir, I could not. This value is largely intangible. It's a matter of personal service.

When Clinton was made to deal in more concrete terms, he managed to impart some salient details. The *Times* was only too happy to print them.

> Clinton's two downtown cafeterias are owned and operated through the medium of two corporations, known as Clifton's Brookdale, Inc., and Clifton's, Ltd., and he owns three-quarters of the stock in the two corporations. He declined to estimate the value of this stock but said that a figure of $500,000 was placed on the capital stock in the articles of incorporation. He disclosed that the corporations are in the process of buying the property at 618 South Olive St. and have paid approximately $25,000, with a balance of $250,000.

The corporations also operate two large hotels in the city, Clinton testified, which made profits in 1939. [These were the Figueroa Hotel, at 939 South Figueroa St., and the Clifton Hotel, on Eighth Place near Francisco Street.] Other real property he owns include the Clinton home at Western Avenue and Los Feliz Boulevard and a vacant lot next door; a four-bedroom lodge at Lake Arrowhead; a lot with two cottages at Mount Hermon; a vacant lot in Oakland; and a few shares of stock. He has two bank accounts [in the Bank of America at Seventh and Olive Streets; and in the Security-First National at Seventh Street and Grand Avenue] in which are deposited approximately $7,000. His net personal income for 1939 was approximately $30,000.

The suit was finally settled on December 18, 1941. Williams agreed to a nominal settlement, namely one dollar, claiming that he was satisfied that he had been heard in court and his name cleared. He was no longer in public service; he was practicing law.

Clinton had won another battle, even if it meant revealing his considerable resources. If he were not wealthy, people asked, how could he afford to pay twelve hundred dollars a month for his broadcasts? And what about his high-handed tactics?

I always felt heartsick when an individual, whether due to apathy, incompetence, or complicity, had betrayed the public trust and was the subject of an attack. But I knew of no other way than to first exhaust legal steps and then hold the individual to the light of public scrutiny.

Clinton was surprised when the object of this scrutiny held a grudge against him, or worse, accused him of Pharisaic hypocrisy. Where was his Golden Rule now? He had an answer:

Our interpretation of "Do unto others as you would have them do unto you" threw the weight of the admonition on the term "others." In our reform work there were two separate and distinct "others." The first "other" was a public official who by dereliction of duty had brought reproach upon himself and discredit to his fellow officials. The second "other" was a citizen who had been betrayed and who was being harmed by the actions of the first "other." If we were to apply the admonition "Do unto others," we felt we had to make a choice. The injured "other" deserved our protection.

Clinton cited the case of the city official he had shepherded into office, only to see him abuse the privilege of an official automobile by taking it on a cross-country pleasure trip. If the officials whom Clinton had identified as miscreants could be brought to justice for not considering the consequences of their actions, so could he.

When efforts to have him reimburse the city failed, CIVIC filed charges against him. He was convicted and removed from office. He had not thought of the "others" who had elected him.

Starting on November 11, 1939, Bernarr Macfadden's popular *Liberty* magazine featured a six-part series by Dwight F. McKinney and Fred Allhoff entitled "The Lid Off Los Angeles." The title was a reference, of course, to Harry Raymond's boast. The last segment ran in the December 16 issue, by which time Frank L. Shaw was furious. The articles portrayed him as a parasite and Clinton as an exterminator. Shaw took longer to marshal his resources than did Williams, but when he struck, Clinton felt it. In early 1941, Shaw filed a libel suit against Macfadden, McKinney, and Clinton. Contending that the series damaged his reputation, Shaw was suing for $500,000 actual, $100,000 special, and $150,000 exemplary damages.

At the preliminary hearing in March 1941, Shaw's attorneys C.L. Clearman and E.J.H. Delorey got press coverage by questioning one of Clinton's former CIVIC assistants, John Joy. The thirty-five-year-old nurse described in graphic detail his work as a bell sheep for Clinton's brothel raids:

> JOY: The most hilarious one was in a hotel in Wilmington. I went up to the second floor as a customer. I was carrying a marked $2 bill. Clinton was outside waiting. He always gave me two minutes. When he burst in, the girl ran stark naked down a long hall and into another room and tried to hide the money. Clinton was right behind us with a photographer. He had his timing worked out pretty well. He yelled: "For God's sake give me the money, quick!"
>
> CLEARMAN: What was his legal authority for these raids?
>
> JOY: His grand jury badge. He kept it pinned on his belt. He told the madams he was a grand jury member, and he told me he had a legal right to take me along.
>
> CLEARMAN: Was Mr. Clinton making these raids on account of a sincere desire to expose vice conditions?
>
> JOY: Clinton was wild to get his name in the newspapers. He said he wanted to keep his program before the public eye.

Joy further testified that Clinton had conferred numerous times with McKinney about his manuscript, and that Clinton traded in his modest 1935 automobile for a brand-new ten-cylinder limousine. "As time went on," said Joy, "he indulged in more and more luxuries, but the more money that came in, the tighter he got." The preliminary hearings ended before any more damage could be done to Clinton's reputation.

Despite Clinton's split with Bowron, he believed the mayor's reelection was necessary to sustain the improved city government. CIVIC worked to defeat city councilmen who opposed Bowron or city charter reform. There was indeed opposition. Disgruntled police officers were desirous of easing new restrictions. Shaw cronies and gambling interests hovered in the background, hoping that Clinton or Bowron—or both—would stumble and make way for the return of the old regime. Clinton was not going to stumble. He and son Edmond used *The People's Voice* to air newly acquired reports of police corruption and city hall graft, with scripts often written by Ernest Chamberlain.

Bowron's opponents in the primary election included Frank Shaw, John Porter, and Councilman Stephen Cunningham, who had a reputation for honesty. Bowron and Cunningham survived the primary. By this time, the mayor had expanded his base of support to include other reformers, organized labor, and the business community. When the general election was held, Cunningham received 149,195 votes. Bowron received 181,582. Clinton and CIVIC were given some credit for Bowron's win, but they had not done much. The mayor's conservative shift had driven the liberal elements of both CIVIC and the FCB into other organizations. The 1941 mayoral election would be regarded as Clinton's last great victory. But there was another attack to ward off.

In December, a large monitoring station was discovered in city hall. Earlier in the year, Clinton, using the deputy badge given him by Chief Davis in July 1937, had gotten a criminal named Paul Loeb to cooperate with a wiretap in order to finger Captain T.J. Mailheau, head of the robbery squad, for taking bribes. The case was thrown out; it also made everyone wire-conscious. When hidden microphones were found all over City Hall, a major scandal threatened the Bowron administration.

There was a precedent for wiretap indictments. In fact, there were several—all contradictory. For years, wiretap evidence had been inadmissible in federal court, and use of it in grand jury indictments could result in federal prosecution. However, in state courts there were instances where it was allowed, and, moreover, if a Dictaphone was involved, the legality became blurred, especially in a grand jury hearing. None of this was of comfort when a rabidly anti-reformer grand jury indicted Bowron, Clinton, Deputy District Attorney Grant Cooper, Chief of Police Jack Horrall, and four officers on various charges. Clinton and Cooper were charged with wiretapping, and Bowron of "willful misconduct in office" for aiding the wiretapping.

If convicted, Bowron faced removal from office plus a fine and jail term. Judge Raymond McIntosh heard the case. Clinton admitted to using a Dictaphone to record conversations in his office.

> I don't see anything wrong with Dictaphoning a conversation. But I see a great deal wrong with bombing citizens who oppose your administration. A public official should be able to be recorded without fear. That would be a fine test of whether or not he tells the truth.

Judge McIntosh cited Section 653 H of the California State Penal Code, which permitted the "use of dictagraphy by salaried police officers or others under the direction of the district attorney when necessary to detect crime." Section 640 of the penal code forbade unauthorized connections to a telephone line, but Clinton had approval for the Dictaphone machine, and, since it was a coil device with no direct connection to the line, these conditions were not met. Judge McIntosh dismissed the case against Bowron and quashed the felony indictments against Clinton and the others.

Even with the turmoil of politics, Clinton kept tabs on both Clifton's and Los Feliz. E.J. was "Mr. Clifton's," the Pattersons were in charge of Los Feliz, and Nelda was official hostess at the Pacific Seas, where she assumed responsibility for training and food inspection.

> Clifton's was rolling along. And Los Feliz was still a haven. It had weathered the bombing, provided recreation and pleasure, and been home and office and meeting place during the long fight.

The Clinton children were growing up. All three were tall and blond. Jean and Don were in high school. Edmond was twenty and finding his way. He was an avid student of electronics, particularly radio, and he had a girlfriend named Maryellen Ferguson.

Ferguson's father was the same Vernon L. Ferguson who had been the chief deputy district attorney under Buron Fitts during Clinton and Edmond's campaign to replace him as district attorney. This Romeo-and-Juliet romance was unknown to the Fergusons for some time after she had started dating Edmond. After meeting him, the Fergusons became fond of him, but were dismayed to learn that Edmond's father was the longtime antagonist of his boss. Vernon forbade Edmond to visit his daughter. With the help of his future mother-in-law, Mae Ferguson, the two continued to visit, clandestinely, often through the back screen door. They eventually married and had six children.

Clinton began to develop health issues, the result of years of long hours and severe nervous strain. A bulwark to family, friends, employees, and fellow citizens, he had endured more than one person's share of stress. He was diagnosed with stomach ulcers, so he embarked on a program of bland foods and milk. And, of course, there was ice cream to keep anxiety at bay. The world was on the brink of another cataclysm.

On December 7, 1941, Clinton was in bed, suffering from a high fever when news came on the radio. "The Japanese have attacked the U.S. Naval Base at Pearl Harbor in Hawaii at seven this morning," said the announcer. "Much of the fleet has been destroyed." A short while later, Clinton called all the members of his family to him and informed them that he had decided to enlist.

> Sometimes, when I am freed of my duties and problems, a picture of unusual clarity comes into my mind. It may be an answer long sought or a vision of my next step. The challenge is not to be alarmed at the boldness of the thought, for such flashes are

turning points in our lives. They come unbidden, when one is relaxed and undisturbed, or in the presence of awesome beauty—sunset on a lake, a work of art, music, theater. A sublime mood provides a clear channel for the Infinite Mind of the Universe.

On January 6, 1942, after a year of legal maneuvering, the Frank Shaw libel case went to court. He claimed that he had been maliciously attacked and subjected to ridicule by the series of articles in *Liberty*. The chief witness would be Clinton, and testimony might require him to spend as many as ten days in the witness box, a daunting prospect for someone so introspective. He tried to prepare himself.

> I found that I need not fear an attorney's attempts to confuse, frighten, or intimidate me if I were convinced I was in the right. With my slow-acting mind, I made sure to answer questions slowly, even when I knew the answer. This set my style and gave me time to ponder trick questions. I gauged each with one question: "What is the truth?" Just remember, I said to myself over and over, *the simple truth*. That kept me calm and prevented my falling into the confusion that can overtake a witness when there are too many details. If I was unsure, I would say, "To the best of my memory" or "I do not remember accurately." If an attorney insisted on a yes or no that might lead to a wrong inference or an incomplete truth, I always found the judge willing to let me qualify that yes or no with an explanation.

In his first days in the box, Clinton did well. He testified that he had spent eighty thousand dollars of his own money on the Shaw recall campaign. He gave detailed testimony about his vice investigation, including houses of prostitution he had visited. He supplied names, dates, and addresses. When he tried to link these to city hall by means of the material he had prepared for the 1937 Grand Jury with Brigham Rose and Harry Raymond, the documents were ruled inadmissible as evidence.

On February 4, he almost fell into a trap when interviewed by Richard Cantillon, one of Shaw's four attorneys:

CANTILLON: Mr. Clinton, you say your efforts were not motivated by self seeking, or by any influence, monetary or otherwise.

CLINTON: That is true.

CANTILLON: Have you ever received directly or indirectly any money from any member of what you call the underworld, that is, from vice interests or from the syndicate?

CLINTON: I believe I have.

CANTILLON, moving closer, eyes narrowing: Please tell this court of any such instance, and the circumstances.

CLINTON: I would like to ask the court's permission to speak to the attorney for *Liberty* magazine, and to Judge Haas—privately.

Cantillon frowned as Judge Charles E. Haas called a recess. In his chambers, the judge listened as Clinton explained that there was money in a safe deposit box and requested that Nelda be allowed to bring it to the courtroom.

When the box was opened in the court, all eyes were fixed on the $3,800 in cash. There was a notarized letter in which Clinton declared that he thought he was being set up and was therefore locking up the money until its source was determined. The serial numbers on the thousand dollar bills were identified; none of them had been used. Then Clinton revealed the identity of the man with the monocle. It had to be James Utley, his underworld contact. Because Utley moved in outré circles and because he had hinted at getting money for CIVIC, Clinton believed that he had donned a disguise and gone to the Western Union office looking like Josef Stalin. This was a bombshell. Spectators gasped, then tittered, then roared with laughter. Shaw's attorneys were befuddled. The evening papers bore the headline: "Green Lettuce Flutters in Courtroom."

On his tenth and last day of testimony, Clinton denied that he had used an axe to widen the hole made by the bomb in his home before sticking his head through it for press photographers. Then Clinton slipped out of court and went to an Army recruiting office.

On March 27, the jury was discharged after voting six to five in favor of *Liberty* magazine. It would be a full year before Clinton returned to court, this time on a furlough. He testified briefly and then went back to war. Then, on April 29, 1943, Judge Emmett Wilson closed the case with a private out-of-court settlement. Letters of apology from both Clinton and *Liberty* were read to Shaw. The ex-mayor came out of the case with a check somewhere in the amount of fifty thousand dollars. And Clinton turned his thoughts to World War II.

19

THE ARMY AND E.J.

O N FEBRUARY 6, 1942, CLIFFORD CLINTON SLIPPED OUT OF THE *LIBERTY* MAGAZINE TRIAL. If he was defeated by a fifty-thousand-dollar judgment in Shaw's favor, he didn't show it. Instead he walked from Spring Street to a Main Street recruiting office and enlisted in the United States Army.

> Our nation, our way of life was at stake. There was no way to evade this challenge.

Clinton was forty-one years old and ready to fight in another world war. He was assigned to anti-aircraft training at Camp Wallace, a thousand-acre base near Houston, Texas. Before the anti-aircraft training came basic training. He had maintained a daily exercise regimen for twenty-five years, so even though he was twice the age of the average recruit, he handled the rigors of the camp without discernible strain.

As Clinton neared the end of the program, his fame caught up with him. But it was not as a crusader that he was recognized. The Camp Wallace News learned of his famed eateries and devoted an article to him. One thing led to another, and a captain assigned him to run the Cooks, Bakers, and Mess Sergeants School on the base. His job was to implement a fourteen-day intensive training program that would teach inexperienced young men how to cook, bake, and organize an Army Mess—and to reduce waste.

No one who knew Clinton was surprised at what happened next. Once he dug into the job, he was at first intrigued, then engaged, and then absorbed. It was a challenge, yes, but he thrived on challenge. He began writing a manual for the course. Its first chapter was "Possibilities of an Army Mess." Using mess tables as classroom desks, Clinton taught soldiers to scramble large quantities of eggs, to roast and carve meat, and to bake cakes with icing that tasted homemade. Men with little experience handling food were baking apple pies and feeling accomplished. "From that time on," said Clinton, "there bloomed a new spirit within these men; their enthusiasm and talents were employed."

The success of Clinton's cooking and baking school drew the attention of a major, who offered him the opportunity to train as a medical administrative officer. After he got letters of recommendation from Mayor Fletcher Bowron and District Attorney Dockweiler, he received orders to report as an Officer Candidate to the Medical Field Service School at Carlisle Barracks in Carlisle, Pennsylvania. Clinton found officer training school demanding, but he was determined. As class work and written exams grew increasingly difficult, half of his fellow candidates dropped out. Coursework included "how to drill and train men, how to set up a plan, how to lead a mission, and how to reach an objective."

In due time, Clinton received his appointment as second lieutenant and was assigned to the Army Medical Administration Corps, which was at the 24th General Hospital in Fort Benning, Georgia. He was discharged as an enlisted soldier and had two weeks' leave before he would re-enlist as an officer. He headed for Los Angeles. World War II was imposing restrictions on Clifton's. Sugar rationing meant that Nelda and Ransom Callicott had to discontinue free limeade and sherbet. Gas rationing forced Clifton's to discontinue free tours of the city. The store's barbershop and beauty parlor closed for lack of staff. The organ music and vocalists that had set the tone of the restaurant were gone. Even so, guests kept coming. Soldiers were given a discount, and Clinton was adamant that all races be served. "If colored skin is a passport to death in defense of our liberties," he said, "then it is also a passport to Clifton's Cafeteria." Soldiers without funds were still fed; some repaid this generosity by sending letters of gratitude and envelopes stuffed with cash.

Clinton was dismayed when Nelda and Callicott told him that meat was being rationed. This had been the major source of protein in the four million meals served to the hungry and needy at the Penny Cafeteria. To do without meat was unthinkable—and yet it was a distinct possibility. Clinton began to think. He wanted to feed the hungry. He had created a subsistence meal and a Community Food Center. Yet how could he realize any plan without animal protein? This question preoccupied Clinton in the coming months as he and his full-time aide and press agent Ernest Chamberlain studied the effect of war on the ability to feed the hungry.

Fort Benning was a much larger base than Wallace, nearly the size of a city. It housed infantry, paratroopers, and armored units headed for service overseas. There were substantial health facilities, including several hospitals. Clinton was assigned to the 24th General Hospital Mess with a staff of sixty under his command. This mess served as many as twelve hundred meals three times daily. Clinton threw himself into his work, but was soon hindered by the pain in his shoulder and the loss of mobility in his arm caused by an accident during basic training. He consulted an orthopedist and was told that the injury had been more severe than previously thought; surgery would probably not be successful.

When Clinton reported back to Fort Benning, he was promoted to Acting Food Service Officer in recognition of his accomplishments at the 24th mess. This position had been introduced by the Army Quartermaster General (QMG) as a way to improve quality in hundreds of messes at the post. Although preparation standards were high, daily performance was not, partly because of morale. Clinton worked on morale first, and then repeated the strategy he had used in the 24th, placing thirty-gallon garbage cans where uneaten food was discarded. Burned meat, soggy vegetables, and inedible puddings were wasting twenty-five thousand dollars a day. His phobia of waste was serving a purpose.

> We appraised the consumption and comeback of each item. We had a barometer of quality, taste, preference, and portion size. In the end, we cut food waste by eighty percent—a savings of one pound of food per man, or 100,000 pounds of food per day.

Clinton's food service plan was ultimately implemented in all branches of the military.

As countries were liberated from Axis powers, they found themselves in desperate need of medical relief and food. This was a need that touched Clinton's heart. He had heard about the United Nations Relief and Rehabilitation Administration (UNRRA). He requested a transfer and got Mayor Bowron to write another letter of recommendation. Clinton was discharged as a military officer and sent to Washington to serve as an unpaid consultant to the War Department with both the Office of the Quartermaster General and with UNRRA. His new responsibilities involved traveling around the country, evaluating posts and private food vendors. This gave him a chance to return home more often.

Clinton had long had a desire to build a meditation chapel in the Olive Street basement. He saw the popularity of both the Rock Chapel at Brookdale and the transparency of Christ praying in the Garden of Gethsemane at 618, but he could not proceed with his plan, first because of political commitments, and then because of the war. As he traveled on assignment, he pondered and visualized and remembered. When he had lived on Haste Street in Berkeley, there was a print on the wall of the Heinrich Hofmann painting *Christ in the Temple*, which depicted the twelve-year-old Jesus expounding to the elders. Clinton had recently visited the Riverside Church in New York and viewed Hofmann's *Christ in Gethsemane*. Whenever he was in New York, he tried to spend time in this special place, where the painting cast "a mood of prayerful meditation."

As Clinton began to plan a chapel at Clifton's, he called on Dr. William Evans, the father of the pastor at Hollywood Presbyterian, Louis Evans. Dr. Evans suggested the theme of Christ in the Garden, which would feature a life-size figure of Christ. Clinton began construction of a Garden of Meditation in the basement of Clifton's. Clinton commissioned Marshall Lakey to sculpt the statue of Jesus, François Scotti to create the rocky environment, and Einar Petersen to paint a mural of Jerusalem. Clinton then left Ernest Chamberlain in charge while he traveled to the California army facilities at the Presidio in San Francisco, Camp Stoneman, and Fort Ord.

Four rooms were fabricated in the Garden; a reception area, a grotto in the rock like an early Palestinian home, a Well Court providing the Waters of Life, and the corner of the Garden of Gethsemane where Jesus prayed on the night he was betrayed by Judas. The Riverside Church lent a print of Hofmann's painting and the Forest Lawn Association's library of religious art provided pictures of two-thousand-year-old olive trees; their gnarled trunks were recreated in molded rubber. The reception room was modeled on the main room of a First-Century Galilee home. Its furniture and light fixtures were created by hand. Patricia Page, who would go on to be the designer for the film *The Pilgrimage Play* (1949) created costumes for its attendants. On its stone wall hung an inspirational message. "The Influence of One Life" was composed by Clinton, Chamberlain, and Louis Evans. In addition, there were the Codices, a large volume of parchment pages with quotations from Jesus, all hand bound by the Huntington Library in San Marino.

Besides the restaurants, there was another responsibility that Clinton had to bear after the war. He had lost contact with his father. E.J. Clinton had been knocked down by the stock market and knocked out by the Bodie fiasco. Deep in debt, he had disappeared. After a long silence, Clinton heard that his father was in Long Beach. Clinton and Nelda drove there, looking for his address. They found a filling station. There was E.J., the former restaurant owner, cleaning a windshield.

> It was a heartbreaking sight. With tears in our eyes, we begged him to come and live with us and join forces with us at the business. E.J. still had his misplaced pride. He declined the offer.

A while later, Clinton heard from Mills and Crist that they had been forced to close two more of the Clinton restaurants in San Francisco. Of the chain, only 1059 Market and 18 Powell remained. Not long afterward, he heard that E.J. was opening a restaurant in one of the closed sites, 725 Market St.

> Much of Father's history revolved around that block of Market. In 1912, the Puritan was at 749. In 1913, the Quaker was in the basement at 731. Later, after he'd gone two blocks up to O'Farrell, he bought 725 and 1059 from the Boos Bros. E.J.'s latest venture also began to fail.

Clinton visited his father at 725 and offered to help.

> "If this does not get better, you have a lasting home with us. You need not work. But if you want to work, you can work with us at Clifton's."

> "But son, I have so many debts."

> "Wouldn't it be better to go through bankruptcy? You can clean the slate and then pay what you can."

> "No, son. I could never face bankruptcy. My friends have trusted me."

The restaurant at 725 Market failed, and E.J. was once again lost to his family for a time. Eventually, he reached out. Even though he was living with Rose, he was lonely for his children. He reestablished contact with his daughters Grace and Esther. He made up with Evangeline, who was in failing health. Then he contacted Clifford. At sixty-four, Edmond Clinton was willing to work for his son.

> It was a changed father who came to work at Clifton's. . . . He was not the man with whom I had failed to establish an understanding in my youth, when he had been the "perfect host" at O'Farrell. Now, freed from the responsibilities, the problems, and the pressures of earlier years, he could give love and receive it. He was the handsome new host of Clifton's, working the busy lunch, resting in the afternoons, and returning to work the dinner. We could see by the brightness of his eyes and the set of his jaw that he was once again a whole man. He became known as "Mr. Clifton," but few guests knew that he was not the owner; still, we called him the "Father of Clifton's."

E.J. Clinton provided wholehearted service to Clifton's guests, listening, helping, and advising. He was finally able to settle with his creditors in San Francisco, sending them something from each paycheck. In 1943, he and Rose moved into the guesthouse at the Clinton home on Los Feliz Boulevard.

Clinton's travels had to be coordinated with orders from the quartermaster general, but he was grateful for the time he could spend with Nelda, his father, the Pattersons, and the Gowanlocks. The nest was empty in 1944. Edmond was serving in the Coast Guard as a signalman on troop ships traversing the Pacific, Jean was at Stephens College in Columbia, Missouri, and Don was in the Navy. When he was in town, Clinton spent time at the Pacific Seas, helping his artisans put the finishing touches on the Garden of Meditation. A dramatic lighting effect was created to simulate clouds passing over Jesus. Wood was hand rubbed for a genuinely antique look. Handmade pottery and oil lamps completed the picture. By pushing a button, visitors to the shrine could hear a recording of "The Influence of One Life," which was written with the help of Ernest Chamberlain. It summed up much of Clinton's philosophy. Dr. Louis Evans, pastor of the First Presbyterian Church of Hollywood, narrated the message, and musical background was provided by the church's vocal quartet. As guests sat in the Grotto of the Rock, they could reflect on these words:

Millions have perished in war and terror. We survive.

Millions are homeless. We are sheltered.

This night in all the world, for every man well nourished, three are hungry. We are fed.

The world's abundance should have blessed mankind with homes, health and competence. Instead, it has been used to destroy all these, to breed pestilence, misery and poverty.

The finger of the bitter past points to a bloody page . . . "meanly lose or nobly save the last best hope of earth."

Each life is tested by its answer to the question first asked in the world's beginning: "Am I my brother's keeper?"

One life was lived in answer. By all the formal measurements of greatness it should have failed. 'Twas such a little span of years in such a far-off lonely little land.

He was born in a village stable. No birth could be lowlier, hence none need despair because of lowly birth. Possessed of profound wisdom, He had but meager education. None, therefore, need despair for lack of schooling; no wife, no child. He showed each lonely heart its deepest need.

For thirty years, near the village of His birth, He grew and learned His simple trade, shaping the native wood to serve the wants of home and craft.

Three years He wandered, teaching, shaping the native hearts to service of truth and love. He was never more than a few hundred miles from His birthplace.

He held no earthly rank or office, wrote no book, no song; painted no picture, built no monument.

His native land was ruled by conquerors and foreign legions. While still in the flush of youth, His own people turned against this Man who strangely taught that evil can only be overcome by good.

He was denied by His close friend, deserted by most, betrayed for thirty pieces of silver by one He had befriended.

One dark hour He knelt in the Garden, His hour of decision.

He gave himself over to His enemies, was tried and condemned in mockery, spat upon and lashed, nailed to a cross between two thieves.

He died asking forgiveness for His persecutors while His executioners gambled for his only earthly possession, His robe.

He was laid in a borrowed tomb.

Nearly two thousand years have passed and none has reigned or wrought, or served, or dreamed who has so touched and molded human life. He is the ideal, the example who has inspired the noblest and the humblest lives, the great unalterable, wholesome, growing influence in a world of blood and tears.

He who was friendless would be Friend of all. Homeless, He dwells in countless homes. Books on His life fill libraries. His Gospels cover the earth. Song and music in his praise fill the heavens. Pictures, spires and monuments proclaim His influence. Scholars, illiterates, rich men, beggars, rulers and slaves; all are measured by His life.

Clifton's and Clifford Clinton

The names of Pharaohs, Caesars, emperors, and kings of all the ages that have come and gone are but ghosts upon a printed page. All their combined and military might are dust upon the land; their proud sea-borne armadas rust upon an ocean floor.

But this one solitary Life surpasses all in power. Its influence is the one remaining and sustaining hope of future years.

Where does such power dwell?

"Be ye not therefore anxious saying: What shall we eat? Or Wherewithal shall we be clothed? But seek ye first His kingdom and His righteousness—and all these things shall be added unto you."

In a Roman court nearly twenty centuries ago, Pontius Pilate asked of the multitudes demanding the death of this young Galilean: "I find no evil in Him. What shall I do with this Man?'"

Today each troubled heart must meet the challenge when the Pilate within us asks: "What shall I do?"

As Clinton walked through Clifton's, he noticed his father taking time off from his post. Later he would find E.J. sitting downstairs in silence before the statue of Jesus.

In November 1944, Clinton and Nelda grew concerned when E.J. did not bounce back from a cold. They offered to take him to a hospital or just to the hospital room in their home; he preferred to stay in the guesthouse with Rose. "I feel more comfortable here," he told them. On a Sunday morning, Clinton found E.J. unconscious and rushed him to a hospital.

"There is no hope," the family doctor reported. "His lungs are filling. It is only a matter of time."

Clinton was caught off guard.

> This was one of the few times I felt helpless. Faced with the impossible, a material problem, I had always found a way to surmount it. Here I had no resource. I felt helpless. I knew I must pray, but I could only pray that God's will be done. E.J. was still alive, but each breath came more slowly. The spark of life faded. At last he was still, at peace.

A MORE PRESSING ISSUE

I N THE YEARS FOLLOWING THE CIVIC CRUSADE, CLIFFORD CLINTON HAD PRAYED THAT ITS ACCOMPLISHMENTS WOULD LAST, BUT IT WAS NOT TO BE. While he was in Washington he received reports that Fletcher Bowron was falling down on the job. There were numerous problems that the mayor was either unwilling or unable to address. These included tourism, transportation, the sewer system, the city charter, and racial disharmony.

One of the few issues on which Bowron had acted aggressively was the internment of Japanese-Americans in camps. In 1942, Jimmie Mitsuhata, an Issei chef at Clifton's, was forcibly removed and sent to Manzanar, a camp near Lone Pine, California. That Bowron should participate in the imprisonment of 110,000 loyal Americans while neglecting civic duties saddened Clinton. He had pushed Frank Shaw and Buron Fitts out of office for indolence as much as for graft. Bowron was making it look as if his work had been in vain. And the slate of candidates for the 1945 mayoral election was utterly uninspiring.

Clinton doubted that he could win an election for mayor. He had neither the funds nor the organization behind him, but he wanted to distance himself from Bowron in the public's mind. In 1944, his operatives engaged Fact Finders, a public opinion pollster, to assess his popularity. There was a favorable response, and Clinton started thinking about running. While serving in the Armed Forces, he had gotten weekly letters from Aldrich Blake, an operative who had joined CIVIC in 1938 as a political organizer. Blake urged Clinton to get involved in city government, asking him if he was going to retire after the war or establish a restaurant chain to finance a run for mayor. When Clinton returned, he and Blake contacted former members of CIVIC and reconstituted the organization.

Bowron had widened his support among key groups in the city, including conservative business and the CIO. Clinton had lost his conservative support, so, at Blake's suggestion, he tried to draw liberal groups to his side. Neither Water and Power nor the American Federation of Labor (AFL) was interested; after all, he had a longstanding anti-labor reputation. John Anson Ford was uncomfortable with Clinton's newly liberal stance and doubted his chances of winning. He told him so and, after dropping out of the race, declined to endorse him. A friendship of ten years' duration was ending.

> Mayor Bowron has been unable to get the cooperation of the City Council, the county, state or federal governments. He is a "lone wolf" type of person and lacks genuine executive abilities. He harbors an attitude of distrust and cannot delegate decisions and responsibilities.

Clinton wanted to reshape his own image.

> I am always cast in the role of being a reformer and bluenose. Although Bowron has been wonderful—as far as he's gone—I take the position that we haven't gone far enough to regenerate our citizens.

By 1944, the Hyperion sewage plant was woefully inadequate to handle the needs of a greatly increased population. Several council plans to expand the plant had been voted down, and Bowron seemed unable to do anything about it. The State Board of Health ordered the city to build a new plant, but there was still no action. By April 1943, raw sewage was being dumped in Santa Monica Bay, so much so that the State Board of Health quarantined the bay. Acting as Clinton's campaign manager, Blake wrote a brochure with Ernest Chamberlain entitled *Sewers of Los Angeles: The Story of Millions in Damages, Disease, Pestilence, Death.*

On January 1, 1945, Clinton published his second brochure, *The Clock Strikes Twelve.* Part of his direct-to-the-people campaign, it presented his blueprint for a "City of Dreams." In a small insert, *If Los Angeles Could Talk,* Clinton spoke directly to Angelenos.

> What is the Voice of the City? You—two million of you—are the Voice of Los Angeles. Not as automatons, but as human beings. What do YOU want? What do YOU think Los Angeles would say if it could talk?

He distributed twenty-five thousand copies and then opened his home to the public every Sunday afternoon.

> Don't knock. Walk right in and make yourself at home. Let's meet in the front room. No back-room meetings. No headquarters.

His campaign slogan was: "We have committed the needs of Los Angeles to memory. Let us now commit them to action!"

To solve the problems of the postwar era and build a Los Angeles of the future, Clinton proposed an affordable citywide transportation system. He was disappointed with the new freeway system. He expressed incredulity that a city would not provide funds for a sewer system when its population was growing exponentially. He disagreed with Bowron on the internment of Japanese Americans and advocated a plan to welcome residents of racially and ethnically diverse backgrounds. Finally, he was critical of the city charter, which he described as a "riddle-ridden jigsaw puzzle."

On January 30, 1945, Clinton submitted his name to the city clerk and officially entered the mayoral race. The primary election would be held on April 3. Other men nominated for mayor by petition included Jim Renfro and Leland Ellis Zeman. Clinton would campaign on three issues: adoption of a city manager form of government; public ownership of all streetcar and bus lines; and immediate action to construct an adequate sewer system. He also proposed a citizens' committee to keep the city council engaged in new projects.

On February 16, Clinton's completed nominating petitions were presented to the City Clerk by Aldrich Blake, who had become his campaign manager. Clinton had modest expectations. He had received contributions from only a few supporters, including Van Griffith and the Mellinkoffs, who had helped him during his anti-Shaw campaign. He made only a few speeches, and these were at sparsely attended affairs. He did not directly oppose Bowron, John Ford, or Roger Jessup. The campaign was low key and focused primarily on the sewage system and the city's structural and political problems.

Typically unorthodox, Clinton proposed a Visitors-and-Greeting Agency where well-known citizens could guide visitors through Los Angeles attractions. The oil industry could make a "glass-walled spiral stairway tubed down into an oil well where viewers could watch the oil processed from the ground." He also proposed the development of the Los Angeles River, which was dry most of the year. He envisioned a "River Showplace" with dams, flood control, and lock systems, which would allow the river to be used for sports, recreation, and rapid cargo transport.

> Along the river could be developed such garden spots as Xochimilco in Mexico. Showboat theaters could provide unlimited possibilities for entertainment.

He even promoted Van Griffith's dream of a revolving restaurant on Mount Hollywood connected to the street below by a funicular railway.

Clinton was a wellspring of ideas, and, even though these were ahead of their time and controversial, press coverage was embarrassingly sparse. Bowron received thousands of lines of newsprint. Clinton received only ninety-six. Was this a fitting acknowledgment of the good work

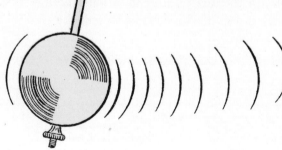

The

Clock Strikes Twelve

A LITTLE JOURNEY INTO LOS ANGELES AS IT WAS, AS IT IS AND AS IT CAN BE ✓ ✓ ✓ GLIMPSES OF THE PHYSICAL, CULTURAL AND SPIRITUAL PROMISE OF THE CITY OF THE ANGELS ✓ ✓ ✓

LOS ANGELES *Unlimited*

THERE IS one thing upon which all the experts and prophets agree:

Los Angeles, in particular, and the West Coast, in general, face the nation's toughest postwar problems.

Today is zero hour for Los Angeles. In the measurable future, either it will astonish the world in physical progress, wealth, fresh mental outlook, bodily perfection, tolerance, beauty, cultural and spiritual depth, or, like most big cities, it will succumb to mere corpulence.

Either the sign posts which now mark its "city limits" will continue to inspire only wisecracks, both at home and among the boys overseas, or the corporate limits of the startling new Los Angeles will be as elastic as the human mind.

Either this new urban empire of the Pacific will exemplify true democratic genius for local government, or it will sink to the levels so common in dense urban life elsewhere in America.

Already, the convulsive struggle of the West for industrial independence from the East is on. Here also, in Los Angeles' boiling postwar cauldron, are brewing all of the ingredients of racial and religious intolerance, industrial strife, civic jealousy and discord which, if allowed to go too far, will destroy both private and public plans for civic development.

It is hoped that those who read this outline will gain new understanding of Los Angeles in the light of its past, absorb fresh inspiration in the prospects which lie ahead, and may be induced to join with others who seek the goal to the city's highest hopes and aspirations.

For it is only by knowing, daring and doing that cities are built and live eternal.

Clifford E. Clinton

BEHOLD...

HARDLY more than a stone's throw from the simple monument which marks the birthplace of the once tiny pueblo, and rising 452 feet into the heavens, stands the massive Los Angeles City Hall, symbol of the growth of the new civilization which began 175 years ago in a dry river bottom, leap-frogged to a mud-flat (now a mighty harbor) 25 miles away, and finally sprawled over fertile valley, undulating hill, sharp mountain side and sandy beach, to form an empire within itself on the ruins of the old Spain.

From the tip of the soaring tower of this rather cold but stately edifice of mixed Greek, Romanesque and American architecture, we look out upon a scene of thrilling beauty . . . deep tranquility . . . sweeping panorama whose outlines fade and reappear in the soft, grey mists . . . Cinderella City for dreams come true . . . incomparable setting for gay fiesta, undying world's fair . . . bit of earthly paradise set apart as if by Divine Providence for the happiness and inspiration of man . . . the Promised Land!

Here, perched far above the seething, restless City of the Angels, drafts-men bend over their work boards and draw the plans which some day, per-haps, will make it possible to erase the dark streaks and patches of ugliness and obsolescence, dimly visible below, which we forget, or fail to observe, in our moment of ecstasy and awe.

But let not the charms and generosity of nature and of climate, nor these fine blue-prints, nor the fascinating exhibits we saw in the shop win-dows, deceive us.

Wishful thinking does not build a city.

Plans are not self-executing.

Cities are but the reflection of the people who live in them. It is the men and women of Los Angeles who must translate the glowing image into the reality.

From atop the City Hall we may well pass to the floors below. For here, in the subdued executive and councilmanic chambers of local government, the official decisions, which determine much of civic destiny, are made.

THE CITY'S BRAIN

It is something more than an odd phenomenon that during the 73 years of its modern existence and growth, Los Angeles, now a city of nearly two million people, and always a feverish political center, has yet to produce its first statesman.

This curious circumstance is a challenge, an ominous yardstick of our genius for democracy.

It is true that many worthy and competent men have stood guard at the city hall. But no mayor or councilman has ever won more than fleeting local acclaim. No City Father, poured in bronze, adorns our parks, and no Angeleno has yet been proposed for the Hall of Fame at the national capitol.

As in nearly all American cities, except for brief intervals, government in Los Angeles has been like "a steam-engine stuck in the mud."

Even as we now plan for the expenditure of huge sums in the postwar years (much of this money to correct mistakes of the past) we shrink from the job of providing ourselves with a modern charter of organic law. This is the one major peace time activity which justifiably could have been undertaken during the crisis of war.

We are late, but, let us hope, not too late!

Yes, we need men—big men—to study the breath-taking plans, pass the laws, appropriate the money, and to devise the means for the orderly execution of these plans and laws.

But must we not also give these men the tools with which to work? Among them a short, understandable, flexible charter of organic law to take the place of the riddle-ridden 125,000 word jig-saw puzzle which currently passes as the city's "constitution" and which has afflicted us since 1925 at such frightening cost?

In the end, nearly all of the trails of civic progress lead directly to the city hall where the nerves of the body politic converge.

By the very nature of democratic institutions, the composite brain of the city is its local government, and our ideals and dreams can be realized only to the degree that we elect unselfish leaders with the ability and vision to preside over public administration.

We might as well understand this before we begin to remodel and redevelop Los Angeles.

BLOOD STREAM

The block-long Angel's Flight incline railway, built a half century ago and linking Bunker Hill to down-town Los Angeles, was a milestone in the city's progress then.

Today it is an uncomfortable reminder that we are no longer a unified community.

Angel's Flight, with its crude cable cars, enabled the people of the nineties to live in what was then the city's most desirable suburb, without isolating themselves from the busy marts and gay social life centering in the alluring Plaza and once famed Pico House.

Now we have many Bunker Hills, scattered over magnificent distances, with no adequate transportation means to make them neighbors, to transport their people from home to factory, beach, valley, mountain, stadium; from quiet suburb to throbbing centers of pleasure and commerce.

Safe, cheap, rapid transit is the blood stream which keeps the heart of the city pumping, its muscles working in perfect coordination.

Today the blood stream of Los Angeles is sluggish. A half century ago, the few hundred feet of iron rails in Angel's Flight quickened the pulse of the growing community.

Now it will require a new conception of rapid transportation, in addition to improved down-town connecting links and the proposed new parkways, to quicken the blood stream of the elephantine metropolis, and to give it that harmonious, reciprocal movement without which life in the big city becomes stale, stagnant and tedious.

New York City recently spent its billionth dollar on its rapid transit system. The City of Los Angeles has yet to spend its first penny on fast electric transport.

Sound government, adequate transportation!

These are two of the absolutely vital conditions precedent to intelligent long range city planning and building.

There is a third.

* * *

"Cities are for people."

The people of a city are its will, spirit and soul.

Los Angeles has always been a community of many kinds and races of people. New tides of migration have buried preceding cultures almost as completely as the whirling sands of Egypt entombed the Pharoahs and their palaces.

In more recent times we have witnessed the mad scramble of hopeful,

A CHALLENGE

aged and middle-aged farmers, merchants and professional people from the frost-bitten middle west, who sold their rich, black soil, closed their stores and offices, to exchange a sure thing for a ray of California sunshine and a fragrant orange blossom.

Today, another epic.

Wave on wave they come, the toilers of the nation:

Mechanic, riveter, welder, white collar workers, Oakies and Arkies— not to live their longer span out of savings, like so many of their predecessors —but determinedly to make their living in the sweat of their brow, to earn larger happiness for themselves and their children in the hopeful atmosphere of the Golden West.

Cities are for people, but people also create problems for cities. To weave a pattern of these tangled human strands which comprise Los Angeles today is one of the most baffling civic problems of the future.

What are some of these strands?

Nearly one-half of Los Angeles' citizenship, born outside the United States, or children of foreign parents. Two hundred nationalities, 40 of them in sizeable numbers, permanently settled, bag and baggage. Seventeen newspapers, mostly printed in foreign languages. Congested Negro population, nearly 150,000 citizens. Protestant, Jew and Catholic, here in great numbers. Practically every cultural badge in the United States worn by Los Angeles' population. Hordes of immigrants from every section of the United States. Veterans marching to tune of "California, Here I Come!" First retired, then middle class, now working-man America—here and here to stay!

Melting pot? Or giant test-tube filled with components which are never to liquefy and fuse?

New and foreboding challenge:

Can we be tolerant enough to appraise every citizen on the basis of his own individuality and worth; wise enough to choose only the best for leadership; civic minded and unselfish enough to become a unified, disciplined, harmonious, fighting force placing overall community welfare first?

This the third and most important condition precedent to healthy outer community growth and real inner community peace and happiness.

Problems to look squarely in the eye!

* * *

Only by evaluating the past can we understand the Los Angeles of today, intelligently plan, and realize our dreams for tomorrow.

Officially founded by royal Spanish decree in the fall of 1781, here was a community which had little to commend it except Bible and Cross.

IN PERSPECTIVE

Unlike other great metropolitan communities, Los Angeles' birth was unpromising. Its site was no logical junction point for overland trade routes to the east, no readily saleable terminus for iron horse. No navigable stream beckoned commerce from distant markets. No natural harbor or bay encouraged commercial development here. No mineral deposits or agricultural hopes lured prospector or farmer.

In its semi-arid climate, even a pure, refreshing drink of water became an elusive luxury as the little pueblo grew.

For well over a century, geography and nature, which now seem so kind to us, resolutely decreed that Los Angeles grow from the outside in, instead of from the inside out, and that its citizenry perform the miracle of moving forward in reverse.

Los Angeles made good!

Amid droughts which ruined choice vineyards, and left only bones where once fine herds of cattle browsed; in the face of recurrent and shocking governmental ineptitude; between resounding boom and crash of real estate values and weird speculation which sent the price of a single Belgian hare, worth fifty cents on the hoof, to as much as $2500; despite a murder a day and wholesale lynchings, the clash of strange personalities, new populations and shifting cultures, there were imagination and enterprise which bore rich fruit.

In succession came the Southern Pacific and Santa Fe, the San Pedro-Wilmington breakwater, long slabs of concrete stretching across the nation, the Owens Valley and Boulder dam aqueducts, linking the rising metropolis with east, west, north and south, and converting dry desert into land of flowers, palm and eucalyptus, pasture and orchard.

The voting of two bond issues, one for 23 million dollars for the Owens Valley aqueduct in 1905 by a 7 to 1 margin, and the other for 220 million dollars for Boulder dam water in 1931 by a 5 to 1 majority, now seem incredible civic achievements. In proportion to population, the Owens Valley gamble was the equivalent to a bond issue of 250 million dollars today; the Boulder dam venture the equal of voting 350 million dollars by the present tax payers of Los Angeles.

Yet now, once dare-devil Los Angeles, transformed into multi-billion dollar city because of its past "reckless spending," hems and haws (for a decade) over the matter of providing the few million dollars necessary to rid itself of the sewage effluent which has closed its once famous beaches.

THE CROSS REMAINS

Despite repeated warnings of ocean pollution, where was leadership? "Make no little plans . . ."

But it was even before Owens Valley that Los Angeles began to grow from the inside out instead of from the outside in, and shifted from reverse into high gear.

At the turn of the century, for reasons we shall soon learn, the world already was moving in, ready for the kill.

Soon old landmarks—priceless heritage of the past—one by one, began to disappear. Colorful adobe gave way to steel and concrete. Gay fiesta, romance, quickly vanished. The bells that rang at Ramona's wedding tolled the death of a gracious tradition. Pioneer hospitality and neighborliness were in retreat.

The free-for-all scramble for a niche in the new empire of the Pacific was on. Modernity could no longer be denied. The practical, enterprising mid-westerner wanted something more than sunshine, ocean, valley and mountain, gaiety and fancy. He sought the conveniences and comforts of material progress.

In the all-out assault on the citadels of the past, one monument was spared—the crude, wooden cross erected by Felipe de Neve in 1781. To this day, on the spot where Los Angeles was born, it stands a silent sentry over most that remains of the old Spain.

Block-long Olvera—Los Angeles' only famous down-town street—at whose entrance this cross was planted, still shelters the old adobe house on the site where Commodore Stockton led his gringo band into the new pueblo.

And, with its clay toys, black paper cigarettes, scented candles, bright pottery, cactus plants, quaint iron forge, artists, wine cellars, cabarets, gaily costumed senoritas, guitars, tile, cobble stones and market place this bit of unadulterated Latin, cloistered in the heart of a great city, still delights the tourist's eye while serving as constant reminder that Los Angeles is now home to many other races whose life and culture need rediscovery in its tomorrow.

May ancient cross, symbol of the city's inner life, and Olvera Street, guardian of the city's romance and early gaiety, be with us always!

Of all the great cities in the world, Los Angeles fell heir to the most living, playing and working room. For this inheritance we must give man as well as nature credit.

When, in 1897, Henry E. Huntington built his 20 million

TRANSITION

dollar interurban system, he gave the City of the Angels its first wings. Henry Ford's tin lizzie accelerated the flight of Angelenos to the wide open spaces.

Previously, Los Angeles had boasted the first electric street car in the United States. Soon, as if Destiny had planned it, began to gestate the only small urban community in the world whose birth as a metropolitan city was to come after the invention of the automobile.

The transition from Model T Los Angeles to Model 1944-45 Los Angeles was inevitable, precisely as adolescence always follows childhood. Aqueduct, harbor, simply had to come.

Quite naturally, the city grew horizontally instead of perpendicularly. It was easier to cultivate the greener tips than to tear down and replant at the aging center. It required less energy and planning to follow any old trail than to blaze new trails.

Like a buzz bomb, Los Angeles, after 1897, exploded where it happened to hit.

And, paradoxically, the very impetus given by the two Henrys to Los Angeles' transmigration is accountable for its three major current problems —grotesque assortment of separate governmental units, tragically inadequate transportation, shocking lack of civic cohesion.

But, first, where did the expanding pueblo go?

For its popular beaches it went to Santa Monica, Manhattan, Hermosa, Redondo; for its yacht harbor to Balboa. Its movie colony discovered Malibu. Several of its most famous motion picture studios located in Burbank, Culver and Universal Cities. For its California Institute of Technology, Huntington Library and Art Gallery, Community Play House, Busch Gardens, Christmas Lane, Rose Bowl, and only famous residential avenue, Orange Grove, it moved to Pasadena. It found its best fishing and finest vacation ground at Catalina; its scenic Riviera at Palos Verdes. It placed its bets at Santa Anita and Inglewood. Many of its writers, sculptors and painters migrated to Laguna. It journeyed to San Gabriel for its Mission Play, to El Monte for its fascinating Lion Farm. Much of its wealth was invested in trees, shrubs and flowers in Beverly Hills. Big Bear and Arrowhead became its winter sports resorts; the valleys below, its orange grove and vineyard. Burbank, Long Beach, Downey, Vernon and other neighboring cities took big bites out of its industrial pie.

And, to cap the climax, Los Angeles decided to cure its sniffles in the bright winter sunshine of swanky Palm Springs, brave the sweltering heat of Yuma for many of its marriage vows.

Small wonder that Los Angeles has been spoken of as "the city which is somewhere else!"

THE PRESENT

In 15 years the assessed valuation of Los Angeles has declined 42 percent, while 57% of its ad valorem taxes are spent by county for out-of-city development. Annual revenues have dropped ten million dollars, and it has become necessary for the city to borrow from the Water and Power Department to pay its bills. An unsound fiscal policy about which nothing is being done, and an injustice to consumers who are thus deprived of lower utility rates.

Yet during this same period of declining assessments and revenues, the city's population has increased by one-half.

The planners have a name for it:

Obsolescence!

The tourist who enters Los Angeles by way of the Union Depot momentarily is charmed. At long last, California! Instinctively, he pauses before the Mission architecture of this low-lying, commodious structure of delicate lines and hue, its lovely patio and semi-tropical plaza which enchant the eye. There is no sensation here of Dreadful Heights, ponderous steel and concrete. Our visitor relaxes in the soft, peaceful atmosphere of archway and palm, slender but graceful tower.

Now he is in his taxi. It will be a long time before he again realizes that he is in fabulous California. No matter where his destination, he must look quickly and intently to discover so much as a tiny patch of the Los Angeles about which he has read and dreamed.

Memories:

As he rides down Central Avenue, he thinks of crowded Harlem. Main Street reminds him of Chicago's honky tonk district. Santa Monica Boulevard, South Figueroa, Sunset, Western, Vermont, East First, Whittier—of shabby streets in the old home town. Here and there on his journey, our new visitor recalls the tenderloins, the squalid slums of other big cities.

And, in between, blocks and blocks of mixed residential and industrial areas, disappointing reminder of the soiled, threadbare, defaced sections of uninviting work-shop America.

San Pedro, Venice—no memories here, only shock. Magnificent natural sites, neglected, abandoned, rotting in spots . . . monuments to picayunish, short-sighted, big city government for many years . . . warning to other incorporated communities that annexation to Los Angeles has not paid those who have tried it . . . psychological obstacles blocking the path to unified metropolitan government and inter-city cohesion.

But perhaps our guest is headed for Los Angeles' pantry and ice box, filled with fruits, jellies, olives, vegetables, poultry and dairy products from

HEIRLOOMS

the thousands of farms and ranches located within Big Town's city limits in the San Fernando Valley—area equal to that of Chicago.

Here, at last, despite the spotty development of these broad acres, is California. But alas! Our passenger imagines he is no longer in Los Angeles!

More than 30 miles from the Union Depot and journey's end. Like acid Henry L. Mencken who called a cab to take him to a friend's home, our tourist pays a $16 fare.

More memories:

Fast, comfortable electric transit or suburban train service in New York City which would have carried him the same distance for exactly one nickel or a few pennies more!

Most first impressions, bad. Others, better. When the growing pueblo went transient, it generously, or absent-mindedly left a few heirlooms in the old homestead:

The Southwest Museum with its sensational discoveries found in Nevada's caves; Los Angeles Museum with its priceless exhibit of prehistoric animals buried in the La Brea pits; Exposition Park with its magnificent rose gardens, Olympic Coliseum, Armory, and Industrial Building housing fascinating dioramas of romantic business and agricultural development—these remain.

Nor did transient Los Angeles walk off with Griffith Park and its Planetarium, Greek Theater, murmuring brooks, dense fern-cooled picnic grounds; nor did it uproot the smaller colleges, St. Vincent's Loyola, Occidental, Pepperdine; nor its larger educational institutions made famous by Trojan and Bruin athlete as well as by scholastic standards. Mercifully, it left us Hollywood Bowl with its ballet, operas, symphonies, Easter Sunrise Service, inspiring spectacles.

The Pilgrimage Play, Pacific League ball parks, Shrine and Pan-Pacific auditoriums, San Pedro breakwater, the old Plaza, the inimitable Japanese Gardens adjoining Pacific Palisades—all remain.

And also—Brentwood Heights, Silver Lake, Mulholland Drive, Cheviot Hills, many, many side streets lined with shady pepper trees, stately palms, proud magnolias, entrancing nooks and corners—are still hiding out in Los Angeles despite outward and inward trek, patiently biding their time, as it were, to prove that Beauty, whether throned in sea, desert, valley or mountain, or in the eyes and lips of movie star, is still the most saleable product in the world.

Actually, Los Angeles is a great deal more than the 452 square miles which comprise Los Angeles City proper. In spirit and concept it extends far beyond its legal limits. The assets of each of the county's 45 separate

WHICH CHOICE?

municipalities and those of Southern California, are the assets of all; the liabilities of each, the liabilities of all. Their problems cannot be divorced.

As of 1944, Los Angeles is still in flux. Because of elbow room, decentralization began early, much too early. The centripetal and centrifugal forces of civic growth have never been in balance. The city has never quite caught up with itself. It has repeatedly tripped over its own rope. First it grew from the outside in; then from the inside out. Since Pearl Harbor its growth has been cancerous.

The big job of civic statesmanship as the war ends is to operate on the cancer, inject financial plasma into the blood stream, and give the patient the power of self-analysis in order to reconcile the conflict between the demands of the dead past and those of a hopeful future.

The pulls must be equalized. Basic re-design of the blighted heart of the city and adequate mass transportation are the best answer. And we must proceed with the speed, determination and social vision which led the city to pioneer in public development of its great water and power utilities.

Which shall we choose? Confused or sensible governmental structure?

Shall we continue as a city of hitch-hikers, back seat drivers, parking lot combatants and tired, jostled street car riders, or as comfortable commuters in fast, modern, adequate suburban trains?

Shall we keep on shuddering at the shrill, piping voices of distraught and befuddled civic leadership, or respond to the massive, irresistibly moving symphonic harmony of a trained community chorus?

Despite the cynic, Los Angeles is no hick town populated by boobs, slickers and fanatics, and composed mainly of hot dog stands, B-girl joints, beano games and merry-go-rounds.

Yet we cannot pretend that it is an ancient democratic shrine like Athens; an Eternal City like Rome; an art and literary center comparable with Florence before the wars; a Peacock Alley like gay Paris of the nineties; a Versailles with its world famed gardens and fountains; an amorous, stunningly beautiful Buenos Aires; an intriguing Mexico City with its limitless passion for pageantry and fun; a Shanghai or San Francisco with their cosmopolitan garb and sophisticated manners.

Nor is Los Angeles like New York, city of Stony Skyscrapers; nor like Chicago with its Big Shoulders; nor like Pittsburgh, huge Boarding House with Workshop in Garage.

Similarities there are—ominous increasing similarities—to commonplace urban America, yet . . .

THE INNER CITY

The City of the Angels is still the City of Promise, its character and pattern not yet, but almost ready, to be cast.

Tomorrow?

But, first, what of Invisible Los Angeles?

Menace:

Mere physical growth of a city unless at the same time this growth enables its people to secure greater bodily health and perfection, and to realize their natural urge for richer, fuller and sweeter lives.

The really great city is the city in which dwell happy people.

Jobs, homes, automobiles, radios—these things help to make people happy. But for most people they are not enough.

There is the desire for music, art and architecture, drama, literature, education, lecture, the tremendous zest for competitive sports.

And above all, there is the vital impulse which craves spiritual satisfaction.

Beyond are still other yearnings.

Hospitality, neighborliness, tolerance and dignification of race and religion, economic and industrial justice, democratic fulfillment. Peace in everyday living.

Without these, no city can become or remain truly great because too many of its citizens will be miserable in mind and spirit. Without inner satisfaction, your multi-billion dollar city will not be worth a plugged nickel in terms of real human happiness.

Tug-of-war between utilitarian and spiritual Los Angeles closely parallels the clash of centripetal and centrifugal forces in the city's physical development. We veer to and fro from the Latin conception of a semi-tropical civilization and the mal-adapted conception of northern cultures.

Especially in the City of the Angels, it has always been a struggle between the census figures and the city's natural heritage and environment; between those who measure civic growth in terms of population increase and area, and those who think of the city as something besides a lot of people mechanically going about their daily chores in a fixed amount of space.

How shall we equalize the pulls, deal with these conflicting mental states? Can we build here the new City Republic whose physical boundaries, neatly marked "Los Angeles City Limits," are as limitless as the mind and spirit of man? Can we tie our expanding industries to civic purposes? Is it

possible for us to keep growing bigger and bigger and at the same time guide and direct the human impulses which either contribute to man's happiness or condemn him to agonizing frustrations?

In short, can we create here an outer and an inner city in proportions which will assure both material well-being and the deeper emotions of life?

It is twelve o'clock midnight!

* * *

When the war ends—cheap, easy over-night hop between cities.

What a choice for the air-minded vacationist!

London, rebuilt, beautified, historical. Versailles with its gardens, terraces, Grand Canal; statues and bronze groups; amazing fountains; Orangery with 1200 orange trees, 300 other kinds of trees; alleys bedecked with sculpture, vases, and lined with neatly trimmed hedges.

Or perhaps the choice will be Stalingrad with its great battle panorama in mile long central park with memorial square, and stunning new architectural design for the entire city; or Moscow with its Kremlin, Red Square, municipal art studios, unbelievably generous subsidies to painter, musician, sculptor, and its eleven new bridges with statues of rare beauty and strength rising 150 feet above the abutment approaches.

There is also Rio De Janeiro with its astonishing new thoroughfare cutting a swath 180 yards wide and more than four miles long, replacing old and ugly down-town business blocks; its 120 foot granite figure of Christ on Corcorado, daily inspiration of a million city dwellers.

And beautiful Buenos Aires with its Plaza Del Congreso and charming French Renaissance architecture, stimulated by the city's annual award for the most attractively designed business and residence building.

Yes, for the vacationist who takes to the skies—Alaska, the Holy Land, the Orient, Africa—all of the marvels of the world from which to choose.

Perhaps Angelenos should begin to think of Pershing Square as something more than a convenient spot for an underground garage, and of their precious seashore as something else than a site for a sewage dump!

What shall we say of leadership which is willing to leave the Hyperion plant on the ocean front despite the recommendation of disinterested eastern engineers, with esthetic vision, that it be moved inland?

Tentative plans already call for spending more than a billion and a quarter dollars for the improvement and redevelopment of Los Angeles in the postwar era—an amount almost equal to the total assessed valuation of the city today.

MANY NEEDS

A low price to pay if by such expenditure Los Angeles can become a ten billion instead of a billion and a half dollar city. Far less than enough to spend if its outer and inner life are to be balanced.

No sensible citizen will complain against the present plans for a municipal auditorium, for parkways, streets, storm drains, sewage disposal, flood control, airports, water and power improvements, better harbor facilities, parks, playgrounds and beaches.

But these things are not enough if Los Angeles is to compete success-fully with its rival cities after the war, and is to be really happy within itself.

There must be money to take over and extend the now privately owned bus and electric transit systems; to establish a medical plan, similar to New York City's; for a real zoo, and an aquarium like Marineland in Florida.

Funds must be available to give initial impetus to a permanent world's fair, with Olvera Streets and Chinatowns revealing life as it is lived by many different peoples; for museums of living art and an arts center; for regular band and symphony concerts in diverse sections of the city; for the development of the city's agriculture; for inexpensive but suitable meeting places in the 300 or more distinct communities—little worlds—which exist within the larger city, so that neighborliness may be promoted and plain citizens may give fuller expression to the democratic process.

And still more money will be needed for real hospitality, to give every incoming tourist a personal and cordial welcome; for the world's finest indoor Sports Garden, appropriate also for grand opera, mass graduations, scientific exhibits; for gay carnival and fiesta; for numerous Community Play Houses to encourage the theater and complement our priceless motion picture drama; for awards for outstanding achievement in science, education, literature, the arts, and, in short, for a program of broad spiritual, cultural and educational enrichment.

No, the tax payer need not swoon!

It will require many years to do these things and the money will come from many sources.

It will come from the revenues of self-liquidating projects; out of profits to be derived from the proper handling of waste materials which the city now allows to be destroyed; from business enterprises which will reap both direct and indirect profits from many of these public under-takings; from the federal government in the form of advances and outright grants of cash; from the state government; from steadily increasing private endowments for public purposes; from the swelling multitude of eager visitors, and a small part, yes, from greatly increased Los Angeles property values.

Over a period of time, no insurmountable fiscal problem here.

Merely perplexing riddles in political leadership and civic will.

It is said that a city is only as great as its citizens. In Los Angeles and environs there is a vast basin filled to the brim with all types of civic leadership which heretofore has shunned the art of politics and government.

Our problem tomorrow is to find the key which will unlock the gates of this huge reservoir and release its walled-in Niagara of brains and character.

Not just *part*, but *all* of the city's reserves of top-rate manpower must be used—drafted, if necessary—for the official and unofficial tasks of civic statesmanship.

To make a new city charter possible; to create some kind of formal but voluntary federation of cities within the county; to solve the sewage and other exasperating municipal problems; to initiate and pursue a plan for fast, cheap electric transit; to take the lead in forestalling zoot suit riots and Sleepy Lagoon cases; to devise means of minimizing industrial strife and of protecting minority groups; to wipe out slums and tackle social issues head-on—these are among the special concerns of local administration.

Busy citizens engaged in arduous tasks of their own must not be asked nor expected to poodle-dog either the executive administrators or councilmen at the City Hall by actually doing much of the work which these officials are paid to do.

Vital to Los Angeles tomorrow:

Colorful, aggressive, bold, imaginative and selfless administration of local government, Leadership which knows its way around Washington as well as around the corridors of the City Hall. Showmanship which gets things done!

Fatal to Los Angeles tomorrow:

A citizenship divided against itself. Pressure groups which prefer no parkway to one which does not pass their doors. Citizens who would rather see others suffer transportation pains than vote for a municipally owned transit system. Men and women who would tolerate slums rather than have them removed by public housing. People who fail to realize that there is an inner as well as an outer Los Angeles. Public sentiment which refuses to jell into any kind of unified action for the creation here of the world's most advanced and happiest civilization.

Which way, Los Angeles?

The same old gutted highway trod elsewhere by metropolitan America? Or smooth open road to open city?

The clock strikes twelve!

he had done? Or was it a payback from Chandler and Hearst for the trouble he had caused them? As he later learned, their new policy was to ignore him. "Don't play him up," they told their editors. "Don't ridicule him. Don't even mention him."

On April 3, 1945, Bowron won the mayoral primary election. This ended Clinton's political career.

On April 5, John Anson Ford broke his silence to write a letter. He knew how disappointed Clinton must be and commended him for a good fight. He felt that he himself would have made a better candidate and that Clinton would have been more effective in a supporting role.

> On the contrary. I am not in the least disappointed. I feel you have failed to understand what prompted me to run. It was to fulfill a personal obligation for supporting Fletcher Bowron. I had no other way of being discharged forever of this obligation. My future plans are to work as a citizen for the things we have advocated so long.

This was the last communication between Clinton and the man who had brought him into politics.

On July 19, Clinton made a presentation to the city council calling for development of the Los Angeles River as a waterway from downtown Los Angeles to the harbor in San Pedro. The "dry concrete canal" could become both a freight route and a resort with floating gardens. On December 6, he proposed a two-million-dollar project to build a four-tier parking area under Pershing Square, which would also include an auditorium, restrooms, and a hospitality house for tourists on the street level. It would be many years before some of these ideas were implemented, and not by Clinton.

When Clinton got Bowron elected in 1938, the links between City Hall and the syndicate were ostensibly severed. As Clinton expected, they were eventually restored. One example was the apparent immunity of the notorious madam Brenda Allen, who had been arrested time and again, only to go free. She had powerful allies, all the way from the cops on the beat to the mayor's office. But she was far from the only one with friends in important places. The brutal gangster Michael "Mickey" Cohen was proven to have a connection to law enforcement when one of his bodyguards was revealed to be an employee of the state attorney general's office. (In his autobiography, Cohen bragged that although he did not socialize with Mayor Bowron, he had his private phone number and could reach him at any time.) The public wanted to believe that Bowron had vice under control and was maintaining a clean administration. In the 1949 mayor's race, he defeated city engineer Lloyd Aldrich. Bowron had barely settled in when a scandal broke. Wiretaps revealed that Allen was involved with a police officer. Then Police Chief C.B. Horrall perjured himself before the grand jury and was relieved of his duties. Citizens demanded that Bowron be recalled.

An electrical inspector named O.K. Jones formed the Ordinary Citizens Committee (OCC) and began to circulate petitions. Not unlike the Shaw recall committee, the OCC had limited funds and was about to disband when someone began to underwrite it. Rumors pointed to Clinton, but he denied it. The committee's future improved as the Democratic Party Central Committee and the Associated Republicans of America joined the fight. After much political maneuvering, a recall election was scheduled for 1950. Bowron was not recalled; he was elected once again. At this point Clinton decided to stay away from politics.

He had accomplishments of which to be proud: an affordable, convenient urban trolley car system for those without automobiles, the use of radio as a medium for informing the public, and ideas to streamline city government all proved to be prescient. No one could deny his unprecedented remarkable achievements. Between 1880 and 1938, many citizens had tried—and failed—to reform municipal government. "You can't fight City Hall," was the legacy of these attempts. Only Clinton succeeded. He had fought City Hall with all its entwined and powerful influences and won. He was tenacious in the pursuit of truth, innovative in the use of radio, willing to unite with those of differing philosophies, and most importantly, he spent his money to prove the depth of his convictions. When his involvement with politics ended, he was not disappointed. He had shifted his attention to a more pressing issue.

NOVEMBER 20, 1969

AFTER WORLD WAR II ENDED IN THE LATE SUMMER OF 1945, THE GREATEST ARMED
CONFLICT IN HISTORY NEEDED THE GREATEST CLEANUP. Clifford Clinton had always
strived to feed the hungry. What was happening in postwar Europe and Asia disturbed
him. Millions were suffering from the ravages of famine. There were crises in Greece, Holland,
India, Poland, Russia, and Indochina. The United Nations Relief and Rehabilitation Administration (UNRRA) had begun relief efforts in 1943, but the major work would not begin until
November 1945 with the founding of the Cooperative for American Remittances to Europe,
better known as the CARE Foundation. "CARE packages" contained food, clothing, bedding,
and tools. The United States also had stores of food that had been prepared as military rations.
These would be sent to Europe by the shipload. In the meantime, millions of human beings
were still imperiled. Clinton had never forgotten the faces of hunger he had seen in China. As
he traveled around the country with UNRRA, he resolved to do something.

In May 1944, Ernest Chamberlain introduced Clinton and Nelda to Dr. Henry Borsook
at the California Institute of Technology (Caltech) to discuss the prospects of inventing a food
supplement that could be used both in the United States and in famine-wracked nations. Dr.
Borsook, a biochemist, was a researcher in protein synthesis and synthetic vitamins. Clinton laid
out the challenge. He told Borsook:

> This is what I must have: a product that will provide one-third of a day's full nutrition in
> each two ounces. It must not offend any religious dietary law and must make no signif-
> icant drain on supplies of accustomed food. Production costs should make it available

to people having little or no income (under five cents a meal). It must have a long shelf life, require no refrigeration, and be palatable whether served hot or cold.

Dr. Borsook was intrigued by the challenge. Clinton paid him a five-thousand-dollar retainer, and work began in earnest. Clinton did not know it, but if it were not for his arch-detractor, Harry Chandler, there would have been no Caltech to help formulate his revolutionary food. In the 1920s, Chandler, Henry E. Huntington, and others raised private funds to transform the university into the world-class institution renowned for aeronautics, but as time went on, it became well known for scientific advancements in many fields. However, had Chandler been alive when Clinton came to Caltech, there could have been no collaboration.

Dr. Borsook hired Mme. Soulange Berczeller, a recognized French chef, to begin the research. By late 1944, the Multi-Purpose Food (MPF) was ready. As formulated by Dr. Borsook, it was made from soybeans that had been toasted and cracked into coarse pieces called soy grits. These were then dehydrated, which gave them a grain-like appearance. It contained sixty-eight percent defatted soy grits along with dehydrated potatoes, cabbage, tomatoes, onions, leeks, parsley, and spices. Borsook added vitamins and minerals to provide the nutrition of a complete meal.

MPF came in three varieties. The first was seasoned, and, after six minutes of cooking, it tasted like turkey dressing. The second was combined with milk powder for babies and invalids. The third was fortified but kept free of inherent flavor so that it could be combined with indigenous food, enhancing nutrition but not competing with native seasonings. MPF was packed in vacuum-sealed tins, which preserved and protected it and allowed for low-cost shipping.

Two ounces of MPF, when reconstituted with water and cooked for six minutes, would provide nutrition equivalent to a meal of beef, potatoes, peas and milk. When Clinton served MPF at Clifton's Cafeterias (at a cost of five cents), he included a dessert wafer that contained enough Vitamin C to satisfy the recommended daily requirements for this vitamin. Dr. Borsook and his team anticipated that when the MPF was shipped to other countries, Vitamin C would come from indigenous fruit. Dr. Borsook explained:

> As long as we think of food in terms of bushels of wheat, we can never have enough food to go around. Wheat and meat are considered food because they provide nutrition. Anything that provides the human body with protein, vitamins, minerals, and calories is food. The body doesn't care if it comes from a farm or a factory.

At Clifton's request, no patents were requested and the formula and know-how were offered at no obligation to any interested party. In the mid-1940s, Clifton's offered the new product for taste testing. When added to a one-bowl rice dish, it got good reviews.

"Nothing more amazing has come out of California," said *Kiplinger's* magazine. "Multi-Purpose Food is the answer to mass relief feeding," said Lee Marshall, head of the President's Famine

Emergency Committee. Everyone agreed that MPF was a "wonder food," but raves were not contracts. Clinton needed to sell MPF to distributors. "No man need starve," was his rallying cry as he traveled to the East Coast with his son Edmond, Ransom Callicott, and Ernest Chamberlain. His MPF team visited CARE headquarters in New York and talked to Mayor Fiorello La Guardia, who was also Director General of UNRRA.

Clinton met with former First Lady Eleanor Roosevelt. In an impromptu demonstration, he set a tin can on the living room floor of her Washington Square apartment. He added two ounces of MPF to water and held the can over a candle. Once the mixture had boiled, a meal was ready. Roosevelt was impressed and described the experience in her syndicated newspaper column "My Day."

Clinton and his son Edmond approached the Salvation Army, the American Red Cross, and various other organizations. "Their eyes glazed and they grew restless when we told them we had hope for the world," he recalled. "They were already carrying too great a burden."

Clinton was starting to feel the same way. He could not get his arms around a solution. He asked Edmond what to do. How should they proceed? One day in a hotel room, they came to a conclusion.

> No matter how small and insignificant we were in ourselves, we were runners in the relay of life. We held a small torch. We could not quit until we had reached a forward runner who could take the torch from us.

Shortly thereafter, Clinton managed to secure a meeting with Pearl S. Buck. The renowned author and her husband, publisher Richard Walsh, had founded the East and West Association to help Americans understand Chinese culture. Buck turned out to be a kindred spirit, sharing many of Clinton's experiences during her own years in China. Her 1931 novel *The Good Earth* had won a Pulitzer Prize for its description of peasant life in China, and in 1938 she became the first American woman to receive the Nobel Prize for Literature. Buck received Clinton warmly and sympathetically, so he felt comfortable enough to launch directly into his topic. "What would you think," he asked, "of forming an organization whose sole purpose is to relieve and prevent starvation?"

"Like a food Red Cross?" asked Buck. "I like it." She agreed to lend her influence if others joined. Clinton made attempts to sign influential individuals but was met with lukewarm responses. Through Buck he met Florence Rose, an East and West director who worked under Margaret Sanger for women's rights. When he first saw her he thought she had an illuminated countenance. He pitched her too. After some thought, she agreed to help create an organization. Clinton had found a torchbearer. In December 1949, Buck wrote an article for *United Nations World* entitled "Mr. Clinton Stops Starvation: By inventing 3-cent meal, a Californian spearheads man's fight against hunger." In 1951 Buck wrote a novel called *God's Men*, which modeled its main character on Clinton.

The Meals for Millions Foundation (MFM) was incorporated on July 5, 1945, in Los Angeles as a private, nonprofit, nonsectarian organization and included Florence Rose, Ernest R. Chamberlain, Ransom Callicott, and Dr. Henry Borsook. To get the ball rolling, Clinton donated office space on the top floor of the Clifton's Brookdale building. The foundation's only endowment was forty thousand dollars; it came from Clinton, his son Ed, and a few others. The C.B. Gentry Company and the F.W. Bolz Company were hired to manufacture the food.

Soon after its formation, MFM began shipping MPF to areas where famine was the most severe. In September 1945, *Reader's Digest* included an article by microbiologist Paul de Kruif, "How We Can Feed Europe's Hungry." He credited Clinton with MPF, the "Friendship Food for a Hungry World."

Eventually General Mills took over production of MPF. The food was shipped in sealed #10 cans both within the U.S. and globally. During the period 1945 to 1955, MFM distributed more than thirty-six million two-ounce meals to eighty-six needy countries through 126 different relief agencies. The renowned Dr. Tom Dooley at his hospital in Laos called MPF "my third arm." From its unpretentious beginnings, MFM had grown into a global presence. Dr. Albert Schweitzer, the esteemed humanitarian, welcomed the Clintons to his hospital in Gabon, Africa:

> The lepers' sores heal more rapidly after servings of MPF, and the patients love the flavor of MPF in crocodile soup.

Meals for Millions saw major changes in the 1960s. As Clinton retired, MFM went from distributing relief to helping others learn to process food and use technology. By 1967, MFM had moved its headquarters to Santa Monica, California, where it continued to expand and diversify. By then, MPF was being manufactured in Japan, Brazil, Mexico, and Korea in plants run by local people with technical assistance from MFM foundation. The Santa Monica facility served as a pilot plant and training center to teach students to process protein-rich supplements from indigenous resources. Over time, MFM evolved into a self-help organization for overseas training in nutrition, food science and agriculture after it merged with the Freedom from Hunger Foundation founded in the 1960s by the United Nations.

(In 1984, President Ronald Reagan awarded MFM the Presidential World without Hunger award for "continued, demonstrated vision, initiative and leadership in the effort to achieve a world without hunger.")

While Clinton was devoting his time to finding ways to feed a starving world, Clifton's Cafeteria had taken on a life of its own. He didn't have to worry about the place that had been his passion for so many years. The restaurant had given him a secure life. In November 1944, *Life* magazine devoted a big, splashy article to the Pacific Seas:

> Los Angeles has appreciated Clifford Clinton's ideas, ideals, and food. In the past fif-
> teen years he has served more than 50 million customers and last year paid an income
> tax of $120,000.

Photographs showed the interiors, which were to say the least unusual—rubber molded palm trees with neon foliage, tiki huts, thatched roof shelters and a mezzanine entertainment bandstand. This article awakened the public who hadn't already discovered this island oasis.

By 1946, Ed, Don, and Jean had all come home to Los Angeles, so Clinton turned the management of Clifton's over to them. Nelda retired shortly after that. As before, the Clinton home was a haven for many.

E.J.'s stepson Robb Crist and his son were living in Los Angeles, and, during the wartime housing shortage, helped Clinton's children find lodging. Out of gratitude, Clinton offered Crist the hospitality of the Los Feliz mansion. Crist accepted and then began treating Clinton to a nightly critique of his philanthropy, and at the dinner table, no less. Clinton accepted Crist's cynicism graciously and even invested his savings in Crist's grain speculations. Then there came a curious flashback to a lesson of years earlier. The mercurial Crist absconded with the money that Clinton had trusted him to invest. Neither Crist nor the money was ever found.

The three Clinton children were appointed vice presidents of the business along with Callicott, but Clinton still retained ownership. In 1947 Clinton and Nelda sold their interest to their children; Ransom Callicott retained a twenty-five-percent share. Clinton remained on the board of directors but only rarely offered advice to the new owners. In 1955, Callicott sold his interest to the Clinton siblings. Clifton's had passed to the fourth generation of Clinton restaurateurs.

At the height of its prosperity, the Clifton's chain operated as many as seven restaurants, although there have been as many as thirteen locations over the years. There were five in the 1930s; the original at 618, the Penny on Third Street, the Brookdale, the Holly Western, and the Whittier. In the flush 1950s, there were stores in Lakewood, Anaheim, and West Covina. In the 1960s, they opened in the old Westlake District and in newly developed Century City. Later, there were additional stores in West Covina, downtown, and Whittier, and a store in Laguna Hills.

With Clifton's in the hands of his children and Meals for Millions doing well, Clinton took on a new project. This was not business, though. He collaborated with architect George F. Wright on the construction of an ultramodern home at 2021 Castilian Drive in the Hollywood Hills. They incorporated unusual design elements, including an elevator from the street to the living room, a television that descended from the master bedroom ceiling, and a fireman's pole. Shortly after the house was complete, Clinton and Nelda sold the house. In 1959, it fetched a price of one hundred thousand dollars. From then on the Clintons chose to live in a co-op apartment on

Wilshire Boulevard between Holmby Hills and Westwood.

By the late 1950s, the suburban shopping centers were pulling people from downtown, and automobiles were changing the way they shopped. The Pacific Seas began to lose momentum. On June 17, 1960, the famed cafeteria served its last meal. Clinton removed religious artifacts from The Garden and watched bulldozers erase thirty years of his life. The company still owned the parcel of land and Clinton still owned the company. Later that year, Ed, Jean, and Don transferred ownership of the vacant lot at 618 South Olive St. to their father in exchange for full ownership of Clifton's.

Clinton kept busy in the 1960s with travel and family. He kept his seat on the Clifton's board of directors but retired from MFM in 1965. He made two tentative attempts to start a small business; one was a Laundromat and the other an art store. Neither one caught on. Clinton was enjoying his retirement and was comfortable in the dual role of retired statesman and perennial paterfamilias. He had thirteen grandchildren, his wife Nelda, his own children who were following in his footsteps, and an enviable list of achievements. His only vice was the prodigious amount of ice cream he consumed nightly.

In 1969, in the midst of his comfortable retirement, Clinton was interviewed by Sharon Fay, a staff writer for the *Los Angeles Times*, which had been handed down to more objective members of the Chandler family than his old nemesis, Harry. A Senate subcommittee had just released findings on hunger in the United States, so it was only appropriate to check in with the by-then legendary food crusader. Fay quoted Clinton on how his early years in China, seeing humans scratching at the ground for roots and finally eating the soil itself, affected his career:

> A child's mind tries to find answers. It seemed to me then that starvation was a missionary problem. I decided to do something about it if I could, but I didn't want to be a missionary in the traditional sense. . . .
>
> A missionary shouldn't go abroad to feed the hungry if his neighbors are starving. There are many little hungry people living in apartments in this city who are less than normal human beings because they are inadequately nourished.

On November 20, 1969, just a few months after his sixty-ninth birthday, Clinton excused himself from a family dinner so he could lie down. He was feeling nausea, chest discomfort, and weakness. Conscious until his last breath, he died just a few hours later. Cause of death was acute myocardial infarction secondary to coronary thrombosis. He had severe coronary atherosclerosis.

The *Los Angeles Times* obituary called him a "Restaurateur, Philanthropist-Reformer."

AFTERWORD

BIOGRAPHERS OFTEN STUMBLE ACROSS NEW INFORMATION ABOUT THEIR SUBJECTS, LONG AFTER THEY THINK THEY ARE FINISHED WITH THEIR RESEARCH. Such was the case for me, when writing about my grandfather Clifford Clinton. Out of nowhere came an article in *L.A. Weekly* that said Clinton had carried on a long-running romance with a woman twenty-one years his junior named Terri Richmond. Although the true nature of their relationship is impossible for me to confirm, Ray Richmond, Terri's son and biographer, wrote that his mother described my grandfather as the "great love of her life." Ray Richmond wrote in detail about their relationship, about knowing Clinton, and about how he and his siblings poured her ashes into the electrical closet of Clifton's Brookdale while the building was under renovation—so she would be a part of the place forever. Terri's offspring also returned a portrait of Clinton to my uncle that Ray Richmond says hung on her wall for years after my grandfather's death.

Fifty-plus years after Clinton died, and months after I had finished his biography, reading this article made me reconsider everything I thought I knew about what my grandparents' lives were really like. And, I asked myself, did Richmond's account of my grandfather having a mistress explain years of whispers and half-heard conversations at family gatherings? I had to ponder it.

As Ray Richmond tells the story, Clinton and Terri's love affair began in 1958, when Terri worked as a "nurse" in the office of a "chiropractor" across from 20th Century Fox Studios in West Los Angeles. Clinton may have been seeking treatment to relieve back and neck pain that had ailed him much of his life, the typical pain that afflicts people who work too hard and remain under stress. But, according to Terri's son, who based his article on what she told him and what he observed as a young boy, his mother, far from being a medical professional, was providing backroom sexual services to an all-male clientele, while dressed up in a crisp white nurse's uniform. Hollywood celebrities and ordinary men from all over the city sought out her brand of therapy. Clinton's visits with Terri, whose son described her as a "squat, buxom, broad-minded Jewish woman from Cleveland," developed into a romantic relationship that lasted for years.

As Clinton's emotional investment in her grew, he suggested Terri abandon her work in exchange for his financial support and guidance in founding a business of her own. According to Richmond, Clinton paid her enough to cover the income she earned from all of her customers, while he remained her exclusive client.

Clinton's attentions to Terri couldn't go unnoticed by his wife, however. Ray Richmond wrote that a confrontation erupted between Clinton and Nelda over his relationship with Terri, and that Clinton was so distraught that he tried to commit suicide by overdosing on medication. Finally aware that her husband would rather kill himself than give up either of his relationships, Nelda relented, allowing Clinton to continue the extramarital liaisons, as long as she was not humiliated.

Clinton, committed to redeeming Terri, included her in his public events and travel, welcoming her into his inner circle with Nelda and other family members—she even joined them on a trip to Hawaii. Terri's family became Clinton's as well, as he befriended and offered a role model for Ray—often taking him for ice cream and tours of Clifton's. Ray Richmond confirmed the camaraderie he enjoyed with Clinton during this period of time.

In addition to financial support and business advice, Ray Richmond reported, Clinton shared with Terri the strength of his Christian faith, with its promise of salvation and redemption. His spirituality was so strong that Terri eventually converted from Judaism to Christianity, accepted Jesus Christ as her savior, and revised her lifestyle to follow a Christian path.

Clinton earned both his wife's forbearance and his girlfriend's admiration as she watched him in his life of charitable deeds and giving. He helped feed the hungry of Los Angeles and told Terri that his life's mission was to ensure that no one go hungry. Richmond wrote that she described Clinton as the only person whom she loved truly. As testimony to his devotion to her, and the closeness they had grown to share, Clinton gave her a "large diamond friendship ring," her son reported.

Initially it seemed to me that the story of Clinton and his mistress was incongruous with his lifelong moralistic point of view. But having written my manuscript, I had come to understand as best I could, Clifford Clinton, the man—not just Clifford Clinton, the revered grandfather. His ardent attempts to redeem Terri dovetailed quite well with his philosophy and faith-based actions. Clinton, the Christian crusader, had accomplished much during his life, all because of his duty as a true believer to love his fellow man.

He fed many millions who otherwise might have starved in the streets during the Great Depression and later. He received checks of reimbursement and letters of gratitude from World War II veterans who had dined for free during the war. He had cultivated a Christ-like sense of peace and comfort and imparted it to many through his cafeterias, even when the outside world was full of tension and strife. And although he could touch many lives a little, in Terri he saw the opportunity to make a major difference to one person's life.

Clinton's decision to include Terri in his life seems a natural extension of his willingness to open his home to individuals of all walks of life. These people were often strangers, but would cross his threshold as welcome guests. Clinton would feed them, give them money, and include them in his life. These days this might be difficult to understand, perhaps because our culture is less conducive to this kind of openness.

One of my treasured pictures of my grandfather, one that resonates with me so strongly, is of him looking out his front door by an inscription: "This Door Is Open and Inside You Can Find Peace and Rest." That door was never locked and stood as a testament to the consistency of a man who espoused Christian values not just in business or politics, but also in his home. From this perspective, there is a certain familiarity to his friendship with Terri, when viewed in the broader context of his life, early experiences, and his unshakeable belief in a living faith. These incongruous elements may be attributed to the reality that Clinton was human and fallible, and seemed to have gotten trapped in a situation in which he had lost control and which he resolved to the best of his abilities via love and Christian compassion.

In keeping with his parents' background in the Salvation Army, Clinton applied the Salvationists' mandate to help the bedraggled masses out of their misery, not just with spiritual guidance and succor, but with tangible aids such as financial support, housing, entertainment, positive experiences, and examples. The idea is that when people are happy and comfortable, they become more open to the Gospel, and they will listen and accept redemption, forgiveness, and joy.

He applied the same philosophy to his restaurant. And he used his money to amplify his message. He spent fifty thousand dollars on his Garden of Meditation. Money, he said, he never regretted spending:

> The Garden was a continuing source of inspiration. Over the years, many visitors returned again and again, leaving the bustle of downtown to seek a few moments of quiet. Men and women, soldiers and civilians wrote to us, telling of its influence and its impact, its soothing effect on their troubled hearts. I never failed to find benediction there. The times I spent there are among my most cherished memories.

Between the Garden's opening in 1945 and its closing fifteen years later, an estimated seven million people visited it. Clinton never charged admission. A plaque outside its portals said it was dedicated to E.J. Clinton.

Clifford Clinton's legacy was his pursuit of the answer to the question all Christians hear posed on Good Friday when Pontius Pilate addressed the crowd who wanted Jesus crucified. "What shall I do?" This implies not turning away from hunger, suffering, or starvation. Not avoiding the horrors of war, murder, and man's inhumanity to man. Most of Clinton's actions were done in response to the needs of his fellow men—those hungry Depression-era Angelenos, the victims of graft and high-official misconduct, the citizens of Los Angeles, and the needy hungry multitudes in America and around the world.

When family members were clearing out his office, they found a quote under the blotter on his desk. It was from Ralph Waldo Emerson:

> God offers to every mind its choice between truth and repose. Take which you please.
> You can never have both.

Clinton's model of learning developed when he was a young man. He came to realize that for himself, experiential learning was the key to his life, not sitting in a classroom and being told about something. By being in the moment in any experience, he learned best. In his attempts to learn the cafeteria business, he learned through on-the-job training—and he put his all into it. When he traveled to Hawaii, he was overwhelmed by the positive feelings that he experienced in this tropical paradise. So, after the recall of Frank Shaw, when he remodeled the Pacific Seas Clifton's, he created an environment that carried these positive feelings into his business life, not just for him, but for his employees and his customers.

Later when he took his grandchildren to San Francisco and Mount Hermon, Clinton created experiences in Chinatown and on the Santa Cruz Boardwalk that thrilled and delighted us. In 1960, Clinton and Nelda each drove a car—his filled with us boys and hers with the girls—to take us all on a driving trip around the United States. We were exposed to cultures and experiences that he felt would make us more fully developed human beings. I still remember the de facto segregation in the South and viewing historic documents in Washington, D.C. We learned about taking responsibility for each other and the whole group, since we grandkids were in charge of the trip—from managing the money to making trip plans each night before we set out the next morning. We ended up sleeping in a gymnasium one night since we didn't arrange for a motel, but we learned a life lesson. And, when we traveled with them in a reconditioned school bus to the World's Fair in Seattle, Clinton and Nelda showed us that attending a fair was a way to learn about science, food, architecture, and other ways of life—as well as to have fun. We ended up in the Pacific Northwest, for the opportunity to experience the beauty and calm of the Canadian Rockies, something we never would have felt in a geography or history class.

During the school year, Clinton and Nelda were actively involved in our education, and on Sundays we shared a tradition of fireside chats, a time when both grownups and children discussed science. Clinton had bought a Zeiss microscope on one of his trips. He showed us microscopic vistas of red blood cells and microorganisms. Years later, as a medical student at USC, I used the same microscope. In fact, my grandparents made it possible for me to attend medical school. They paid my tuition.

In June 1968, Clinton and Nelda attended my wedding. The last time I saw him was one year later, on our anniversary. Before the year was out, he died.

My grandparents had a profound influence on my siblings and me. They felt that the role of grandparents was as important as that of parents. We learned many lessons from them, and we were fortunate that they lived as long as they did. Very few people I know have had the opportunity to grow up with such role models.

Clifford Clinton continues to inspire me. I only hope I have done justice to his story.

Dedicated to their grandchildren's lives and education, Clifford and Nelda Clinton took the youngsters on trips, providing them experiences that would benefit them for their whole lives. Here, the grandparents, on the right, pose with eleven of their thirteen grandchildren on a trip to Lake Louise in 1962. The author Edmond J. Clinton III, the eldest grandchild, is next to Nelda.

BIBLIOGRAPHY

Abell, Aaron Ignatius. *The Urban Impact on American Protestantism: 1865–1900*. Cambridge, Massachusetts, Harvard University Press, 1943.

Ambrose, Stephen E. *Nothing like It in the World: The Men Who Built the Transcontinental Railroad, 1863–1869*. New York: Simon & Schuster, 2000.

Bean, Walton. *Boss Ruef's San Francisco; the Story of the Union Labor Party, Big Business, and the Graft Prosecution*. Berkeley: University of California Press, 1952.

Bellamy, Edward. *Looking Backward, 2000–1887*. Boston: Houghton, Mifflin, 1888.

Bonelli, William G. *Billion Dollar Blackjack*. Beverly Hills: Civic Research Press, 1954.

Bowron, Fletcher. *Fletcher Bowron Collection, 1934–1970*. Huntington Library, San Marino, California.

Buck, Pearl S. *God's Men*. New York: John Day, 1951.

Buntin, John. *L.A. Noir: The Struggle for the Soul of America's Most Seductive City*. New York: Harmony Books, 2009.

Cage, Crete. "Leader Urges Grand Jury Divorce from District Attorney's Office." *Los Angeles Times*, February 1, 1937.

Caplan, Jerry Saul. "The CIVIC Committee in the Recall of Mayor Frank Shaw." Master's thesis, UCLA, 1947.

Carr, Harry, and E. H. Suydam. *Los Angeles, City of Dreams*. New York: D. Appleton-Century, 1935.

Caughey, John Walton. *California*. New York: Prentice-Hall, 1940.

Chamberlain, Ernest R. *The CIVIC Committee of Los Angeles: Its Background, Activities and Accomplishments*. Clifford E. Clinton papers, UCLA Charles E. Young Research Library, Los Angeles.

Clinton, Clifford E. *Clifford E. Clinton Papers 1934–1969*. UCLA Charles E. Young Research Library, Los Angeles.

___. *Clifford E. Clinton, Biographical Sketch*. Clifford E. Clinton papers, UCLA Charles E. Young Research Library, Los Angeles.

___. "Has Los Angeles a New Boss?" *American Mercury*, May 1941.

___. Unpublished personal memoirs. Los Angeles.

Clinton, Donald H. Oral history, personal communications, and photo scrapbooks. Los Angeles.

"Clinton Gives Statement: Clinton Asks Gambling Tax, Vice District." *Herald of Decency* (Los Angeles), March 19, 1938.

"Clinton's Raiders Uncover Busy House of Ill-Fame." *Los Angeles Evening News*, October 11, 1937.

Cooper, Courtney Ryley. *Here's to Crime*. Boston: Little, Brown and Company, 1937.

Creel, George. "Unholy City." *Collier's Magazine*, September 2, 1939.

Dawes, Amy. *Sunset Boulevard: Cruising the Heart of Los Angeles*. Los Angeles: Los Angeles Times Books, 2002.

Demarest, Gary, and Marily Demarest. Personal communications.

Ebner, Michael H., and Eugene M. Tobin. *The Age of Urban Reform: New Perspectives on the Progressive Era*. Port Washington, New York: Kennikat Press, 1977.

Featherhoff, Grace. *The Experience of a Member of the Young Voter's League in the 1934 Campaign for Supervisor in the Third Los Angeles County District*. John Anson Ford papers, Huntington Library, San Marino, California.

Finney, Guy Woodward. *Angel City in Turmoil*. Los Angeles: American State Press, 1945.

"Fitts Unmoved By Charge." *Los Angeles Times*, January 30, 1934.

Fogelson, Robert M., and Robert Fishman. *The Fragmented Metropolis: Los Angeles, 1850–1930*. Berkeley: University of California Press, 1967.

Ford, John Anson. *John Anson Ford Papers 1832–1971*. Huntington Library, San Marino, California.

___. *Thirty Explosive Years in Los Angeles County*. San Marino: Huntington Library, 1961.

Fox, Stephen R. *Blood and Power: Organized Crime in Twentieth-Century America*. New York: Penguin Books, 1990.

Friedman, Benjamin M. *The Moral Consequences of Economic Growth*. New York: Knopf, 2005.

"Gamblers Flee Inquiry." *Los Angeles Times*, August 2, 1937.

Garrigues, Charles Harris. *You're Paying for It! A Guide to Graft*. New York: Funk & Wagnalls, 1936.

Gottlieb, Robert, and Irene Wolt. *Thinking Big: The Story of the Los Angeles Times, Its Publishers, and Their Influence on Southern California*. New York: Putnam, 1977.

Handy, Robert T., and Washington Gladden. *The Social Gospel in America: 1870–1920*. New York: Oxford University Press, 1966.

Henstell, Bruce. *Sunshine and Wealth: Los Angeles in the Twenties and Thirties*. San Francisco: Chronicle Books, 1984.

___. "When the Lid Blew Off Los Angeles." *Westways*, November 1977.

"High Gaming Chiefs Called in Inquiry." *Los Angeles Times*, August 1, 1937.

Hofstadter, Richard. *The Age of Reform; from Bryan to F.D.R.* New York: Knopf, 1955.

Hopkins, Charles Howard. *The Rise of the Social Gospel in American Protestantism 1865–1915*. New Haven: Yale University Press, 1940.

Horne, Gerald. *Class Struggle in Hollywood*. Austin: University of Texas Press, 2001.

Howe, Daniel Walker. *What Hath God Wrought: The Transformation of America, 1815–1848*. New York: Oxford University Press, 2007.

Kazin, Michael. *A Godly Hero: The Life of William Jennings Bryan*. New York: Knopf, 2006.

Kooistra, AnneMarie. "Angels for Sale: The History of Prostitution in Los Angeles, 1880–1940." Ph.D. dissertation, University of Southern California, 2003.

Lewis, Oscar. *The Big Four; the Story of Huntington, Stanford, Hopkins, and Crocker, and of the Building of the Central Pacific*. New York: Knopf, 1938.

"*Life* Visits Clifton's Cafeteria." *Life*, November 27, 1944.

MacWilliams, Carey. *Southern California: An Island on the Land*. Salt Lake City: Peregrine Smith, 1983.

McGreevy, John T. "Farmers, Nationalists, and the Origins of California Populism." *Pacific Historical Review* 58, no. 4 (1989).

McKinney, Dwight, and Fred Allhoff. "The Lid Off Los Angeles." *Liberty*, six issues from November 11–December 16, 1939.

Mowry, George E. *The California Progressives*. Berkeley: University of California Press, 1951.

___. *The Era of Theodore Roosevelt 1900–1912*. New York: Harper, 1958.

Norris, Frank. *The Octopus: A Story of California*. New York: Doubleday, 1901.

Older, Fremont. *My Own Story*. San Francisco: Call Publishing, 1919.

Orsi, Richard J. *Sunset Limited: The Southern Pacific Railroad and the Development of the American West, 1850–1930*. Berkeley: University of California Press, 2005.

Rayner, Richard. *A Bright and Guilty Place: Murder, Corruption, and L.A.'s Scandalous Coming of Age*. New York: Doubleday, 2009.

Richardson, James Hugh. *For the Life of Me; Memoirs of a City Editor*. New York: Putnam, 1954.

Rose, Alice Madeleine. "Rise of California Insurgency Origins of the League of Lincoln-Roosevelt Republican Clubs, 1900–1907." Ph.D. dissertation, Stanford University, 1942.

Rudd, Hynda. *The Development of Los Angeles City Government: An Institutional History, 1850–2000*. Vol. 1. Los Angeles: City of Los Angeles Historical Society, 2007.

Schlesinger, Arthur M. *A Critical Period in American Religion, 1875–1900*. Philadelphia: Fortress Press, 1967.

Sitton, Tom, and William Deverell. *Metropolis in the Making: Los Angeles in the 1920s*. Berkeley: University of California Press, 2001.

Sitton, Tom. "Another Generation of Urban Reformers: Los Angeles in the 1930s." *The Western Historical Quarterly* 18, no. 3 (1987).

___. "The 'Boss' Without a Machine: Kent K. Parrot and Los Angeles Politics in the 1920s." *Southern California Quarterly* 67, no. 4 (1985).

___. *John Randolph Haynes, California Progressive*. Stanford: Stanford University Press, 1992.

___. *Los Angeles Transformed: Fletcher Bowron's Urban Reform Revival, 1938–1953*. Albuquerque: University of New Mexico Press, 2005.

___. *Urban Politics and Reform in New Deal Los Angeles: The Recall of Mayor Frank L. Shaw*. Ph.D. dissertation, University of California, Riverside, 1983.

Smith, Richard Norton. *Thomas E. Dewey and His Times*. New York: Simon and Schuster, 1982.

Starr, Kevin. *The Dream Endures: California Enters the 1940s*. New York: Oxford University Press, 1997.

___. *Endangered Dreams: The Great Depression in California*. New York: Oxford University Press, 1996.

___. *Inventing the Dream: California through the Progressive Era*. New York: Oxford University Press, 1985.

___. *Material Dreams: Southern California through the 1920s*. New York: Oxford University Press, 1990.

Steffens, Lincoln. *The Shame of the Cities*. New York: Sagamore Press, 1902.

Stevens, Errol Wayne. *Radical L.A.: From Coxey's Army to the Watts Riots, 1894–1965*. Norman: University of Oklahoma Press, 2009.

Stoker, Charles. *Thicker 'n Thieves*. Santa Monica: Sidereal, 1951.

Taft, Clinton J. "City of Fallen Angels." *Forum Magazine*, May 1938.

Tygiel, Jules. *The Great Los Angeles Swindle: Oil, Stocks, and Scandal during the Roaring Twenties*. New York: Oxford University Press, 1994.

U.S. Congress, Senate, Special Committee to Investigate Organized Crime in Interstate Commerce. *Investigation of Organized Crime in Interstate Commerce. Hearings before the United States Senate Special Committee To Investigate Organized Crime in Interstate Commerce* (Eighty-First Congress, Second Session and Eighty-Second Congress, First Session, on November 15–18, 20–22, 27, December 13, 1950, February 27, 28, March 2, 3, 1951). By Estes Kefauver. S. Rept. Washington: U.S. G.P.O., 1951.

Vale, Rena. "A New Boss Takes Los Angeles." *American Mercury*, March 1941.

Viehe, F. W. "The Recall of Mayor Frank L. Shaw: A Revision." *California History* 59, no. 4 (Winter 1980).

Vollmer, August. *Law Enforcement in Los Angeles*. New York: Arno Press, 1974.

White, Ronald C., and Charles Howard Hopkins. *The Social Gospel: Religion and Reform in Changing America*. Philadelphia: Temple University Press, 1976.

Whitehall, Richard. "When the Mobsters Came West: Organized Crime in Los Angeles Since 1930." In *20th Century Los Angeles: Power, Promotion, and Social Conflict*, by Norman M. Klein and Martin J. Schiesl. Claremont, California: Regina Books, 1990.

Wilkman, Jon, and Nancy Wilkman. *Picturing Los Angeles*. Salt Lake City: Gibbs Smith, Publisher, 2006.

Willard, Charles Dwight. *The Herald's History of Los Angeles City*. Los Angeles: Kingsley-Barnes & Neuner, 1901.

Wolsey, Serge G. *Call House Madam: The Story of the Career of Beverly Davis*. San Francisco: Martin Tudordale, 1941.

Woods, Joseph Gerald. *The Progressive and the Police Urban Reform and the Professionalization of the Los Angeles Police*. Master's thesis, UCLA, 1973.

Zimmerman, Tom. *Paradise Promoted: The Booster Campaign That Created Los Angeles, 1870–1930*. Santa Monica: Angel City Press, 2008